The Life and Death of Yukio Mishima

HENRY SCOTT STOKES

The Life and Death of

Yukio Mishima

PETER OWEN · LONDON

ISBN 0 7206 0123 1

PL
833
I7
Z874
1975

PETER OWEN LIMITED
20 Holland Park Avenue London W11 3QU

First British Commonwealth Edition 1975
© Henry Scott Stokes 1975

Printed in Great Britain by
Bristol Typesetting Co Ltd
Barton Manor St Philips Bristol 2

To my parents

CONTENTS

ILLUSTRATIONS

ACKNOWLEDGMENTS

I should like to thank the following for their kind permission to quote from the works of Yukio Mishima: Messrs. Secker & Warburg Ltd for *After the Banquet, Death in Midsummer and Other Stories, Five Modern No Plays, Forbidden Colours, Runaway Horses, Spring Snow, Sun and Steel, The Temple of the Golden Pavilion, Thirst for Love*; *The Hudson Review* for the extracts from Edward Seidensticker's translation of *Runaway Horses* which appeared first in *The Hudson Review*, Vol XXIV, No. 2; *The Times* for 'A Problem of Culture'; *Harpers/Queen* for an extract from *Queen*, January 1970; *Sports Illustrated* for extracts from 'Testament of a *Samurai*'; Shinchosha Publishing Co. for *Niniroku Jiken to Watakushi* and 'Isu'; Kodansha Publishing Co. for *Watakushi no Henreki Jidai*; the Tobu Department Store for extracts from the catalogue to their Mishima exhibition. For other works the following must be thanked: *Shokun* magazine, *Bungei* magazine for recollections of Mishima; *Asahi Shimbun* for extracts from articles, interviews and letters; *Mainichi Shimbun* for extracts from articles and interviews; *Pacific Community* for extracts from Edward Seidensticker's article on Mishima in their April 1971 issue; and Messrs. Secker & Warburg Ltd for extracts from *Landscapes and Portraits* by Donald Keene.

Yukio Mishima published more than 100 books. Only a small part of his work has been translated and published in English. I was therefore most dependent on my assistants—Michiko Shimizu, Michiko Murasugi and Kanji Takamasu—not only for translation of Mishima's works but also for criticism of my understanding of his untranslated books. A few of the translations of Mishima's essays were condensed by my staff in the course of translation, in order to save space; a scholar who compares Mishima's originals with my versions in English will at once note this fact. I would like to thank also the friends, translators of Mishima and scholars in the field of Japanese literature who helped me with this book, in particular Professors Ivan Morris and Donald Keene. My research was partly financed by grants from two British companies: the Swire Group and Phillips and Drew. Finally, I must express my thanks to my editor at Peter Owen, Dan Franklin, and to Gilbert de Botton for his encouragement.

H.S.S.

Beauty, beautiful things, those are now my
most deadly enemies.

YUKIO MISHIMA, *The Temple of the Golden Pavilion*

INTRODUCTION: A PERSONAL IMPRESSION

I first saw Yukio Mishima–the name is pronounced Mi-shi-ma with short vowels and equally stressed syllables–in April 1966, when he made an after-dinner speech at the Foreign Correspondents' Club in Tokyo. He was spoken of as a future winner of the Nobel Prize for Literature, hence his invitation to the 'press club'. He came with his wife, Yoko, and after having drinks with members of the board, the Mishimas took their seats at the top table, flanking the Associated Press journalist, John Roderick, who was then president of the club. I was seated a little distance from the top table but I could see that Mishima had a remarkably mobile face for a Japanese, with heavy black eyebrows and a crew-cut, and he conversed fluently in English. His wife seemed meek and retiring, but she was pretty, and had somewhat heavier lips than other Japanese women.

In his introduction that night, John Roderick described the career and achievements of Yukio Mishima. He was born Kimitaké Hiraoka in 1925, the eldest son of an upper-middle-class family in Tokyo; he had a brilliant record in school and received an award from the Emperor when he graduated at the top of his class from the *Gakushuin*, or Peers' School, in 1944. After the war he became famous with the publication of his first major work, *Confessions of a Mask*, in 1949, being hailed as a genius although he was only twenty-four. His important novels thereafter were *The Sound of Waves* (1954) and *The Temple of the Golden Pavilion* (1956), both of which had been translated and published in English. But Mishima, said Roderick, was much more than a novelist. He was a playwright, a sportsman, and a film actor; he had just completed a film of his short story 'Patriotitsm', in which he directed himself in the part of an army lieutenant who commits *hara-kiri*. Mishima was a man of many talents, the Leonardo da Vinci of modern Japan.

Mishima's speech interested me. He made several references to his war experiences. His peroration, which followed a jocular reference to his wife ('Yoko,' he said, 'has no imagination whatsoever'), went as follows, in his forceful but often incorrect English:

15

But sometime, sometime during such a peaceful life [Mishima had spoken of his married life]—we got the two children—still the old memory comes to my mind.

It is the memory of during the war and I remember one scene which happened during the war when I was working at the airplane factory.

One motion picture was shown there for the entertainment of the working students which was based on the novel of Mr Yokomitsu [a famous writer]. And it was maybe May-time of 1945, the very last of the war, and all students—I was twenties [twenty-years-old] —couldn't believe that we could be survived after the war. And I remember one scene of the film. There was a street, a street scene of Ginza, before the war, a lot of neon signs, beautiful neon signs; it was glittering and we believed we couldn't see all in my life, we can never see it all in my life [for the rest of my life]. But, as you know, we *see* it actually right now, in the Ginza street, there are more and more neon signs on it. But sometimes, when the memory [of] during the war comes back to my mind, some confusion happens in my mind. That neon sign on the screen during the war and the *actual* neon sign on the Ginza street, I cannot distinguish which is illusion.

It might be our . . . my basic subject and my basic romantic idea of literature.

It is death memory . . . and the problem of illusion.

Mishima spoke slowly in English, enunciating his words. That he made mistakes in English did not seem to bother him. He was remarkably un-Japanese in this respect. His pronunciation, meanwhile, was idiosyncratic; he said 'urtist' instead of 'artist'.

After the speech, the foreign correspondents asked questions. I wanted to know what Mishima—who had spoken more freely about the war than any other Japanese I had met—thought about the causes of Japanese entry into the Pacific War. His answer, which consisted of a long explanation of the most spectacular of the *coups d'état* of the 1930s (the *Ni Ni Roku coup* of 26 February, 1936), was hard to follow. Another journalist asked him about the tradition of *seppuku* (as *hara-kiri* is known in Japan). Mishima replied, and I have corrected his English here:

Once I was asked that question by the English cineaste, Mr Basil Wright, and I replied to him in a letter: 'I cannot believe in Western sincerity because it is invisible, but in feudal times we believed that sincerity "resided" in our entrails, and, if we needed to show our sincerity, we had to cut our bellies and take out our *visible* sincerity. And it was also the symbol of the will of the soldier, the *samurai*; everybody knew that this was the most painful way

to die. And the reason they preferred to die in the most excruciat-
ing manner was that it proved the courage of the *samurai*. This
method of suicide was a Japanese invention and foreigners could
not copy it.'

As Mishima spoke his words were punctuated by laughter from the
audience in which he joined. He had an odd, hoarse way of laughing.
'Huh-huh-huh.' He sounded, sometimes, as if he were about to
vomit.

Two years later, when working in Tokyo as correspondent for *The
Times*, I came to know Mishima personally. I have reconstructed a
picture of our friendship from diaries and notes made between 1968
and 1970, the last three years of his life.

March 1968. Met Yukio Mishima for the first time. We had a
rendezvous at the Okura Hotel. I mixed up the meeting place. He
was waiting in the Oak Bar, I was downstairs in the Orchid Bar.
After half an hour I had a message via the waiter: 'Mr Mishima
is waiting for you in the Oak Bar.' I went up there and spotted
him at once, sitting in an armchair facing the entrance. First
impression: irritated at having been kept waiting; he sprang to
his feet at once, though, and came forward to shake hands,
with a broad smile on his face. Mishima came up to my shoulder
only; he must be six inches shorter than me. Hair cut very short.
A charming and captivating man. Quite un-Japanese; fluent in
English; gestures and manner of speaking Western; funny way of
laughing, deep down in his throat, very hoarse . . . went on and
on, 'huh-huh-huh'; embarrassing laugh. Loved attention from
others; very conscious of others looking at him (bar waiters knew
him well, other customers were aware of his presence). Wore
Western suit, shirt and tie. Very formal in a way; didn't talk about
himself. Intrigued by Japanese politics and international defence
problems; not well informed. After a while we retired to my room
(at the Okura) and drank most of a bottle of brandy. His face
darkened and went red with the alcohol, at least Japanese in that
respect. Smoked Churchill cigar with much gusto. Gave impression
of titanic energy. He declined brandy after eleven (has the habit of
working at night) and returned home, promising to keep in contact
in future. Could anyone be less Japanese? A forthright man, he
looks directly at his interlocutor. Seemingly very confident and
contented with his life.

May 1968. Invited by Mishima to his home for dinner. Other guests:
Takeshi Muramatsu, literary critic, expert on French literature
(*Action Française* type), and senior man from *Jietai* (the armed
forces or 'Self-Defence Forces' (SDF)). Surprised by luxury in which
Mishima lives. Modern, three-storey home set back from road in

quiet suburb; Magome; garden with lawn and outsize figure of Apollo on plinth. Solid house with thick walls. Maid at door with cap and apron! Mishima challenges me: 'Why are you interested in dangerous rightists like us?' Screams with laughter. Dinner served by Yoko, who does not sit with us.

July 26, 1968. Had not seen Mishima much this summer but letter arrived from him today. Suggested that I come down to Shimoda to visit him during summer holidays; said he always stayed at Shimoda Tokyo Hotel for his holidays with his family (wife, two children). Strange letter. Mishima said that the critic Rintaro Hinuma had died; added that Hinuma had kept saying that Mishima should commit suicide as soon as possible; this would be, according to his friend, the only solution to Mishima's career as a novelist. Since Hinuma's death, he added, this remark about suicide had come to seem a serious comment. Am confused by this letter; do not know what Mishima wants. Am not prepared to get into suicide scenario with Mishima; will not answer letter.

September 25, 1968. Mishima has published strange article in *Chuo Koron* (monthly magazine) in which he states that the Emperor should once again present regimental colours in person. Cannot follow this article, entitled *Bunkaboeiron* ('On the Defence of Culture'). Have written piece for *The Times* in which I criticize the essay.

October 29, 1968. Nobel prize has gone to Kawabata. Picture published in papers showing Mishima greeting Kawabata at his Kamakura villa; latter has huge forehead and melancholy eyes; a generation senior to Mishima. First Japanese to win Nobel for literature.

It was about this time that I heard that Mishima had founded some kind of 'private army'. A report to this effect was published in a Japanese magazine, the *Sunday Mainichi*. Mishima himself was responsible for the report. I could hardly believe it at first. For what purpose did a Japanese novelist require a student 'army'? When I met him I found him vague on the subject. He talked about the need for a 'civilian militia' in Japan, and made reference to *The Chrysanthemum and The Sword*, the classic book about Japanese society by Ruth Benedict. He said that there was too much emphasis in modern Japan on the chrysanthemum (the arts) and not enough on the sword (defence, army matters). I could not understand what Mishima was driving at, not least because he made a joke of the whole exercise. The uniforms of the *Tatenokai* ('Shield Society'), as he had named his private army, were 'fantastic'; as he said this, he roared with laughter.

His clowning amused me greatly. And when, in early 1969, he phoned me one afternoon and asked me whether I would like to take part in a *Tatenokai* 'all-night exercise' on Mt Fuji I at once agreed to do so. Shortly before this took place he invited me to a separate occasion –*karate* training at the gym at Suidobashi in Tokyo where he did his regular work-outs. I went to this too, and I had an opportunity to see Mishima in action. His *karate* style was not good but he put an enormous amount of effort into the sport. His problem was that he was physically too stiff, at the age of forty-four, to be able to kick his legs swiftly into the air in the *karate* style.

March 16, 1969. Just returned from Mt Fuji and the *Tatenokai* 'all-night exercise'. Cannot understand the thing. We paraded about the slopes of Mt Fuji like a crew of idiots. At least the weather was lovely–sun and powdery snow. Longed to go ski-ing and climb the big mountain. We marched for hours through the snow. The *Tatenokai* has no fieldcraft and little training. Have written piece for *The Times* but feel a bit bored by 'private army' lark. Can't see where it leads. Fantastic uniforms–yellow-brown with rows of shining, brass buttons which give wasp-waists to Mishima's young men. Mishima's taste for *kitsch* exemplified. Is this a homosexual club? Can't really see anything in the *Tatenokai* exercise beyond the uniforms. Met Morita, student leader of 'private army', and found him a dull boy, 23, not bright; devoted to Mishima and confuses him with the Emperor. What is this all about? Mishima drove me back to Tokyo in hired car; he went to sleep in the back. At last saw him tired.

April 1969. Had a call from Philip Whitehead at Thames TV in London. Sent out a team to film Mishima after reading my article in *The Times*. Went up to Mt Fuji, where Mishima was still training with the *Tatenokai*, with Peter Taylor, reporter for Thames TV. He wouldn't let us see the 'private army' as my article has stirred up hornets' nest in *Jieitai* ('Self-Defence Forces'); talk of firing a general for negligence; problem was that *Times* headline used the expression 'right-wing' (fair enough). This is first time that *Jieitai* come under fire for training *Tatenokai*. But so they should be! *Jieitai* a bit cuckoo for training *Tatenokai* with arms when this is strictly forbidden. By way of compensation Mishima arranged a showing of his film *Patriotism* to the Thames people and also invited Taylor and I to dinner at his home. Stayed there until midnight, drinking brandy and smoking Mishima's cigars. Man hands round Churchill cigars like most generous tycoon in the world.

Strange scene upstairs after dinner at Mishima's home (dinner served by Yoko, who did not sit with us). Went upstairs to Mishima's private sitting room and he asked us if we'd like to see his swords. Said yes. He went downstairs again and came bouncing back with a bundle of weapons wrapped up in cloths; he had a dozen knives and swords—short and long. Mishima was excited about their blades and knows a good deal about sword pedigrees. All the weapons very sharp and in good condition: subtle, tempered patterns on the blades. In the end Mishima asked Taylor if he'd like to know how the classical *hara-kiri* was performed; made me kneel on the floor and pretend to cut open my stomach. Meanwhile he swished the sword over my neck. Seemed he wanted to cut my head off! He laughed his laugh. Scrambled to my feet and found Mishima shouting with laughter and holding a yard of razor sharp steel in his hands. A long sword with a double-handed hilt: inlaid in black and white. Old weapon. Sixteenth-century. Much too sharp. As for film of *Patriotism*, there was much swordwork in that too; only 20-minutes-long, set to dirge from *Tristan*. Shut my eyes tight and did not watch Mishima sawing his stomach in half with his sword—played the role of army lieutenant who commits *hara-kiri* during February Incident (*Ni Ni Roku*). Horrible taste!

Mishima was usually a most charming companion but later that summer I had another illustration of his taste for blood. He invited me to the *première* of a feature film called *Hitogiri* in early July; it was a conventional *samurai* film and Mishima played the part of a famous nineteenth-century *samurai*, Shinbei Tanaka, who, as chance would have it, had committed suicide in the house of an ancestor of Mishima, Naonobu Nagai. Mishima proved to be a good actor but once again I removed my eyes from the screen when the time came for Shinbei Tanaka to commit *hara-kiri*.

Later that month I went down to Shimoda, the historic port and summer resort in the Izu peninsula, where the Mishima family were once again spending their summer holidays. I had asked Mishima to write an article for *The Times*, which was about to publish a special supplement on Japan. He invited me to go down to Shimoda to collect the piece and discuss it with him, and also to spend a few days on the beach with him and his family.

August 15, 1969. Have returned from Shimoda. I swam in the hotel pool with the Mishimas. Teased Mishima about his 'masculinity', body-building and the rest. He is small but has well-developed shoulder and leg muscles and is slim. Replied that he didn't like fat men; fat men were spiritually lazy, etc. I approached close to him in the pool and had him put his arms on my shoulders, saying 'Feel and see, I have no muscles at all!' He did what I said then turned away, as if embarrassed. Shy. Didn't like touching someone else, or being touched .

He and Yoko had two rooms in the hotel. Yukio had a little room where he slept and worked during the night. Madman still works at night while he's on holiday. His room is tiny. We changed in there into our swimming trunks and talked about A. E. Van Vogt. Both of us like him. 'Ah, my favourite SF writer,' he said.

I picked up Mishima's manuscript. The Japanese characters are written so clearly that I could read some of them myself. He has the most amazing hand. So plain and upright, easy for a foreigner to read. I wonder if any other Japanese writes like this: clear, straight and simple. The article itself was not too interesting. He praises the *samurai* of the Shinpuren Incident (1877), [the last occasion on which real *samurai* went into action with swords. They made an attack on an army camp; most of them were killed and the survivors committed *hara-kiri*]. Mishima seems to share the Western illusion that Japan is still a nation of *samurai*. No wonder he gets on well with foreigners. In him they find a Japanese who *is* a *samurai*. That's part of Mishima's fun.

We went out to dinner together one night at Shimoda. Lobsters. A marvellous little place on the sea. We went over by taxi, and had a little room perched over the waves. The coast there was 'Japanese': pine trees sticking out of islands at improbable angles; a heavy sea crashing into the rocks below us. Got quite drunk on *saké*, which takes some doing, and watched insects like men-of-war (*funemushi*), about an inch long, dashing back and forth on the balcony by our feet. Disgusting creatures. Strange combination: staggering view and these horrible insects crawling about our ankles.

Ate a pair of kicking, raw lobsters, scooping out their insides with chopsticks; delicious. Plenty of rice and pickles to follow. Mishima and I went home by taxi. What a lot of trouble he takes with his guests!

Still have talked to him little about his writing. Can't get into *The Temple of the Golden Pavilion*, probably my fault. Still like only *Confessions of a Mask*. Asked Mishima about Sonoko, the heroine of *Confessions*. Said that he had an affair with her. He announced this in the manner of one who hadn't enjoyed it, programmed himself. Hagiwara (a historian friend) says that many Japanese believe Mishima to be homosexual. Asked me whether I agreed. Don't know. Have never discussed subject with him.

During the next twelve months I continued to see Mishima, about once every two months on average. At one point he seemed to be suggesting that I should help him with a book on the poetry of Byron, but I did not take up the idea. Our tastes were in fact quite different. On the few occasions when he came to my house I would usually play rock music. He did not care for the Cream and I was not interested in Byron. Meanwhile my interest in the *Tatenokai* had declined. I attended its first anniversary parade, which was held on 3 November, 1969, on the roof of the National Theatre, but I wrote nothing further on the subject for my newspaper.

It was not until the summer of 1970, when I once again went down to Shimoda, to spend a short holiday with the Mishimas, that I saw Mishima for more than a couple of hours at a time. There was on this occasion no specific reason for my going down to Shimoda–it was simply a holiday–and I took along with me my girl-friend, Akiko Sugiyama. I remember one particular day on the beach. We were at a place known to Western people in Tokyo as the 'Secret Beach'. It has dazzling, white sand and magnificent cliffs with dense green foliage and creepers. There was scarcely anyone else there and we–the Mishima family, some friends of theirs, Akiko and I–had the beach to ourselves. Mishima, who was burnt a deep brown, was wearing a skimpy pair of bathing trunks, two tiny triangles of black knitted cotton, which hung perilously from a pair of large brass buckles at the hips. He lay back on the hot sand while the sun beat down on him, listening to pop music on the radio and leafing through a batch of cheap magazines full of stories about Japanese film stars. Akiko, who was twenty, was wearing a swimsuit similar in design to Mishima's, and the two of them chatted about their swimsuits, Mishima asking Akiko where she had bought hers. The rest of the family interrupted. Where had *he* got such a funny pair of trunks? And would he do a strip-tease for us? Mishima, his narcissism exposed, rolled on his back on the white sand, roaring with laughter.

August 15, 1970. Just back from Shimoda. Same scene as last year, only more people around, including Donald Keene [the American scholar]. A whole party of family friends. Saw something of Yoko. She runs the family, takes the decisions about daily life, when the family is going to the beach and so on. Mishima playing role of hen-pecked husband. Liked that. Loaded himself up with nets and balls for the children and trooped off to the beach. Yoko drove the bright blue American car. Yukio doesn't drive at all.

According to Yoko he is scared of the sea. Swims out only a few yards with his son, Ichiro, on a rubber mattress; doesn't go out into the waves very far. Ichiro a barbaric little boy with strong white teeth, very sunburnt tiny body; only Yoko can control him. Little girl, Noriko, two years older at 11, is beautiful child, quiet and very feminine.

One night Mishima suggested we go to see a gangster (*yakuza*) film. Waited for him outside dirty little cinema in Shimoda, having walked over from an inn a mile away. After a while Mishimas arrived, Yoko driving the big car. We all trooped in. M. got the tickets–the host as usual–and walked in with Yoko. Grimy hall almost totally empty, just a few fishermen and lay-abouts. Air-conditioning much too strong. Vast air-conditioning machine shooting icy air into hall at the side at ninety mph. Placed myself right at back of hall. Was shattered to see Mishima seat himself right in front of the machine, so that the icy gale played on his body –he wore only a black shirt with string front. Yoko sat there for a moment and then moved out of path of icy typhoon, with shawl over her shoulders. Film was odd. I had never seen *yakuza* film before. Bit like a Western. The hero acts with reluctance; finally, under provocation, goes roaring into action. His weapon: a sword! That is kinky part of *yakuza* films–use of swords. At denouement mighty splattering of villains' blood all over screen. Mishima engrossed. Still sitting in front of air-conditioning machine after two hours. At end of the film he didn't stir. Wondered if he'd got lumbago sitting there. Finally, rose to his feet; walked back towards us, very slowly, shrugging his shoulders, head down; seemed to be in dream.

September 3, 1970. Yukio came to dinner. Looking healthy and strong as usual. Sat on the floor on cushions drinking Scotch. Drank steadily in his usual way: measured and slow. He never gets drunk. It's control, control, control.

He was in a very curious mood. Talked in melancholy fashion about heroes in the Japanese tradition. I was critical but he ignored my hostility and went on about Heihachiro Oshio, the nineteenth-century hero, and what a great man he had been. 'The body is a vase full of empty spaces,' he said, 'Oshio touched emptiness and died'. Couldn't understand him. Usually Mishima very easy-going and cheerful; but very solemn this time. I made the steaks for us and underdid them. Put off by something in Yukio. Steaks had to go into the pan again, bloody red. After dinner he struck his pessimistic note again: said that Japan was under a curse, all Japanese ran after money, materialism; no spiritual values. Yukio used an odd image: said that Japan was under the curse of a 'green snake'; there was a 'green snake in the bosom of Japan'. Said this with a straight face. Green snake indeed!

September 1970. Bolshoi in town. Went to see *Boris Godunov*. Accompanied by Donald Keene. Had good, expensive seats obtained by Hagiwara. During interval went out to foyer; suddenly Donald crossed over the foyer–Yukio was there, chatting with Yoshie Fujiwara, doyen of Japanese opera. Chatted. Guessed that Yukio would enjoy scene in Polish court, with rococo frills, and went out of theatre to have a smoke. Polish scene very *kitsch* in comparison with rest of opera. Tackled Mishima afterwards and accused him of enjoying the court scene and its slushy music. He confessed, bursting into laughter. Glad to find him cheerful again.

October 4, 1970. Letter from Mishima. Says that finishing 'the long novel' (*The Sea of Fertility*) is 'like the end of the world'.

After receiving what I interpreted as a second letter hinting that he was contemplating suicide (the first had been in late July 1968) I wrote to Mishima and when he did not reply I phoned him. It was early November 1970. He at once suggested that we should meet for dinner and invited me to go to a newly-opened restaurant, the Fontainebleau, at the Imperial Hotel.

November 12, 1970. Mishima in most aggressive mood. Charming as usual but flashes of great aggression. He implied that I might as well pack my bags and leave Japan as 'no foreigner could ever understand Japan;' made a joke of this but was serious at the same time. He also criticized the 'Western scholars', saying that they appreciated only the 'soft' side of the Japanese tradition, ignoring the 'dark' element in Japanese culture. Had never heard him speak so sharply. Also made strange remarks to Janie [an Irish friend whom he had included in his invitation]; complimented her lavishly on her white skin and red hair, and encouraged her to write more. Also rambled on about prostitution in Japan, stating that the price of a virgin *geisha* was two million yen (about £3,000)—seemed rather to insist on this. Yukio wants me to go to an exhibition devoted to Mishimalia at the Tobu department store and gave me a free entrance ticket with an embarrassed smile. Doubt if I'll go. He seemed in a terrific hurry at the end of the evening and went shooting out of the restaurant, bowed at on all sides by white-coated waiters. He crushed a note into the hands of the lift-boy as he left; wondered what on earth he was doing. [Tipping is very much the exception in Japan.]

This was my last sight of Yukio Mishima—tipping a lift-boy, looking flustered. Normally he would have waited to accompany us down in the lift, but he seemed in a great hurry—to keep another appointment, or perhaps not to have a lingering good-bye.

I had an assignment in the Philippines in November 1970. The Pope was visiting Manila. But things did not go according to plan. A typhoon forced me to cancel my arrangements and so I was still in Tokyo on 25 November, when the first news came.

It was a lovely, sunny day, typical of autumn in Tokyo, when a north wind blows the polluted air of the Japanese capital south over the bay. I worked at home during the morning and was at my desk when I received a telephone call from Sam Jameson, a friend at the *Chicago Tribune*, shortly before noon. I heard from him the news that was just being announced on the radio: that Yukio Mishima had taken an army general hostage at the *Jieitai* military base at Ichigaya and that he was threatening to kill himself. When I heard this, I broke down. I was sure that Mishima would act on his threat; he was not one to leave an action uncompleted. If he had announced that he might kill himself, then he would do so, willy-nilly. I had completely ignored Mishima's warnings of his intentions. Regardless of whether this was a 'rightist' action or not, I was appalled by my neglect of a friend.

I found a taxi and twenty-five minutes later I was at the gates of the base at Ichigaya. There was a small crowd outside and I shouldered my way through it; I showed my press pass to the guards and ran up the steep drive. This led to the top of a hill. In front of me stood a long, utilitarian building–a structure built after the Great Earthquake of 1923, to judge by its ugly lines. In the centre of the building was a balcony. A pair of white streamers dangled from it and waved in the breeze. A steady November sun warmed the parade-ground on which I stood.

It was almost deserted, but at the entrance to the headquarters building I found some soldiers. From one of these bystanders I learned that Mishima had died minutes earlier; no one knew exactly what had happened. Five minutes later, just after 12.30 p.m., I heard that Mishima and Morita, the student leader of the *Tatenokai*, had both committed *hara-kiri* in the office of the commanding general of the Eastern Army, a General Mashita. The office was on the second floor of the headquarters building, just above us. We were not allowed to see the bodies.

What vast, immoral courage had enabled Mishima to kill himself in this manner? In 1960 he had written a short story, 'Patriotism', in which he had glorified *hara-kiri*; and five years later he had made a film of 'Patriotism' in which he had taken the part of the hero of the story, an army lieutenant who disembowels himself. In 1968 he had completed *Runaway Horses* (the second volume of his tetralogy, *The Sea of Fertility*), in which the protagonist, a right-wing terrorist, also commits *hara-kiri*. And in the following year he had taken the role of a *samurai* in a feature film, *Hitogiri*; once again he had played the part of a man who cuts open his belly. Thus Mishima endlessly rehearsed his own death.

PART ONE

Kimitaké Hiraoka

I

Hara-kiri

1

Yukio Mishima rose early on the morning of 25 November, 1970.[1] He shaved slowly and carefully.

He took a shower, and put on a fresh, white cotton *fundoshi*, a loin-cloth. Then he dressed in his *Tatenokai* uniform.

His wife, Yoko, had gone out with the children, taking them to school. He had the house—a large, Western-style home in the south-west suburbs of Tokyo—to himself.

Mishima checked the items he was taking with him that day. He had a brown attaché case, containing daggers, papers and other things; he also had a long *samurai* sword and scabbard.

On a table in the hall he placed a fat envelope. It contained the final instalment of his long novel, *The Sea of Fertility*, on which he had worked for six years. The envelope was addressed to his publishers, Shinchosha, who would send someone for it later that morning.

At ten o'clock he made a couple of short phone calls. He spoke to reporter friends, whom he wanted to be on hand to witness the events of the day.

Shortly after ten he saw a *Tatenokai* student walk up the path through the garden from the front gate. This was Chibi-Koga, a short youth with a pointed nose. Mishima went out of the house to greet him.

He gave three envelopes to the student. They were addressed to Chibi-Koga, to Furu-Koga, a second student in their small group, and to Ogawa, the tall, pallid boy who was the standard-bearer of the *Tatenokai*.

'Take these out to the car,' Mishima said to Chibi-Koga. 'I will be out in a moment. Read the letters now!'

The student went back down the path.

Mishima gathered his belongings—the attaché case and the sword. He fixed the sword to his belt on the left side. Then he left the house.

An elderly man with silver hair—Azusa Hiraoka, Mishima's father—looked out of his house, next-door to that of his son.

'Ah! So he's off to another *Tatenokai* parade,' thought the father, disapprovingly.

Mishima went down the steps into the quiet suburban street.

The *Tatenokai* party had come in a white Toyota Corona, a medium-size saloon car. It was parked down the street.

Mishima climbed into the front seat, next to the driver, Chibi-Koga. He turned to face the others—Furu-Koga and Ogawa. With them was a third student; he was a stolid, thick-set youth with heavy jowls—Masakatsu Morita, the leader of the *Tatenokai* under Mishima, and a close friend.

'Have you read the letters?' Mishima asked. 'You follow? *You* are not to kill yourselves. That's clear? Just take care of the general. See that he doesn't commit suicide. That's all.'

Mishima and Morita were to commit *hara-kiri*. The three younger members of the party were to stay alive. At their trial, according to Mishima's letters, they were to expound the principles of the *Tatenokai*; they were to follow the slogan of *Hokoku Nippon* ('The Imperial Reconstruction of Japan'), a war-time, imperialist slogan.

Mishima had put into each of the envelopes a sum of about £50, three 10,000 yen notes for each of the students. The money was for initial expenses.

'All right, let's go,' said Mishima. 'Start up!'

2

The Fight in General Mashita's Office

The car with Mishima and his four students arrived at the Ichigaya base of the *Jieitai*, in the heart of Tokyo, just before 11 a.m.

The guards at the gate saw Mishima in the front and waved Chibi-Koga through. They telephoned up to the HQ of the Eastern Army at Ichigaya, to let the staff know that Mishima and his group had arrived.

Chibi-Koga drove up the steep road leading from the front gate to the top of the little hill on which the HQ stood. He parked at the edge of a big parade-ground in front of Eastern Army HQ.

The men got out of the car. Mishima led the way toward the building, carrying his attaché case. His sword swung at his side.

The army HQ building was yellow-grey in colour and three storeys high. In the centre of the box-like building was the main entrance, which had a large, squat portico. On top of the portico was a spacious balcony; it faced the parade-ground across which Mishima and his men walked.

An aide-de-camp to General Kanetoshi Mashita, the commander of the Eastern Army, came out of the main entrance. He was a major, dressed in the blue-grey uniform of the *Jieitai*.

'Do come in,' he said to Mishima. 'General Mashita is waiting for you.'

The officer, Major Sawamoto, led the way. The *Tatenokai* party followed him into the dark entrance-hall. They went up a circular flight of stairs to the first floor.

'I won't keep you a moment,' said the major to Mishima. He disappeared into Room 201, the general's office, just at the top of the stairs.

The *Tatenokai* group stood outside.

To left and right there were long, dark corridors with high ceilings. Senior officers of the Eastern Army, responsible for Tokyo and the surrounding Kanto plain, worked on this floor.

On either side of the door of Room 201 were opaque glass windows. Thus, glass alone separated the corridor from the general's office beyond.

Major Sawamoto reappeared at the door.

'Do come inside,' he said, 'the general is ready.'

Mishima went through the door, followed by his men.

The major pointed to four chairs lined up close to the door.

'You sit here,' he said to the students. Major Sawamoto then withdrew from the room, shutting the door behind him.

Mishima went forward to greet General Mashita. The latter was a dignified officer with grey hair. He was fifty-seven and had served through the Pacific War; he had a quiet, unpretentious manner.

'How nice to see you again,' he said to Mishima.

The office was not large, no more than twenty by twenty-five feet. It had a high ceiling and tall windows facing south over the balcony outside. Bright sun streamed through the windows.

Access to the office was from all four sides: from the entrance door, from the balcony, and from two tall doors set in the panelling, on either side of the room. One door led to the Chief of Staff, the other to the office of his deputy, a Vice-Chief of Staff.

'Please come and sit over here,' the general said to Mishima.

He gestured towards a low table, around which were set armchairs.

Mishima took a seat next to the general.

'Please sit down,' said Mashita to the students. At Mishima's suggestion they had brought their chairs up to the middle of the room; they sat in a row in their mustard-brown uniforms.

'I brought these *Tatenokai* members to meet you, General,' said Mishima. He introduced them one by one.

Mashita nodded.

'We have just finished an exercise at Mount Fuji. During the exercise some of our men were injured. These four with me today distinguished themselves by carrying down the wounded men from the mountain.'

'Ah, is that so?'

Mishima continued: 'I wanted them to have the honour of meeting you, that's why I asked for today's meeting. Later today we will have a regular *Tatenokai* meeting at which these four will receive a commendation.'

'Mm, I follow.'

'The reason why we are in uniform today is that we are holding our monthly meeting.'

'I see,' said the general.

Mishima had taken off his sword before he sat down. The weapon was propped up against one of the chairs where Mashita could see it.

'Tell me,' said Mashita, who had been eyeing the weapon, what is this sword that you have with you? Did anyone ask you about it on the way in? I am not very clear about the rules on swords, as we don't carry them any more ourselves.'

'It's all right to carry this sword,' replied Mishima. 'It is a military sword. An antique. I carry an expert's authentication.'

Mishima produced a piece of paper. 'The sword was made by Seki no Magoroku, according to this. It's a genuine sixteenth-century blade. The Seki school.'

The general glanced across at the sword. The hilt was inlaid; it had diamond-shaped panels with mother-of-pearl inlay. It was an altogether exceptional piece.

'Would you like to see it?' asked Mishima.

'Yes,' replied the general. 'It has *sambon sugi*, hasn't it?' He referred to the smoky, wavy pattern of the tempering of a sword of the Seki school.

'Let me get it out,' said Mishima. He stood up and picked up the sword. He drew the blade from the scabbard with a practised motion. He held the glittering weapon upright.

He and Mashita studied the blade for a moment. Its surface was obscured by grease.

'Koga,' said Mishima to Chibi-Koga, 'a handkerchief!'

The words, 'Koga, a handkerchief!', were a cue for Chibi-Koga.

The small student got up from his chair and came towards the two men by the table. In his hand he carried a *tennugui*, a thin, strong towel.

This was the 'handkerchief'. Chibi-Koga was to use it to gag General Mashita. His instructions were to slip the *tennugui* over the general's face, from behind.

At that moment, however, the general walked away. He went to his desk to fetch some tissue to wipe the sword.

The student was in a quandary. He could not wait where he was; that was not in the plan. And he was incapable of improvisation.

Chibi-Koga handed the towel to Mishima and went back to his seat.

Mishima methodically wiped the blade. He held it up, admiring its razor-sharp edge. It was in flawless condition.

The general, who had returned to the table, stood with Mishima, who handed the weapon to him. He pointed the sword upright and caught the light in it.

'Yes, I see them,' he said to Mishima, as he glimpsed the semi-circular, smoky shadows which ran along the blade.

'It's superb,' said Mashita. 'I've never seen anything like it in private hands before.'

He handed the sword back to Mishima and sat down. It was 11.05 a.m.

Mishima glanced at the row of students, sitting on their chairs close by. Chibi-Koga came forward for the second time. Mishima gave him a look of silent command.

The youth stepped one pace forward, going behind Mashita, and thrust his hands suddenly, clumsily around the general's neck, throttling him.

B

Chibi-Koga's action was the cue for the others to move.

Furu-Koga and the lanky Ogawa came forward to help him. From their pockets they took two lengths of rope; with this they bound Mashita's arms and legs and tied him to the chair.

Mishima moved to the centre of the room, holding the sword in his hands, high in the air.

Morita's task was to fasten the doors. Using wire and pincers he worked quietly, securing the door handles. There was nothing solid to which to fix the wire and he did not make a good job of it. With the help of the other students he moved Mashita's heavy desk to block one of the doors; the second door they barricaded with tables and chairs, sticking in a potted palm tree as well.

Mashita, gagged and bound, observed these activities. At first he had thought that this was a commando exercise of Mishima's. When he looked him in the eyes, however, he realized that Mishima was not rehearsing.

Mishima stood in the middle of the office, eyes blazing, sword aloft.

Unknown to him there was a peep-hole into the room. The peep-hole was close to the entrance door, in the opaque glass window on the left-hand side. It was composed of a small piece of transparent tape, stuck onto the glass on the corridor side; with this device it was possible to see through into Mashita's office, dimly.

Shortly after Mishima's group had struck, their action had been discovered.

Major Sawamoto had come out from an adjoining office, and had looked through the peep-hole. He had wanted to see whether the men were sitting down and ready to take *ocha* (green tea).

At a first glance he had thought that a *Tatenokai* student was giving General Mashita a shoulder massage. He had looked again, realized that something was up—seeing the rope and the gag—and had dashed off to fetch his immediate superior, Colonel Hara.

The two men, having tried the main door into the office and found it blocked, had informed General Yamazaki, the Chief of Staff, who had been in conference with a dozen officers in the room next to Mashita's.

One by one the officers had peeped through the hole and had seen Mashita. Then they assembled in Yamazaki's office again.

From there they could hear furniture being moved about next door, while they prepared a plan of action.

'What kind of a game is this?' asked one officer.

'We will go in and find out,' said the general.

By this time the *Tatenokai* party inside had done their best with the barricades. Mishima was about to move to the next stage of his plan: to compel the general to order his men to summon the garrison at Eastern Army Headquarters, about 1,000 men. He wanted the soldiers to assemble on the parade-ground in front of the HQ building; he would make a patriotic speech to them from the balcony outside.

His plan was already beginning to go wrong.

At 11.20 a party of men beat on the door leading into Mashita's room from the office of the Chief of Staff. 'Open up!' they shouted, 'Open up!'

Mishima gestured to the students to stand behind him and moved towards the door, sword held high. Chibi-Koga stood by Mashita with a dagger, taken from the attaché case. His orders were to remain by the hostage.

The army officers beat on the door with their fists. 'Open up! What's going on? Open up!'

One turned the handle and shoved. The weak barrier collapsed instantly and five army men, three colonels and a pair of master sergeants, rushed into the room. Colonel Hara was in the lead.

Mishima barred their way. 'Out!' he screamed at them.

The men were very close to Mishima. They hesitated, facing him. None had weapons. Colonel Hara had an old wooden sword, which he had snatched up outside.

'Out!' screamed Mishima once again.

The men facing him made no move.

Mishima swung the sword at them, swishing over their heads. Some moved, others flinched. The sergeants edged towards him, with a colonel leading the way.

'Out! Out! Out!'

Suddenly Mishima attacked. He aimed glancing blows at the men. A colonel ducked away. Mishima slashed him in the back. The man raised an arm in self-defence and Mishima hit him again.

A sergeant came at Mishima, who struck him on the wrist, almost severing the hand.

'Out!' screamed Mishima again.

He stared wildly at the men.

He slashed at a second colonel, three blows in succession on the arms and in the back, while Colonel Hara sought to parry the blows with his wooden sword.

The two uninjured men in the party helped the others out of the room. The door slammed shut behind them. The wounded men were bleeding profusely.

Orderlies were summoned and a second conference ensued. The officers were excited and unable to think clearly; the sudden emergency was too much for them. Their main concern was for the safety of General Mashita, but they were also worried about their careers; a major scandal was in the making. Who would take responsibility for the fracas? What did Mishima want out of it? Failure to appreciate the importance of the last question led General Yamazaki to act unwisely; he decided to lead a second party into Mashita's office without making a plan of action and without arms, not even staves. He quickly chose six officers and men to accompany him.

The men forced the door leading into Mashita's room from the Vice-Chief of Staff's office. Yamazaki went at the head of the party and entered the room first.

Mishima was immediately in front of him, holding his blood-stained sword in the air. The general hesitated. Behind Mishima was his commanding officer, tied in a chair; Chibi-Koga held a knife to his right side.

At Mishima's elbow stood three other students. The pallid Ogawa had drawn a black truncheon. Furu-Koga was behind him, a heavy ash-tray in his hand. Close to Mishima stood Morita; he had a dagger.

Yamazaki had expected a situation like this. Still, he could not believe his eyes.

Mishima saw the half-dozen men behind Yamazaki. How many more would there be? With his sword he kept them bunched in the corner of the room, not allowing them to deploy to either side of him. His own men were not strong.

'Well!' shouted Mishima. 'Now you've seen! Take a good look! If you do not leave I will kill the general.'

Yamazaki looked past Mishima at his commanding officer. He wanted guidance.

'I repeat,' screamed Mishima, 'get out or else!'

'Stop this fooling,' Yamazaki said loudly. 'Calm yourself.'

'Out!' screamed Mishima once more. He took a short step towards Yamazaki, holding the sword at the general's neck.

'Stop this play-acting,' said Yamazaki.

'If you don't leave,' repeated Mishima, 'I will kill the commanding general.'

The army officers continued to edge forward. The men at the front had climbed over the barrier of furniture and those behind were following. Then there was a crash and a tinkling of glass. Other *Jieitai* men had smashed the opaque glass window between Mashita's office and the corridor outside. They peered in.

Suddenly Mishima backed. He wanted room to use his sword.

Yamazaki spoke again: 'We do not understand what you want. Tell us.' It was a parley.

Mishima suspected a manoeuvre. The army officers kept on advancing, seven altogether, including Yamazaki. Mishima had only three men; Chibi-Koga had to stay with the general.

Mishima swung the blade at Yamazaki, deliberately missing: 'Out!'

The officers behind Yamazaki moved. One jumped towards Morita.

Mishima had taken up a posture with the sword held back over his shoulders again. He took a step to the rear and aimed a blow at Yamazaki. The general ducked and Mishima slashed him in the back. It was a light wound.

Yamazaki staggered. An officer behind him supported the general for a moment. Others jumped forward.

One man in the lead grappled with Morita, trying to wrench the knife from his hands.

Three men came at Mishima simultaneously.

Striking back and forth, chopping down, right, left, right, left, he beat the men about their arms, shoulders and backs with the open blade.

Blood stained the uniforms of three colonels.

Morita had lost his knife to his opponent.

'Out!' Mishima screamed at the officers. 'Out!' He swung the sword over their heads. 'Out! Or I will kill the general!'

Yamazaki and his men had no time to work out whether Mishima was bluffing.

'Out!' he shouted again, slashing at a colonel who had come too close. He hit him on the arm.

The *Jieitai* men could not understand what Mishima wanted. Had he gone completely mad?

Mishima gave them no more time to reflect. Prodding the men with his sword and administering broad strokes to their buttocks, he herded them out of the office.

The seven men tumbled back into the Vice-Chief of Staff's room as the door crashed shut behind them. They heard Mishima's party moving furniture again.

Yamazaki, though not badly injured, was in a state of collapse. The deputy, Colonel Yoshimatsu, Vice-Chief of Staff, took over command. He called for orderlies again and conferred with his officers.

Meanwhile, Colonel Hara, watching the proceedings in the commanding general's office from the corridor outside, took an initiative.

'What are you demanding?' shouted the colonel, staring through the broken window at Mishima, who stood a few feet away from him.

The two men began to shout at each other. Mishima insisted that the *Jieitai* officers summon a parade in front of Eastern Army HQ, and Hara responded that he would do nothing of the kind. Mishima then passed a hand-written note to Hara, specifying his demands in detail; the colonel dashed off to confer with his senior officer, Colonel Yoshimatsu, in a staff room close by. The men phoned the *Jieitai* main headquarters in the Defence Agency a mile away and asked for instructions; they were told to handle the situation as they saw fit.

In Mashita's office, Mishima forced the pace. He was behind schedule as a result of the two *Jieitai* attacks. He had intended to start his speech at 11.30, having compelled Mashita and his men to summon the garrison to parade in front of the Eastern Army HQ.

It was already 11.30. Mishima felt a danger that control of the situation would slip from his hands.

He wiped the sword. Then he walked towards Mashita, raising the weapon in the air. He held the sword over the general.

'Take the gag off,' he said to one of the students.

'Now listen, general,' Mishima began. 'I have some demands to make. If you accept them, I guarantee your safety. If you do not, I shall kill you and then commit *hara-kiri*.'

'What is this folly?' asked Mashita.

'Read the demands to the general,' Mishima broke in. One of the students took a piece of paper from the attaché case. It was a short list of the conditions on which Mishima would spare Mashita's life.

'Read!'

All soldiers at Ichigaya—a garrison of 1,000 men of the 32nd

Infantry Regiment, a signals unit and the HQ staff—were to gather in front of the HQ building by midday.

Mishima would make a speech to them from the balcony outside the general's office.

There must be no interruption of the speech. He must be heard in complete silence.

The *Jieitai* must summon a group of forty *Tatenokai* members, who were waiting at Ichigaya Hall, a *Jieitai* centre just outside the gates of the base. They must be present to hear Mishima's speech.

There would be a period of truce, lasting ninety minutes. During this time the *Jieitai* must guarantee not to attack Mishima and his group.

At the end of the truce Mishima would hand Mashita over to his own men. If, however, the truce were broken, or there was a danger that it might be, Mishima would kill the general and then commit suicide.

He wanted instant action.

'This is foolish,' replied Mashita. 'What is there to gain?'

Mishima ignored him. 'I have given these demands to your officers. You will order them to obey me,' he said.

He wasted no more time on the general. It was late.

Mishima walked over to the broken windows looking out into the corridor beyond.

'Who is in command?' he shouted. 'Bring him here.'

A soldier rushed off to inform Yoshimatsu. The officer appeared a moment later: 'I have taken over as Yamazaki is injured. What is it?'

The two men faced each other through the broken window. Yoshimatsu saw the sword in Mishima's hand.

'I have made my demands,' replied Mishima. 'If you do not comply I will kill the general and commit suicide.'

The officer looked through the broken window. On the far side of the room was Mashita, tied to his chair.

'The general orders you to carry out my orders,' said Mishima.

Mashita nodded.

'When?' asked Yoshimatsu.

'Now,' replied Mishima, 'hurry!'

It was 11.35.

Yoshimatsu went back to his office. He told his officers of the development. They made up their minds to call in outside help.

The Eastern Army staff telephoned a police station near the gates of the Ichigaya base. They asked for ambulances as well. They also communicated their decision to the *Jieitai* headquarters at Roppongi, two miles away. Finally, they decided who should make the announcements to the garrison, summoning the soldiers to parade; they would do this after the police had arrived.

Mishima, meanwhile, was relaxing quietly with his men. He had no notion that the police were being summoned.

The students took out a set of *hachimaki* from the attaché case. The headbands were dyed with red circles—The Rising Sun—and emblazoned with a patriotic slogan in black Chinese ink: *Shichisho Hokoku* ('Serve the Nation for Seven Lives'), a medieval *samurai* battle sign.

'Loosen your collars and tie on the *hachimaki*,' said Mishima to the students.

The movements of the men were watched by soldiers posted outside, by the broken window. Mishima did not care. He took a cigarette from a pack he had brought in his case and puffed away cheerfully.

The loudspeaker announcement summoning the garrison to parade would be made at any moment. In the meantime Mishima and his group had nothing to do but wait.

At 11.38 there was a sound of police sirens. At first it was faint, coming from the main road which ran below the hill on top of which stood the Eastern Army HQ. The sirens came closer; the cars must be coming up the hill, inside the base.

A cavalcade of vehicles came to a halt in front of the HQ building on the parade-ground outside.

Helmeted men in white jumped out of ambulances and ran into the building, under the portico. Armed police accompanied them.

'What a lot of people for the party!' said Mishima.

A moment later an announcement was made on the camp loudspeakers. All troops were to assemble in front of Eastern Army HQ. Men ran to the parade-ground from all over the base. In a short time nearly 1,000 soldiers had assembled.

Within the building, the police were taking charge. Men in dark-blue uniforms appeared at the broken window and peered in at Mishima.

'What weapons do they have?' the police wanted to know.

'A sword. Mishima has it. And a dagger, with the student next to Mashita.'

The police calmly accepted the truce.

They posted men on the stairs, in the corridor and at the doors leading into Mashita's office.

They had no thought of using their weapons. Mishima was trapped.

Police cameramen were posted at the broken window. Their photos would be useful in court. Both Mishima and Morita were in full view.

Reports were made to the *Jieitai* headquarters at Roppongi and to Metropolitan Police Headquarters at Sakuradamon near the Imperial Palace, also two miles away.

At 11.45 the first helicopters arrived.

They flew northward from the direction of the Palace. Some were from the police and landed on a pad at the back of Eastern Army HQ. Others were from the newspapers and TV stations and circled above the building; at once they started to film the crowd of soldiers standing around on the parade-ground. They filmed the HQ building and the large balcony in front of it and also the ambulances into which injured men were being carried on stretchers.

The *Tatenokai* party of forty students, however, was not in sight. Their leaders had refused to obey *Jieitai* orders to assemble on the parade-ground at Ichigaya; they had not understood that the orders came from their leader.

Shortly before midday, Morita, a squat figure, appeared on the balcony, followed by Ogawa. The two students came out of one of the windows of Mashita's office and walked towards the front of the balcony carrying papers and cloths in their hands.

The balcony was large. It was thirty feet from the windows of the general's office to the front of the balcony.

The students, with the ends of their *hachimaki* trailing over their bright mustard uniforms, came up to the parapet.

Leaning over the edge of the balcony they threw out long cotton streamers, facing the crowd. They fastened the banners to the parapet so that they dangled over the parade-ground; on them were written the series of conditions which Mishima had made under which General Mashita's safety was guaranteed.

One of these conditions was that Mishima's speech should be heard in silence. However, the noise at that moment was tremendous.

Soldiers were shouting excitedly at one another. Police bicycles, cars and ambulances were all running their engines on the parade-ground. And more cars were arriving all the time, including press vehicles flying company flags. The helicopters made the most noise, as they came in close to film.

Meanwhile the two *Tatenokai* students were dropping papers over the edge of the balcony on the crowd below. Some were caught by a light breeze and drifted out over the parade-ground.

The papers were copies of Mishima's *gekibun*, his last manifesto, a document modelled on statements made by rebel army officers in the numerous abortive *coups d'état* of the 1930s in Japan.

The *gekibun* read:

> We, members of the *Tatenokai*, have been handsomely treated by the *Jieitai*. Why are we biting the hand that fed us?
>
> It is simply because we revere the *Jieitai*. The armed forces are the soul of Nippon.
>
> We have seen the *Jieitai* treated as a toy by the nation's leaders. And thus the *Jieitai* protects the very instrument which denies its right to exist: the Peace Constitution.
>
> Opportunities to rectify this dreadful error have been missed. On 21 October, 1969, the *Jieitai* should have been mobilized and thrown into the battle against anti-war demonstrators. The *Jieitai* should then have taken power and demanded revision of the Constitution.
>
> The chance was missed. The honour of the nation is at stake. The *Jieitai* is unconstitutional; and no steps are being taken to save it.
>
> Our fundamental values, as Japanese, are threatened. The Emperor is not being given his rightful place in Japan.
>
> We have waited in vain for the *Jieitai* to rebel. If no action is taken, the Western powers will control Japan for the next century![2]

The manifesto ended with this appeal:

> Let us restore Nippon to its true state and let us die. Will you value only life and let the spirit die? . . . We will show you a value which is greater than respect for life. Not liberty, not democracy. It is Nippon! Nippon, the land of history and tradition. The Japan we love.

The soldiers on the parade-ground picked up copies of the *gekibun*. Some read the document. Others stuffed the papers into their pockets. The men were puzzled. Most of them were young and had had no experience of the war. For twenty-five years Japan had been at peace, and the alliance with America, the cornerstone of Japanese foreign policy, had been challenged only by the Left. Nothing in the experience of these young men had remotely prepared them for this assault from the Right. Many of them knew of the existence of the *Tatenokai*; but they had no notion of its purpose. Nor did they understand why Mishima–a famous novelist–had involved himself in this enterprise. Adding to their bafflement was the spectacle of wounded men being carried from the building. Why had Mishima attacked and injured their officers?

At midday precisely, Mishima himself appeared on the balcony.

He strode forward to the front of the balcony, a small figure in the mustard uniform of the *Tatenokai*.

The men below saw only his head, with a *hachimaki* bound around it, the symbol of the Rising Sun in the centre of his forehead.

He leapt up onto the parapet. His small, wiry frame came entirely into view. The buttons of his uniform shone brightly in the November sun. He wore white gloves on which bloodstains were visible.

He braced himself, shoulders back, his hands on his hips.

3

Tenno Heika Banzai!

'It is a wretched affair,' Mishima began, 'to have to speak to *Jieitai* men in circumstances like these.'

The helicopters were making a great noise. Many in the crowd could not hear Mishima's words.

'I thought,' Mishima continued, 'that the *Jieitai* was the last hope of Nippon, the last stronghold of the Japanese soul.'

His words were blotted out by the helicopters.

'But . . . . Japanese people today think of money, just money. Where is our national spirit today? The politicians care nothing for Japan. They are greedy for power.'

'The *Jieitai*,' Mishima continued, 'must be the soul of Nippon. The soldiers! The army!'

'But . . . . we were betrayed by the *Jieitai*!'

There were shouts from the crowd.

'Cut it out now!'

'*Bakayaro!*' (An untranslatable swear-word.)

'Arse-hole!'

Mishima became excited at once. 'Listen! Listen! Hear me out! Listen! Listen! Listen to me!'

He resumed. 'We thought that the *Jieitai* was the soul of national honour!'

There were shouts.

'Come down from there!'

'We don't agree with you!'

Mishima went on, 'The nation has no spiritual foundation. That is why you don't agree with me! You don't understand Japan. The *Jieitai* must put things right!'

There was violent hooting.

'Listen!' shouted Mishima. 'Be quiet will you! Listen!'

'*Bakayaro!*'

Mishima struggled to carry on.

'Kiss your arse,' shouted a soldier below.

'Don't you hear?' Mishima shouted back. 'I ask you to be quiet! Listen! Hear me out!'

'Stop playing the hero!' shouted another heckler.

'Just listen to me,' Mishima hurled back. 'What happened last year? On October 21? There was a demonstration, an anti-war demonstration. On October 21 last year. In Shinjuku. And the police put it down. The police! After that there was, and there will be, no chance to amend the Constitution.'

'So what?'

'So the *Jiminto* [the Liberal Democratic Party], the politicians, decided that they could just use the police. The police would deal with the demonstrations. Don't you see?'

'Hooray. Call the police. Dial 110 somebody!'

Mishima fought on. 'Look! The government did not use the *Jieitai*. The armed forces stayed in their barracks. The Constitution is fixed forever. There will be no chance to amend it. Do you understand?'

'No, no. Absolutely not!'

'No, we don't follow you.'

'No!'

'All right,' Mishima continued. 'Listen! Since last October 21, since that time, it is you who protect the Constitution. The *Jieitai* defends the Constitution. There will be no chance to amend it. Not for twenty years! The *Jieitai* waited for that chance, with tears in their eyes. Too late!'

'Japan is at peace!'

Mishima looked at his watch. He had been speaking for less than five minutes.

'Why don't you understand? Think about October 21 last year! Since that time I have waited for the *Jieitai* to act! When would the *Jieitai* come to its senses? I waited. There will be no further chance to revise the Constitution! The *Jieitai* will never become an army! It has no foundation, no centre!'

He continued. 'The *Jieitai* must rise. Why?'

'Come down! Come down!'

'To protect Japan! You must protect Japan! To protect Japan! Yes, to protect Japan! Japanese tradition! Our history! Our culture! The Emperor!'

His audience exploded with shouts and jeers.

'Listen! Listen! Listen! Listen!'

Mishima resumed. 'A man appeals to you! A man! I am staking my life on this! Do you hear? Do you follow me? If you do not rise with me, if the *Jieitai* will not rise, the Constitution will never be amended!'

He paused. 'You will be just American mercenaries. American troops!'

'*Bakayaro!*'

'Stop talking!'

'Come down!'

Mishima could not make himself heard above the din.

'I have waited for four years! Yes, four years! I wanted the *Jieitai* to rise! Four years!'

'I have come to the last thirty minutes,' he went on. 'Yes, the last thirty minutes. I am waiting. I want. . . .'

His words were lost in the noise of helicopter engines.

'Are you *bushi*? Are you men? You *are* soldiers! Then why do you stand by the Constitution? You back the Constitution that denies your very existence!'

There were mock cries of alarm from the crowd.

'Then you have no future!' roared Mishima. 'You will never be saved! It is the end. The Constitution will remain forever. You are finished!'

He hammered the point. 'You are unconstitutional! Listen! You are unconstitutional! The *Jieitai* is unconstitutional! You are all un-constitutional!'

There was no reaction from the crowd.

'Don't you understand?' he asked. 'Don't you see what is happening? Don't you understand that it is you who defend the Constitution?

Why not? Why don't you understand? I have been waiting for
you. Why don't you wake up? There you are in your tiny world. You
do nothing for Nippon!'

'Is that why you injured our men?'

'They put up a resistance.'

'Don't be stupid! What do you mean "resistance"?'

Mishima appealed to the men once more. 'Will any of you rise
with me?' He waited for ten seconds.

'*Bakayaro!*'

'Who would rise with *you*?'

'Madman!'

'No one?' Mishima asked.

'Are *you* a man?'

'You say that! Have you studied *Bu*?[3] Do you understand the way
of the sword? What does the sword mean to a Japanese? . . . I ask
you. Are *you* men? Are you *bushi*?'

Mishima's voice grew calmer. 'I see that you are not. You will not
rise. You will do nothing. The Constitution means nothing to you. You
are not interested.'

He added: 'I have lost my dream of the *Jieitai*!'

'Come down!'

'Drag him down from there!'

'Why does no one stop him?'

'*Bakayaro!*'

Most of the crowd looked on silently, while the heckling continued.

'I salute the Emperor!' cried Mishima.

'*Tenno Heika Banzai! Tenno Heika Banzai! Tenno Heika Banzai!*'
('Long live the Emperor!')

As he shouted the traditional salute Morita, who had been standing behind him—only his head visible to the men below—joined in.
The two *Tatenokai* leaders raised their hands thrice as they shouted.

'Shoot him!'

'SHOOT HIM!'

Mishima jumped down from the parapet onto the balcony behind.
With Morita at his heels he retraced his steps to the general's office.
He stooped at the low window and went down into the room beyond,
out of sight of the TV cameras. Then Morita too disappeared. The
window was closed.

4

Hara-kiri

Mishima came down a little flight of red-carpeted stairs that led back into the general's office.

'They did not hear me very well,' he remarked to the students. Morita followed him into the room.

Mishima started to undo the buttons of his jacket. He was in a part of the room, close to the door of the Chief of Staff's office, from which he could not be seen through the broken window by the men in the corridor.

The general's gag had been taken off. He watched as Mishima stripped off his jacket. Mishima was naked to the waist; he wore no vest.

'Stop!' cried Mashita. 'This serves no purpose.'

'I was bound to do this,' replied Mishima. 'You must not follow my example. You are not to take responsibility for this.'

'Stop!' ordered Mashita.

Mishima paid no attention. He unlaced his boots, throwing them to one side. Morita came forward and picked up the sword.

'Stop!' cried Mashita once more.

Mishima slipped his wrist-watch from his hand, and passed it to a student. Then he knelt on the red carpet, six feet from Mashita's chair. He loosened his trousers, slipping them down his legs. The white *fundoshi* underneath was visible. Mishima was almost naked. His small, powerful chest heaved.

Morita took up a position behind him with the sword.

Mishima took a *yoroidoshi,* a foot-long, straight-bladed dagger with a sharp point, in his right hand.

Ogawa came forward with a *mohitsu* (brush) and a piece of paper. Mishima had planned to write a last message in his own blood.

'No, I do not need that,' said Mishima. He rubbed a spot on his lower left abdomen with his left hand. Then he pricked the knife in his right hand against the spot.

Morita raised the sword high in the air, staring down at Mishima's neck. The student's forehead was beaded with perspiration. The end of the sword waggled, his hands shook.

Mishima shouted a last salute to the Emperor. *'Tenno Heika Banzai! Tenno Heika Banzai! Tenno Heika Banzai!'*

He hunched his shoulders and expelled the air from his chest. His back muscles bunched. Then he breathed in once more, deeply.

'Haa . . . ow!' Mishima drove all the air from his body with a last, wild shout.

He forced the dagger into his body with all his strength. Following the blow, his entire face went white and his right hand started to tremble. Mishima hunched his back, beginning to make a horizontal cut across his stomach. As he pulled at the knife his body sought to drive the blade outward; the hand holding the dagger shook violently. He brought his left hand across, pressing down forcefully on his right. The knife remained in the wound, as he continued to cut cross-wise. Blood spurted from the cut and ran down his stomach into his lap, staining the *fundoshi* a bright red.

With a final effort Mishima completed the cross-cut, head down. His neck was exposed.

Morita was ready to strike with the sword and cut off the head of his leader. 'Do not leave me in agony too long,' Mishima had told him beforehand.

The student clenched his wrists on the hilt of the sword. As he watched, Mishima toppled forward on his face onto the red carpet.

Morita brought the sword crashing down. Too late. The force of the blow was great, but the sword smacked into the red carpet on the far side of Mishima. He received a deep cut in the back and shoulders.

'Again!' shouted the other students.

Mishima lay groaning on the carpet, smothered in his own blood and twisting from side to side. Intestines slid from his belly.

Morita struck once again. Once more his aim was poor. He hit Mishima's body, not the neck. The wound was a terrible one.

'Once more!' shouted the other youths.

Morita had little strength left in his hands. He lifted the glittering sword for the third time, and struck with all his might at Mishima's head and neck. The blow almost severed the neck. Mishima's head cocked at an angle to his body; blood fountained from his neck.

Furu-Koga came forward. He had experience in *kendo* (Japanese fencing).

'Give me the sword!' he said to Morita.

With a single chop he separated body and head.

The students knelt.

'Pray for him,' Mashita said, leaning forward as best he could to bow his head.

The students silently said a Buddhist prayer.

The only sound in the room was the sobbing of the young men. Tears ran down their cheeks. There was a bubbling from the corpse; blood pumped from the neck, covering the red carpet.

A raw stench filled the room. Mishima's entrails had spilled onto the carpet.

Mashita lifted his head. The students had not finished. Morita was ripping off his jacket. Another student took from the hand of Mishima, which still flapped in a pool of blood, the *yoroidoshi* dagger with which he had disembowelled himself. He passed the weapon to Morita.

Morita knelt, loosened his trousers and shouted a final salute, as Mishima had done: *'Tenno Heika Banzai! Tenno Heika Banzai! Tenno Heika Banzai!'*

Morita tried without success to drive the dagger into his stomach. He was too weak. He made a shallow scratch across his belly.

Furu-Koga stood behind him, holding the sword high in the air. 'Right!' said Morita.

With a sweep of the sword Furu-Koga knocked off Morita's head, which rolled across the carpet. Jets of blood spurted rhythmically from the severed neck, the body had slumped forward.

The students prayed, sobbing.

Mashita watched them: 'This is the end!' he said.

'Don't worry,' said one of the students. 'He told us not to kill ourselves. We have to hand you over safely. Those were his orders.'

'You must stop,' repeated Mashita, 'you must stop.'

The students unbound Mashita. He rose to his feet, massaging his wrists. On one hand he had a deep cut. Otherwise he had been uninjured in the scuffle.

'Make the bodies decent,' he ordered the students.

They went over to the corpses. They took up the discarded jackets and spread them over the torsos. Then they lined up the bodies on the floor, with the feet pointing towards the main door of the office.

Next they took the heads. They placed them, necks down, standing upright on the blood-soaked carpet. The headbands were still in place.

The students prayed for a third time, before the two heads.

Then they rose to their feet and walked towards the main entrance door. They dismantled the barrier there and pulled open the door.

The students stood there, looking out. The police looked back. The uniforms of the youths were lightly spotted with blood, their cheeks tear-stained.

No one moved.

An officer rushed forward to Mashita. 'Are you all right, sir?'

The general nodded. But he was on the verge of collapse.

The police still did not move.

'Well,' cried out an inspector finally, 'arrest them!'

The police doctors went into the room. At 12.23 they confirmed that Mishima and Morita had died by *hara-kiri* and by beheading.

An announcement was made downstairs to the press. A crowd of about fifty reporters and TV camera men were standing together in a small room; I was the only foreigner amongst them.

A *Jieitai* officer stood on a low rostrum at the front of the room. 'They are dead, Mishima and one other,' he announced.

'What do you mean "dead"?'

'Their heads are off, yes, off, their heads are off, off, I tell you, off.'

5

'Out of His Mind'

The first reaction to Mishima's action was complete incredulity. There had been no case of ritual *hara-kiri* in Japan since immediately after the war; most Japanese had assumed, if they ever thought about the subject, that the practice was extinct. And Mishima had been one of the best-known men in the country.

The police were very confused. Officers at the Metropolitan Police Headquarters in Tokyo did not believe the first reports that Mishima had committed *hara-kiri* and had been beheaded. A senior officer was despatched with the orders: 'If the body is still warm, do your utmost to save his life.'

The Japanese press were also at a loss. A reporter for the *Mainichi Shimbun*, a leading daily paper, phoned his story from Ichigaya, just in time for a late afternoon edition. 'Go back and check your facts,'

said the desk editor who took the call; he drafted this headline:
'INJURED MISHIMA RUSHED TO HOSPITAL.'

At his home in the suburbs Azusa Hiraoka, Mishima's father, had
been having a quiet smoke and watching television when the first
report of the 'Mishima Incident' had flashed on the screen.

'Yukio Mishima . . . made an attack on the *Jieitai* camp at Ichigaya.'

Azusa thought: 'Now I will have to go and apologize to the police
and everyone else involved. What a bother!'

The next line read: '*Kappuku*' (cut his stomach). Azusa worried
that his son's right hand might have been injured too. Modern
surgery would take care of him otherwise.

The characters that followed were those of '*kaishaku*'. Mishima had
been beheaded.

'I was not particularly surprised,' Azusa said later. 'My brain rejected the information.'

The first official comment on the affair was made by Prime Minister
Eisaku Sato.

Sato, a stocky, handsome figure in a morning coat, emerged from
the Diet (Parliament). He had been making a speech at the opening of the autumn session, in the presence of the Emperor. Sato had
known Mishima personally and had helped him, indirectly, to have his
Tatenokai trained by the *Jieitai*.

Reporters gathered round the Prime Minister.

'Would you comment on the Mishima Incident, Prime Minister?'

'He must have been *kichigai*, out of his mind,' Sato said. Then he
got into his big, black President car and was driven away to his
office.

Shortly afterwards the police announced the results of the autop-
sies on the bodies of Mishima and Morita. The former had a cut
five-inches-long in his lower abdomen; intestines protruded from the
wound which was up to two inches deep in places. Morita had only
a light scratch across his stomach, having not had the great strength
required to drive the dagger into his body.

What had led these two men to perform *hara-kiri*? The answer was
not as simple as the Prime Minister had suggested.

II

Early Life (1925-39)

> But my heart's leaning toward Death
> and Night and Blood would not be
> denied.
>
> YUKIO MISHIMA, *Confessions of a Mask*[1]

1

One of the last remarks made to me by Mishima was that it was virtually impossible for a non-Japanese person to understand Japan. We in the West, he went on, consistently underrated the importance of the 'dark' side of Japanese culture and chose instead to concentrate on the 'soft' element in the Japanese tradition. This was a theme which we had discussed from the beginning of our friendship; Mishima had illustrated his point then by saying that there was too much emphasis in Japan itself on 'the chrysanthemum' (the arts) and an insufficient understanding of 'the sword' (the martial tradition). And in this context he had referred approvingly to the work of the American sociologist Ruth Benedict, *The Chrysanthemum and the Sword*[2], a book known to all non-Japanese interested in the culture of Japan. Many times he would insist upon the duality of the Japanese tradition, and he praised Benedict for having understood the nature of this duality.

I accept Mishima's point. Before and during the Second World War, Western commentary on Japan was almost exclusively preoccupied with the martial aspect of the Japanese tradition; it was said that the Japanese were soldiers at heart—ruthless, barbaric men who would not hesitate to commit the gravest atrocity as at the 'rape of Nanking' in 1937. After the war, Western scholars changed their thinking and most writing about Japan since 1950 has dwelt upon the Japanese aesthetic. Writers on a variety of subjects—the classical literature of Japan, Zen Buddhism, the tea ceremony—have delineated the Japanese sense of beauty. Neither school of thought gives a complete picture

52

of Japan, however; the Japanese, as Mishima insisted, have a dual tradition of the literary and the martial arts.

Nonetheless, I see Mishima as a writer and not as a soldier. If one wants to understand the man, one must study his aesthetic; his exploits in the field of military endeavour are intriguing and reveal that he had *something* of the soldier in him; but he devoted almost all his adult life to writing, not to the *Jieitai* and the *Tatenokai*. My purpose here is to explain Mishima's idea of beauty, which he developed during his adolescence.

My study of Mishima's early life relies heavily on a single source, his autobiographical masterpiece, *Confessions of a Mask*[3]. This novel is, I think, the best of Mishima's many works. It also reveals more of his character and of his upbringing than anything else he wrote; it gives a crystalline account of his aesthetic. *Confessions of a Mask* describes the genesis of a romantic idea which impinges directly on his eventual decision to commit suicide: the notion that violent death is ultimate beauty, provided that he who dies is young. This is a particularly Japanese idea and recurs often in the classical literature, for example in the ancient chronicles, the eighth-century *Nihonshoki* and *Kojiki*, and in the monumental eleventh-century novel *The Tale of Genji*. Mishima, however, gave a romantic twist to the classical tradition; he had as much in common with contemporary culture in the West—for example, the cult of violence in Western rock songs and in films—as with classical Japan. One of the most striking features of his early life was the influence upon him of Western literature, from the fairy tales of Hans Christian Andersen to the novels of Raymond Radiguet and the plays of Oscar Wilde. Mishima knew a great deal more about Western culture than his contemporaries in Japan; that is one reason why he could make friends with foreigners so easily.

2

Birth

Yukio Mishima was born Kimitaké Hiraoka on 14 January, 1925, in the Tokyo home of his grandparents, Jotaro and Natsuko Hiraoka, with whom his parents lived. The Hiraokas were an upper-middle-class family—Jotaro had been a senior civil servant and his only child, Azusa, Mishima's father, was also a government official; and in Japan, which has a Confucian tradition, government service is considered the most honourable employment. The high social standing of the Hiraokas had been underwritten by Jotaro's marriage to Natsuko, who came from an old family; Kimitaké's grandfather was the son of a farmer but his humble origin had not counted against him in the late nineteenth century when there had been great social mobility following the Meiji Restoration of 1868. The Meiji Restoration, in which Japan opened her doors to the West (as the cliché has it), had ushered in a period of social instability and great commercial and industrial progress. In this new era men of ability had been promoted regardless of birth and Jotaro had attained a high rank, serving as a provincial governor in Japan and as the first civilian governor of Karafuto (Sakhalin), the island to the north of Japan which has since reverted to the Soviet Union.

A week after the birth of Kimitaké, the first child of Azusa and Shizué Hiraoka–Mishima's mother was the twenty-year-old daughter of a Tokyo school principal–the family held the traditional naming ceremony, the *Oshichiya*. 'On the evening of the seventh day,' Mishima recorded in *Confessions of a Mask*, 'the infant was clothed in undergarments of flannel and cream-coloured silk and a *kimono* of silk crepe with a splashed pattern. In the presence of the assembled household my grandfather drew my name on a strip of ceremonial paper and placed it on an offertory stand in the *tokonoma*.'[4] (The *tokonoma* is the alcove in the traditional Japanese room and is reserved for precious objects.) Almost all of Mishima's childhood memories, however, were unhappy. He did not like the house where he was born, which was in the Yotsuya district of Tokyo: 'There were two stories on the upper slope and three on the lower, numerous gloomy rooms and six housemaids.' He blamed his grandfather. Jotaro had resigned from his post as governor of Karafuto, taking responsibility for a scandal in the administration, and 'thereafter my family had begun sliding down an incline with a speed so happy-go-lucky that I could almost say that they hummed merrily as they went—huge debts, foreclosure, sale of the family estate, and then, as financial difficulties multiplied, a morbid vanity blazing higher and higher like some evil impulse.'[5]

Mishima's grandfather attempted to be a businessman after his return to Japan but he was not successful; he was obliged to sell his ancestral estates at Shikata, near Kobé, where his forefathers had farmed since the seventeenth century. By the time of Kimitaké's birth in 1925, the Hiraokas had been reduced to living 'in not too good a part of Tokyo, in an old rented house'. Mishima described this residence, which no longer stands, as 'a pretentious house on a corner, with a rather jumbled appearance and a dingy, charred feeling. It had an imposing iron gate, an entry garden, and a Western-style reception room as large as the interior of a suburban church.'[6]

Mishima was undoubtedly gloomy about his childhood. The causes of his unhappiness were not limited to Jotaro's failures and the decline in the Hiraoka fortunes. The fundamental problem was the tension in the family home, which is to be attributed to Natsuko, Mishima's grandmother; she 'hated and scorned my grandfather. Hers was a narrow-minded, indomitable and rather wildly poetic spirit.' Natsuko was much the strongest personality in the Hiraoka family and she overrode not only Jotaro but her son Azusa. Her hate of her husband was generated by scorn for his lack of pride; he lacked the *samurai* spirit of her ancestors; he was a jolly man with a frivolous streak, which Mishima inherited. Natsuko had a second reason for detesting Mishima's grandfather: 'A chronic case of cranial neuralgia was indirectly but steadily gnawing away her nerves and at the same time adding an unavailing sharpness to her intellect. Who knows but what those fits of depression she continued having until her death were a memento of vices in which my grandfather had indulged in his prime?'[7] Natsuko, according to Takeo Okuno, a Japanese biographer of Mishima, had contracted syphilis from Jotaro; her brain was affected by the disease. The unfortunate woman also had a gouty hip and had to use a stick to walk.

The birth of Kimitaké galvanized Natsuko. Disappointed by the commonplace success of her son—Mishima's father had obtained a post in the Ministry of Agriculture and Forestry and was nothing more than a highly competent civil servant—she pinned all her hopes on her first grandson. She resolved to take personal responsibility for his upbringing and virtually kidnapped the little boy from his mother: 'My parents lived on the second floor of the house. On the pretext that it was dangerous to bring up a child on an upper floor, my grandmother snatched me from my mother's arms on my forty-ninth day'.[8] In a traditional Japanese family, a mother-in-law had powers of life and death over her son's wife; and Shizué, only twenty years of age and frail in health, could not rescue the baby, whose bed was placed in his grandmother's sickroom, 'perpetually closed and stifling with odours of sickness and old age, and I was reared there beside her sickbed.' A nursemaid changed his nappies and saw to his needs during the night.

Shizué's position had not been entirely usurped. She still fed the child, but Natsuko kept her in her place, as Mishima's mother recalled after his death. 'We lived upstairs, while Mother [Natsuko] kept Kimitaké with her all the time, ringing an alarm every four hours, loud enough for me to hear upstairs. Kimitaké's feeding times had to be precisely every four hours; and the duration of the feeding sessions was exactly fixed in advance.'[9] Then Shizué was sent upstairs again. This situation existed for a year and her hopes of winning back the child were dashed when an accident of precisely the kind her mother-in-law predicted actually happened.

'One day,' according to Shizué, 'Mother was out at the *Kabuki* and Kimitaké fell down the stairs, banging his head and losing a good deal of blood. We took him to the hospital and called Mother on the telephone. When she returned home she shouted out: "Is he past help?" Still to this day I cannot forget the terrifying look on her face.'[10] Mishima describes the scene only a little differently in *Confessions of a Mask*:

> When she arrived my grandfather went out to meet her. She stood in the hallway without taking her shoes off, leaning on the cane she carried in her right hand, and stared fixedly at my grandfather. When she spoke it was in a strangely calm tone of voice, as though carving out each word:
> 'Is he dead?'
> 'No.'
> Then, taking off her shoes and stepping up from the hallway, she walked down the corridor with steps as confident as those of a priestess . . .[11]

Natsuko had occult powers and thereafter she frustrated all Shizué's plans for regaining possession of her child. Curiously, she brought up Kimitaké as a little girl, not as a boy. He was always attended by a nursemaid, although this annoyed him greatly; he was not allowed to run about in the house, and he was forbidden to go out; and he must stay on the ground floor all the time, usually with his grandmother or the maid. He was not permitted to play as he wanted. 'Kimitaké liked to brandish rulers and other long things but Mother always confiscated these on the grounds that they were dangerous. Kimitaké would obey her meekly. I felt so sorry for him.'[12]

These restrictions were imposed for Natsuko's sake: 'Mother's

hip made her very nervous of sounds, especially when the pain
started. Toys like cars, guns which clicked mechanically, and so on,
were all banned.' But she reacted with hostility to any threat to her
control of the child: 'When it was bright outside, I would try to take
him out. But it was always in vain. Mother would wake up like
a bolt and forbid it. So Kimitaké was kept inside her dark, gloomy
room, full of sickness and ill health.'[13]

In February 1928, Mishima's mother had a second child, a girl
whom they named Mitsuko; Natsuko made no attempt to take over
the girl and it was nonsensical that one child should be confined
to the ground floor and the other to the second floor; that, however,
is what happened.

If Shizué had hopes of recovering Kimitaké, they were destroyed by
the onset of a grave illness. On New Year's Day 1929 the little boy
had a sudden collapse. According to his mother, 'Kimitaké became ill
with "auto-intoxication" [*jikachudoku*] . . . the illness was critical
and all our relatives gathered at the house. I put together his toys
and clothing, ready to go into the coffin. My brother, a doctor at
Chiba Medical University, came in at that moment; and he suddenly
exclaimed: "Look! He's urinating; maybe he'll be all right." And after
a while he urinated a lot more and my brother said: "He will live
now." '[14] 'Auto-intoxication' is not a Western medical term, only a
direct translation of *'jikachudoku'*. Kimitaké's symptoms and treatment were these: 'I vomited something the colour of coffee. The
family doctor was called. After examining me he said that he was not
sure I would recover. I was given injections of camphor and glucose
until I was like a pincushion. The pulses of both my wrist and my
upper arm became imperceptible.'[15] According to a Japanese pedia-
trician, Dr Kiyoshi Nakamura, 'the illness is usually found in children
who are sensitive, intelligent and over-protected, who have been
trained by their mothers to be "good" boys or girls.'[16] The cause of
Kimitaké's illness is unknown, but my guess is that Natsuko, who had
a violent temper, was responsible for the attacks which the child
suffered thereafter at regular intervals.

He grew into an uncommonly weak child, as one may see from a
photograph of him in the summer of 1929. Kimitaké has been taken
out for a rare treat, an outing to a park. He is seated on a donkey
and appears strangely absent and collapsed, like a balloon running out
of air; he lolls forward, dressed in a sailor suit, his chin on his chest.
The child looks as if he will topple off his perch any second.

3

Fairy Tales and Fantasies (1929–31)

Mishima described how his illness 'struck about once a month, now lightly, now seriously.'[17] There were many crises. 'By the sound of the disease's footsteps as it drew near I came to be able to sense whether an attack was likely to approach death or not.' Natsuko rarely allowed him out of the house; and his brief encounters with the world beyond the iron gates of the Hiraoka home assumed great importance. The tiny, pale boy was preternaturally sensitive and he endowed anyone he met, however briefly, with significance. 'My earliest memory, an unquestionable one, haunting me with a strangely vivid image, dates from about that time [when he was four]. . . . It was a young man who was coming down toward us, with handsome, ruddy cheeks and shining eyes, wearing a dirty roll of cloth around his head for a sweatband. He came down the slope carrying a yoke of night-soil buckets over one shoulder. . . . He was a night-soil man, a ladler of excrement. He was dressed as a labourer, wearing split-toed shoes with rubber soles and black canvas tops, and dark blue cotton trousers of the close-fitting kind called "thigh-pullers". . . . The close-fitting jeans plainly outlined the lower half of his body, which moved lithely and seemed to be walking directly toward me. An inexpressible adoration for those trousers was born in me. . . . His occupation gave me the feeling of "tragedy" in the most sensuous meaning of the word.'[18]

The tragedy was Kimitaké's. He was eternally excluded from the lives of ordinary men and women—for example, the drivers of *hanadensha* (trams decorated with flowers) and the ticket collectors with rows of gold buttons on their tunics, whom he saw on his rare excursions. His grief for the night-soil man was, in reality, profound concern about himself. 'The so-called "tragic things" of which I was becoming aware were probably only shadows cast by a flashing presentiment of grief still greater in the future, of a lonelier exclusion still to come.'[19] Later in life, Mishima was to struggle against his alienation; he would identify himself with ordinary Japanese men—taxi-drivers, bar-tenders and soldiers. But he could not escape his upbringing; as a Japanese proverb has it: 'A man's character is determined by the age of three.' Kimitaké was brought up with a false impression of Japanese society;

being much influenced by Natsuko's talk of her 'old family' and by the snobbishness of other members of the household, he did not know how egalitarian Japan was. He had a picture of Japanese society in which families such as the Matsudairas, from which Natsuko's mother was descended, and the Tokugawas, who had ruled Japan for 250 years, were pinnacles surrounding the Emperor, the highest being.

Another of Mishima's early memories was of a picture book: 'I had several picture books about that time, but my fancy was captured, completely and exclusively, only by this one—and only by one riveting picture in it.'[20] This was an illustration which he gazed upon for hours and which he felt he ought not to adore. 'The picture showed a knight mounted on a white horse, holding a sword aloft. . . . There was a beautiful coat of arms on the silver armour the knight was wearing. The knight's beautiful face peeped through the visor, and he brandished his drawn sword awesomely in the blue sky, confronting either Death or, at the very least, some hurtling object full of evil power. I believed he would be killed the next instant.'[21] The thought of the imminent death of the beautiful knight captivated the child. Great was the disillusionment of Kimitaké when the nursemaid told him the 'knight' was a woman—Joan of Arc. 'I felt as though I had been knocked flat. The person I had thought was a *he* was a *she*. If this beautiful knight was a woman and not a man, what was there left?'[22] He had to be a man or his death could not be moving; he quoted Oscar Wilde to make his point:

> Fair is the knight who lieth slain
> Amid the rush and reed . . .

Kimitaké was fascinated by death. 'Yet another memory: it is the odour of sweat, an odour that drove me onward, awakened my longings, overpowered me. . . . It was the troops passing our gate as they returned from drill. . . . The soldiers' odour of sweat—that odour like a sea breeze, like the air, burned to gold, above the seashore—struck my nostrils and intoxicated me.'[23] He was not at an age when the smell of sweat had a sexual quality. 'But it did gradually and tenaciously arouse within me a sensuous craving for such things as the destiny of soldiers, the tragic nature of their calling . . . the ways they would die . . .' Mishima attached great importance to his odd images that stood before him from the beginning 'in truly masterful completeness'. There was not a single thing lacking. 'In later years I sought in them for the wellsprings of my own feelings and action.'[24]

The beauty of the violent or excruciatingly painful death of a handsome youth was to be a theme of many of his novels, from *Chusei* ('The Middle Ages', 1946) to *Spring Snow* (1969). Mishima thought that the more violent, the more agonizing a death, the more beautiful it was; he made a cult of a Christian martyr, St Sebastian, and he invested the ancient *samurai* rite of disembowelment, *hara-kiri*, with supreme beauty. A plain youth, Isao, the protagonist of *Runaway Horses* (1969), qualified as a hero by committing *hara-kiri*.

As a child Mishima felt the desire to play-act. The period of childhood was for him 'a stage on which time and space become entangled . . . I could not believe that the world was any more complicated than a structure of building blocks, nor that the so-called "social community", which I must presently enter, could be more dazzling than the world of fairy tales. . . . Thus, without my being aware of it, one of the determinants of my life had come into operation. And because of my struggles against it, from the beginning my every fantasy was tinged with despair.'[25] He had a fantasy of 'Night' in which he saw 'a shining city floating upon the darkness that surrounded me. . . . I could plainly see a mystic brand that had been impressed upon the faces of the people in that city. . . . If I could but touch their faces, I might discover the colour of the pigments with which the city of night had painted them.'[26] Then a female magician, whom Kimitaké had seen on the stage, appeared before his eyes: 'Presently Night raised a curtain directly before my eyes, revealing the stage on which Shokyokusai Tenkatsu performed her magic feats.' He was fascinated by this woman who 'lounged indolently about the stage, her opulent body veiled in garments like those of the Great Harlot of the Apocalypse.'[27]

The little boy decided to dress up as Tenkatsu. 'From among my mother's kimonos I dragged out the most gorgeous one, the one with the strongest colours. For a sash I chose an *obi* on which scarlet roses were painted in oil, and wrapped it round and round my waist. . . . I stuck a hand mirror in my sash and powdered my face lightly.'[28] Thus attired, the child rushed into his grandmother's sickroom; she was receiving a visitor and his mother was also there. Running about the room he shouted at the top of his voice: 'I'm Tenkatsu!' Mishima said: 'My frenzy was focused upon the consciousness that, through my impersonation, Tenkatsu was being revealed to many eyes. In short, I could see nothing but myself.' For a moment the child's eyes met those of his mother; she had lowered her head and was pale. Tears blurred the little boy's eyes. 'Was the moment teaching me how grotesque my isolation would appear to the eyes of love, and at the same time was I learning, conversely, my own incapacity for accepting love?'[29] Kimitaké's passion for dressing up continued until he was about nine. Once, with his younger brother and sister as accomplices (Chiyuki, the younger brother, was born in 1930), he dressed up as Cleopatra; he had seen the Queen of Egypt on the stage, making her entry into Rome, 'her half-naked, amber-coloured body coming into view from beneath a Persian rug.'

Kimitaké learned to read when he was five. He read every fairy story he could lay his hands on, but he 'never liked the princesses'. He was fond only of the princes. 'I was all the fonder of princes murdered or princes fated for death. I was completely in love with any youth who was killed.'[30] He read works by Japanese authors such as Mimei Ogawa, and also the tales of Hans Christian Andersen. 'Only his "Rose-Elf" threw deep shadows over my heart, only that beautiful youth who, while kissing the rose given him as a token by his sweetheart, was stabbed to death and decapitated by a villain with a big knife. . . . My heart's leaning toward Death and Night and Blood would not be denied.'[31] He was also fascinated by a Hungarian fairy tale in which a prince, clad in tights and a rose-coloured tunic, is torn to pieces by a dragon, miraculously revived, 'caught by a great spider and, after his body has been shot full of poison, eaten ravenously'; the prince was once more brought back from the dead only to be 'flung bodily into a pit completely lined with there is no saying how many great knives.' Kimitaké also imagined himself dying in battle—here were shades of the fantasy which led him to his own death—or being murdered. 'And yet I had an abnormally strong fear of death. . . . One day I would bully a maid to tears, and the next morning I would see her serving breakfast with a cheerfully smiling face. . . . Then I would read all manner of evil meanings into her smiles. . . . I was sure she was plotting to poison me out of revenge. Waves of fear billowed up in my breast. I was positive the poison had been put in my bowl of broth.'[32]

All his life, Mishima was worried about being poisoned. A friend who was with him in Bangkok in 1967 told me that he was forever on the look-out for danger. 'He would never eat anything more than an ome-lette in the local restaurants. No Thai food. And he brushed his teeth with soda-water in the hotel. Vigorously.' His grandmother, who put him on a strict diet after his illness, may have created his phobia about poisoning: 'Of fish, I was allowed only such white-flesh kinds as hali-but, turbot or red snapper; of potatoes, only those mashed and strained through a colander; of sweets, all bean-jams were forbidden and there were only light biscuits, wafers and other such dry confections; and of fruit, only apples cut in thin slices, or small portions of mandarin oranges.'³³ His mother, Shizué, has described Natsuko's strict rules:

> When he was about five or six, I was allowed to take him out of doors, but only if there was no wind. This was a concession won by my husband, who had great arguments with her about the matter on a number of occasions.
> Mother arranged for a group of three girls to come to the house to play with Kimitaké. They were ushered into her room and were allowed to play only such games as *mamagoto* ['houses'], *origami* [folding paper] and *tsumiki* [bricks].
> I almost gave up everything in the end and would read to him and draw pictures. That is how he became interested in drawing . . . and he started to write, too, at the age of five, much to our surprise.³⁴

Mishima says in *Confessions of a Mask* that 'the slightest noise affected my grandmother's neuralgia—the violent opening or closing of a door, a toy bugle, wrestling, or any conspicuous sound or vibration whatever—and our playing had to be quieter than is usual even among girls.'³⁵ No wonder Kimitaké took refuge in his fairy tales and preferred to be by himself reading a book, or playing with his building blocks or 'indulging in my wilful fancies or drawing pictures.' Shizué thought him a little odd: 'We brought him a small record-player and he put on the same tune over and over again for two hours.' Natsuko must have been out on the day the child received the record-player; she would never have tolerated the noise. Kimitaké had learned by this time to obey her in every detail. A photograph taken in the summer of 1930, when he was five, shows the boy standing with a small cart while Natsuko looms above him, her hand on his shoulder. The grandmother has a sombre expression, no doubt her illness was severe; she has a strong jaw and powerful eyes—it is a frightening face. But little Kimitaké stands there grinning, his eyes sparkling, seemingly at ease with her. His sister and brother were not given over to his grandmother's care and were reared with the freedom befitting children. 'And yet I did not greatly envy them their liberty and rowdiness.'

In the early spring of 1931, when the boy was six and was about to start school, he went on a visit to his cousins' house. They were two little girls and Natsuko allowed him to play freely with them. 'I had many times more freedom at the house of Sugiko [his cousin] than at my own. As the imaginary enemies who must want to steal me away—

my parents, in short—were not present, my grandmother had no qualms about giving me more liberty.'[36] It was a difficult experience. 'Like an invalid taking his first steps during convalescence, I had a feeling of stiffness as though I were acting under the compulsion of some imaginary obligation. I missed my bed of idleness. And in this house it was tacitly required that I act like a boy. The reluctant masquerade had begun.'[37] Kimitaké proposed that he and his cousins play war, and the trio ran about the garden shouting, 'Bang-bang,' until he escaped into the house and collapsed on the floor. 'I was enraptured with the vision of my own form lying there, twisted and fallen. There was an unspeakable delight in having been shot and being on the point of death. It seemed to me that since it was I, even if actually struck by a bullet, there would surely be no pain.'[38]

Mishima's comment on this scene is a reflection of his entire life and on his death. 'What people regarded as a pose on my part was actually an expression of my need to assert my own true nature and . . . it was precisely what people regarded as my true self which was a masquerade. It was this unwilling masquerade that made me say: "Let's play war." '[39]

4

School and Adolescence (1931–9)

The 1930s was a decade of violence in public affairs in Japan, but the Hiraokas were little affected by the events of these years. Kimitaké's father continued in his ministry post and received a promotion; and the boy knew little of the upheavals which took place in Tokyo. One morning in 1936, when he was on his way to school, he heard bugles in the far distance—the start of the *Ni Ni Roku* Incident, the greatest of the numerous *coups* that shook Japan in the 1930s. The boy remembered that there was snow on the ground—it was in February; and later in life Mishima associated snowy streets with revolution. The Hiraokas, however, were secure in their upper-middle-class existence; life went on as before.

Kimitaké began school in April 1931, when he entered the *Gaku-shuin* (Peers' School). He was still under the control of his grandmother; Natsuko showed no inclination to surrender him to his mother. According to Shizué: 'After Kimitaké had entered elementary school, I was allowed to take him there myself every day. I was so happy to be with him, picking up acorns in the park and singing songs with him in the park at Yotsuya.'[40] She bought him ice cream, to which he was partial; and she induced him to go to the dentist, by offering him ice cream before each visit. Natsuko set the daily programme of her grandson; when he came back from school with his mother he had to have his *osanji* [three o'clock tea] with Natsuko, and he must then do his homework by her bedside. She was particular about being given priority over his mother. 'If he called out to me *"Okasama"* [Mother] before speaking to her first, addressing her as *"Obasama"* [Grandmother], she would be most unpleasant. At other times she would criticize both of us if he showed an inclination to do something with me.'

The *Gakushuin*, a school for the children of the rich and the aristocracy–it was also attended by members of the Imperial family–had a liberal tradition. There was swimming at the beach in the summer, a luxury by the austere standards of pre-war schools. But Natsuko would not allow the boy to go on these excursions; he expressed his disappointment in a composition he wrote in 1932:

Enoshima Excursion

I did not go on the school outing.
When I woke up that day I thought: 'Now everyone must be at Shinjuku Station, on the train.'
I easily think of things like that.
I went to my grandmother and my mother. I wanted so much to go. Just at that moment they would all have arrived at Enoshima.
I wanted to go so much because I had never been there.
I was thinking of it from morning until evening.
When I went to bed I had a dream.
I *did* go to Enoshima with everyone else, and I played there very happily. But I could not walk at all. There were rocks.
Then I woke up.[41]

According to his mother, his first school excursion was to Kashima Shrine. 'He was so happy that time. He sent a card to Mother, but he rarely sent cards to me.' All his life Mishima was to take delight in going to places that he had never visited before; he loved to go to newly-opened restaurants, to climb to the top of new skyscrapers in Tokyo–if possible, before anyone else he knew. His child-like enthusiasm, suppressed when he was a child, burst out in later years. When teased about this, he would become angry. 'Oh, don't say that,' he would say and turn away.

Life at home was often difficult. The boy, as told in Mishima's auto-

biographical short story 'Isu' ('Chair', 1952), which describes the unhappy home life of a nine-year-old, would run crying to his mother
when scolded by his severe grandmother. Ruthless scolding terrified
and depressed him; but his grandmother would not let him stay with
his parents and would insist that he return to her sickroom. Shizué
could hardly bear the situation; on the morning of one such day she
drew up her chair to a window on the second floor of the house and
looked down at the sickroom where she knew her son must be sitting
obediently beside his grandmother's bed. 'I saw his small head for a
moment while he was waiting for his grandmother and her nurse
to return from the lavatory.' The boy's attitude was a little different
from his mother's: her sympathy for him (how he must long to run
about and be active like other children) was mistaken in some ways; he
liked being with his ill grandmother, who loved him so desperately.
He had many of the instincts of a child, 'but something within me
responded to the darkened room and the sickbed—even now I work at
my desk all night long and wake up around noon.' As Mishima has it,
while his mother was looking down at him and the nurse from the
floor above, he was not sad; in fact, he was content. Only sometimes he
felt a sudden hatred of the nurse, who 'would play obscene jokes on
me' (he does not say what these were); it frightened him that his
mother might see. 'It is hard for me to account for my hatred, for we
usually want those close to us to know our pains and sorrows. I tried
to hide the pleasure which I took in my pain.'[42]

Shizué resolved to take her son back from his grandmother, who was
increasingly bedridden; and one day she asked a manservant to smuggle
the boy out of Natsuko's room while she was sleeping. It was late
December 1934 and there was a cold wind; these were conditions under which the boy was not supposed to go outside, as he was
still frail. Shizué took him to a photographer's studio to have his picture
taken. 'Afterwards her hands were clammy with sweat and she spoke
in an unusually pathetic voice. It seemed that she had made a plan to
do something and then changed her mind on the way home.' A picture
taken of the boy at nine shows a little fellow with a shaven head and
the look of a wizened old man, preternaturally aged; he has a sweet,
sad expression.

The following year, the Hiraokas moved house. The family split up.
Kimitaké went with his grandparents to one home, and the rest of the
family moved into a separate residence a few streets away. The practice
in Japan is for parents to move out of their children's homes at a

C

certain age; Jotaro and Natsuko were following this tradition, known as *inkyo*. The time was approaching, however, when Natsuko's health would no longer permit her to care for the boy. Two years later, in March 1937, when he completed elementary school at the *Gakushuin*, he rejoined his parents. They had moved to another house closer to the middle school of the *Gakushuin*, which is in a different part of Tokyo from the elementary school. Natsuko fought to the last. 'Day and night my grandmother clasped my photograph to her bosom, weeping, and was instantly seized with a paroxysm if I violated the treaty stipulation that I should come to spend one night each week with her. At the age of twelve I had a true-love sweetheart aged sixty.'[43]

After moving away from his grandmother, the boy honoured the arrangement that he come and stay with her once a week; he was also taken on outings by her. Natsuko invited him to accompany her to the theatre, and for the first time he went to the *Kabuki*, where he saw *Chushingura*, the story of the 'Forty-Seven *Ronin*' who committed *hara-kiri* in 1704. They also went to the *No*. Kimitaké had an instinct for the theatre which his family had encouraged, but until this time Natsuko had refused him permission to go to the *Kabuki* or to the *No*, on the grounds that they were unsuitable for a young boy; the scenes of blood-letting in the *Kabuki* may have been what she had in mind. These visits to the theatre taxed Natsuko's strength; she was in her early sixties and years of illness had taken their toll. Gradually her health declined and Kimitaké's visits to her home became less frequent. In the autumn of 1938, her condition became serious, and she died early in the following year at the age of sixty-four.

Her influence on her grandson had been great. She had brought him up like a little Japanese girl but she had also taught him to be proud, instilling in him the *samurai* spirit of her ancestors. One of her sayings was: 'You must be as haughty as you can be.' Mishima showed her influence in his formal manner. Even later in life he found it hard to unbend; he taught himself to smoke and trained himself to drink but he did not greatly enjoy tobacco and alcohol, which perhaps reflected Natsuko's wish to see him a paragon. But her enormously strong personality also repressed him; even as a successful adult Mishima was vulnerable and sensitive behind his *samurai* mask. He was easily injured and easily influenced by others, and although apparently unable to love, he demanded love from other people; yet, when there was a response, he sheered away.

His grandmother shaped a dual personality. One Mishima had a strong character, with a capacity for making decisions; he directed his body like a machine, made plans for it, sought sexual gratification and achievements in the world. The other Mishima was in retreat from life. I knew a little of both sides of him, but nearly always it was the strong Mishima that one saw, not the shy, retreating child. On the last day of his life, he cast himself in the role of the strong *samurai*-like figure, but of course there was another side to his personality, or he would not have written *Confessions of a Mask*, a work which reveals weakness, a morbid imagination, and a decadent sense of beauty in which eroticism and 'blood' are joined.

Mishima's account of his aesthetic has a quality of desperate humour. He suffered in his adolescence from 'the anguish of a child provided with a curious toy.' At the age of twelve or thirteen he began to have erections, and Kimitaké's 'toy increased in volume at every opportunity and hinted that, rightly used, it would be quite a delightful thing.' He was excited by muscular men, by the sight of swimming teams at Meiji pool, and by 'the swarthy young man a cousin of mine married.' One is reminded of his summary of his aesthetic, 'Death and Night and Blood', by many later passages in *Confessions of a Mask*, such as the series of images which excited his adolescent imagination : 'Gory duelling scenes . . . pictures of young *samurai* cutting open their bellies, or of soldiers struck by bullets, clenching their teeth and dripping blood . . . photographs of hard-muscled *sumo* wrestlers of the third rank, and not yet grown too fat.'[44]

Kimitaké turned his talent for drawing to strange ends when he was alone at home: 'When the composition of a picture in an adventure-story magazine was defective, I would first copy it with crayons and then correct it. . . . Then it would become the picture of a young circus performer dropping to his knees and clutching at a bullet wound in his breast; or a tight-rope walker who had fallen and split his skull open and now lay dying, half his face covered with blood.'[45] The boy hid these illustrations in a drawer at home, but sometimes, as he sat in class at the *Gakushuin*, he had the horrifying idea that someone in the house might discover them; this blotted out all thought of school-work.

Kimitaké moved back into his mother's house at a delicate stage in his life. A family friend, who has known the Hiraokas for thirty years, described to me the effect upon the boy of being handed over to his mother at the very moment that his adolescence was beginning: 'When Mishima started to live with his mother he fell in love with the poor, beautiful woman who had been so cruelly treated by her awful mother-in-law. As they had been separated for such a long time the reunion between mother and son was scarcely normal. Mishima was at a most sensitive age, the start of his adolescence.' Later in life, Shizué would refer to her son as her 'lover'. (After his suicide she said, 'My lover has returned to me.') Kimitaké reciprocated her feelings; he loved her deeply and probably never had a really close relationship with any other person. His mother, he said, 'protected me ever since I was a child,' taking his manuscripts to established writers and giving him secret encouragement to pursue his writing. She hid her actions from her husband, as Azusa wanted his sons to follow the family tradition of government service and thoroughly disapproved of literature as a career for the boy. Shizué, the protector, aroused these feelings in her son: 'My mother has been very good-looking since her youth. It may sound odd if I say so, but I was proud of her youth and beauty. I felt superior to others, when I compared my mother to those of my friends.'[46]

After his death, Shizué wrote these impressions of her son's relationship with her after World War II:

> If ever I was in bed with flu or something, Kimitaké really worried about me, as if I were on the point of dying. He brought *hanebuton* [feather cushions] and ordered dishes from Hamasaku and Fuku-daya [the best restaurants in Tokyo], proposed that I should have a Western-style lavatory or wanted to buy a new air-conditioner instead of the noisy one we had. While he was still single, he would sit by my bedside, working at his papers and taking care of me.
>
> Whenever flowers were sent to him, he would have the maid bring them over to me [from his house next-door]. One day he admired one of my flower arrangements greatly; it was 'Seven Flowers of Autumn'.
>
> If he went on a trip he would never fail to bring back *omiyage* [presents] for the family and for the maids. When he was travelling in Japan he would phone from wherever he was, on arrival, chat about the trip and say exactly when he was coming back.
>
> Once he proposed that we should go to Nara for the *Saegusa Matsuri* [a festival] saying that there would be masses of *sasayuri* [lily decorations]. [I could not go and] I was delighted when he brought back a single, thin, pink lily all the way from Nara, carrying it himself although he had masses of luggage that day.
>
> Kimitaké invited me to plays, foreign operas, interesting exhibitions and so on, every month, and also to new restaurants. I saw all these places thanks to him.[47]

His mother was the first person to see his writing, which appeared regularly in the school magazine, *Hojinkai Zasshi*, after the boy had entered the middle school in 1937. He got on there much better than he had in the junior school, where his teachers had regarded his compositions as adventurous (he used rare characters and unusual constructions); and as his health improved steadily, his academic results got better. He was no longer an absentee at the *Gakushuin*.

His father, however, resisted Kimitaké's literary ambitions and thus came in conflict with the boy's mother. Azusa's ministry had sent him to Osaka for two years, where he lived apart from his family, and on his return to Tokyo in 1939 he was disturbed to find how quickly his elder son's interest in writing had developed. On one occasion Azusa stormed into Kimitaké's room and seized the manuscript he was working on, tearing it into pieces, which he scattered about the room. The boy wept and his mother comforted him with tea; thereafter Kimitaké hid his stories so that his father would not find them.

Shizué was literally her son's 'protector'; it was not just a matter of encouraging him to write. Her own interest in literature stemmed from her scholarly family. She did not write herself but would have liked to, and Kimitaké was her proxy. Shizué did not have the pronounced character and definite literary taste of her mother-in-law (Natsuko had had a high regard for the ghostly, mysterious tales of Kyoka Izumi, a turn-of-the-century writer), but she was far more attuned to literature and the arts than was her husband. Azusa still wanted his son, who showed intellectual promise, to make a career in government. He could not imagine that anyone could make a living by literature, and in fact before World War II this *was* virtually impossible; writers needed patrons. Relations between father and son were never close, yet Azusa had an influence on the boy and exerted a steady pressure on him in his teens. As the oldest, and most gifted child, Kimitaké was intended by his father to take the lead in the family; the other two children—Mitsuko, a strong, cheerful, unimaginative tomboy of a girl, and Chiyuki, a quiet, gentle boy—were supposed to follow. Such is the role of the elder son in a traditional Japanese family.

One may only conjecture what would have been the reaction of his father had he known the thoughts and adolescent dreams of his oldest boy—who was to all appearances a normal, even exemplary, child. Ironically, Azusa played a part in Kimitaké's discovery of an image that haunted him all his life, St Sebastian on the tree of martyrdom. 'One day, taking advantage of having been kept from school by a slight cold, I got out some volumes of art reproductions, which my father had brought back as souvenirs of his foreign travels. [Azusa had been to Europe, to represent his ministry on fishery problems; and, like most educated middle-class Japanese, he was a sampler of Western culture.] . . . Suddenly there came into view from one corner of the next page a picture that I had to believe had been lying in wait there, for my sake.'[48] It was a reproduction of a late Renaissance work, Guido Reni's 'St Sebastian'.

Mishima described the painting in *Confessions of a Mask*: 'A remarkably handsome youth was bound naked to the trunk of a tree. His crossed hands were raised high, and the thongs binding his wrists were tied to the tree. No other bonds were visible, and the only covering for the youth's nakedness was a coarse white cloth knotted loosely about his loins. . . . Were it not for the arrows with their shafts deeply sunk into his left armpit and right side, he would seem more a Roman athlete resting from fatigue. . . . The arrows have eaten into the tense, fragrant, youthful flesh, and are about to consume his body from within with flames of supreme agony and ecstasy.'[49] The boy's hands embarked on a motion of which he had no experience; he played with his 'toy'. 'Suddenly it burst forth, bringing with it a blinding intoxication. . . . Some time passed, and then, with miserable feelings I looked around the desk I was facing. . . . There were cloud-white splashes about. . . . Some objects were dripping lazily, leadenly, and others gleamed dully, like the eyes of a dead fish. Fortunately, a reflex motion of my hand to protect the picture had saved the book from being soiled.'[50] This was the first occasion on which Kimitaké had an ejaculation. How deep an impression the image of St Sebastian made on him! Twenty-five years later, Mishima posed for a photographer as St Sebastian: he had 'a coarse white cloth knotted loosely about his loins' and three arrows planted in his suntanned torso, one of which was embedded in his armpit.

Mishima described his 'first love' at the *Gakushuin*. It was an older boy, 'Omi'[51]; as *Confessions of a Mask* has it, 'he surpassed us all in physique, and in the contours of his face could be seen signs of some privileged youthfulness excelling ours by far. He had an innate and lofty manner of gratuitous scorn.' Omi, according to a school rumour had 'a big thing'; Kimitaké duly reflected on this report: 'It was like fertilizer poured over a poisonous weed of an idea deeply planted in me.' The boy, who was fourteen, looked forward impatiently to summer: 'Surely, I thought, summer will bring with it an opportunity to see his naked body. Also, I cherished deeply within me a still more shamefaced desire. This was to see that "big thing" of his.'[52] He could not be the only admirer of Omi's person; the older boy filled his school uniform, a 'pretentious' copy of a naval officer's uniform, 'with a sensation of solid weight and a sort of sexuality.' And 'surely I was not the only one who looked with envious and loving eyes at the muscles of his shoulders and chest. . . . Because of him I began to love strength, an impression of over-flowing blood, ignorance, rough gestures, careless speech, and the savage melancholy inherent in flesh not tainted in any way with intellect.'[53] He worshipped all 'those possessors of sheer animal flesh unspoiled by intellect–young toughs, sailors, soldiers, fishermen'–but he was doomed to 'watching them from afar with impassioned indifference.'

One encounter with Omi led to Kimitaké's discovery of a fetish: white gloves. It was the custom at the *Gakushuin* to wear white gloves on ceremonial days. 'Just to pull on a pair of white gloves, with mother-of-pearl buttons shining gloomily at the wrists and three meditative rows of stitching on the backs, was enough to evoke the symbols of all ceremonial days . . . the cloudless skies under which such days always seem to make brilliant sounds in midcourse and then collapse.'[54] In the grounds of the *Gakushuin* stood a swinging-log and the boys often had fights for possession of the log. One day Omi stood on the log waiting for someone to challenge him; he seemed 'like a murderer at bay' to Kimitaké, rocking back and forth and wearing his white gloves. The boy was drawn towards the log: 'Two contrary forces were pulling at me, contending for supremacy. One was the instinct of self-preservation. The second force–which was bent, even more profoundly, more intensely, upon the complete disintegration of my inner balance–was a compulsion toward suicide, that subtle and secret impulse.'[55] He darted forward and attacked and the two boys struggled, white-gloved hands interlocked, and crashed to the ground together; during that brief struggle they exchanged a single look and Kimitaké felt that Omi had surely understood that he loved him. The two boys sat close together in the school ceremony that followed and time after time Kimitaké looked across at Omi, his eyes resting on the stains on his gloves; both boys had dirtied their white gloves on the ground. Kimitaké, however, after a short time, looked forward to the ending of this Platonic affair; he even felt an intense pleasure deriving from the foreknowledge that his love would be shortlived.

The end came in the late spring (of 1939). There was a gymnastics

class outside, from which Kimitaké was excused because of ill-health—
he had had a touch of tuberculosis and had a continual cough. The
boy went out to watch the class, at which Omi, a favourite of the gym
instructor, was the star. He was called upon to show the class how to
swing on a horizontal bar; the day was warm and Omi wore only
a light undershirt. Kimitaké reflected that his strong arms were 'certainly worthy of being tattooed with anchors.' A surge shot through
Omi's body and in a moment he was suspended from the bar, on which
he did a series of pull-ups. There were admiring exclamations from the
class and from Kimitaké, who had observed with astonishment that
Omi had a plentiful growth of hair under his arms: 'This was probably
the first time that we had seen such an opulence of hair; it seemed
almost prodigal, like some luxuriant growth of troublesome summer
weeds. . . . Life-force . . . it was the sheer extravagant abundance of
life-force that overpowered the boys. . . . Without his being aware of it
some force had stolen into Omi's flesh and was scheming to take
possession of him, to crash through him, to spill out of him, to out-
shine him.'[56]

Kimitaké, sensing the reaction of the other boys, was filled with
consuming jealousy; he told himself that he was no longer in love
with Omi. The boy then felt the need for a Spartan course of self-
discipline and became obsessed with a single motto: 'Be strong!'
Riding to school by tram in the morning, he fixed other passengers
with his gaze and stared them down, to prove his 'strength'. And
yet the spectacle of Omi on the bar had made a deep impression
on him; the sight of armpit hair became erotic and when he took
a bath, Kimitaké would look for a long time in the mirror, survey-
ing his scrawny shoulders and narrow chest and willing that one
day he too would have luxuriant armpits. He was still small and
undeveloped, weighing less than seven stone at the age of fourteen.
But slowly his armpits budded, 'becoming darker and darker,' and
they soon became bushy enough to serve as an erotic image for the
boy; when he indulged in his 'bad habit' (masturbation) he would gaze
fixedly on that portion of his anatomy.

Toshitami Bojo, a senior student at the *Gakushuin* when Kimitaké
arrived in middle school, remembered him as 'a rather puny, pale
boy. He already had his famous laugh. He read the classics and we
were struck by his ability. Despite the difference of eight years in
our ages Mishima could follow everything that I said, and would
point out weaknesses in my remarks. In a sense he has been ageless

since then.'[57] Bojo was a member of the *Bungei-bu*, a literary circle
at the school, and he became acquainted with Kimitaké when the boy
submitted his first pieces to the school magazine, which the *Bungei-
bu* controlled. Kimitaké's poems and short compositions won the
admiration of his seniors in the *Bungei-bu* and he sought out their
company. He was a snob and befriended boys from good families:
Bojo, whose ancestors had served at the Imperial Court for genera-
tions; Takashi Azuma, who was his closest friend at the school; and
Yoshiyasu Tokugawa, a descendant of the family which had ruled
Japan between 1603 and 1868, which is known as the Tokugawa
Era in Japanese history. Academic brilliance–his marks had continued
to improve greatly since he left the junior school–and precocious
literary ability enabled Kimitaké to stand almost on an equal foot-
ing with these older boys, who published his work in every issue of
Hojinkai Zasshi, their magazine.

One can see in these writings–in the short story 'Sukanpo' ('Sorrel',
1938), for instance–the characteristics of Mishima's mature work:
irony and elegance; alienation from the working class and preoccupation with the upper classes; and an insane delight in cruelty.
Bojo was right when he said : 'In a sense he has been ageless since
then'; his tastes changed little after his early teens. The white gloves
which he wore on the last day of his life, and which became slightly
soiled with blood during the battle in General Mashita's office (one
can see it in the photographs of Mishima speaking from the balcony on that day), were like those he and Omi wore the day of their
fight on the swinging-log.

The descriptions of Omi in *Confessions of a Mask* remind me of
Masakatsu Morita, the student leader of the *Tatenokai*. 'Something
about his face,' wrote Mishima of Omi, 'gave one the sensation of
abundant blood coursing richly throughout his body; it was a round
face, with haughty cheek-bones rising from swarthy cheeks, lips that
seemed to have been sewn into a fine line, sturdy jaws, and a broad
but well-shaped and not too prominent nose.'[58] The fate suffered
by Omi in the book is not so different from that of Morita; he was
made a human sacrifice, according to Kimitaké's fantasy. 'Omi . . .
had been betrayed and then executed in secret. One evening he had
been stripped naked and taken to the grove on the hill. . . . The
first arrow had pierced the side of his chest; the second, his armpit.'[59] The deaths of Omi (in the style of St Sebastian) and Morita
both offered the spectacle of blood pouring forth, and so did the

hara-kiri of Mishima. Blood gave him a sexual thrill–this was one of his most important 'confessions' and the core of his aesthetic. The beauty of the spilt blood of the *samurai* has been endlessly poeticized by the Japanese, who liken the short-lived blossom of the cherry tree to the life of the *samurai*. Mishima, however, romanticized death and blood in a manner foreign to the Japanese classical tradition.

The young Mishima's taste for the decadent is evident from his work 'Yakata' ('Mansion', 1939). In this story, almost the only one he left uncompleted during his life, he describes, in the setting of medieval Japan, a struggle for power between a satanic aristocrat, whose sole pleasure is murder, and his wife, who represents God. In 'Yakata', Kimitaké attempted to develop his idea of a 'murder theatre', a fantasy that he subsequently described in *Confessions of a Mask*: 'There in my murder theatre, young Roman gladiators offered up their lives for my amusement; and all the deaths that took place there not only had to overflow with blood but also had to be performed with all due ceremony. I delighted in all forms of capital punishment and all implements of execution. But I would allow no torture device nor gallows, as they would not have provided a spectacle of outpouring blood. Nor did I like explosive weapons such as pistols or guns. So far as possible I chose primitive and savage weapons–arrows, daggers, spears. And in order to prolong the agony, it was the belly that must be aimed at.'[60]

In Mishima's aesthetic, blood was ultimately erotic. His imagination was aroused by images of blood and death: 'The weapon of my imagination slaughtered many a Grecian soldier, many white slaves of Arabia, princes of savage tribes, hotel elevator boys, waiters, young toughs, army officers, circus roustabouts. . . . I would kiss the lips of those who had fallen to the ground and were still moving spasmodically.'[61] He contrived a special machine for executing his victims: 'A thick board studded with rows of upright daggers, arranged in the shape of a human figure, which would come sliding down a rail upon a cross of execution.' He also had a fantasy of cannibalism; his most terrible dream was of the sacrifice of a boy–he chose an athletic contemporary from the *Gakushuin*–who was stunned, stripped and pinned naked on a vast plate, on which he was carried into a banqueting room. There, Kimitaké began the feast: ' "This is probably a good spot to begin on." I thrust the fork upright into the heart. A fountain of blood struck me full in the face. Holding the knife in my right hand, I began carving the flesh of the breast, gently, thinly, at first. . . .'[62]

This aesthetic owed as much to the West as to classical tradition in Japan–perhaps much more. In *Confessions of a Mask* Mishima says that he took his idea of the 'murder theatre' from the descriptions of the Colosseum in *Quo Vadis*. Mishima sought to incarnate a similar vision and found himself on a path that could lead only to death: to save himself he would have to abandon his romantic notion of beauty.

III

Kimitaké and the War (1940-49)

> I shuddered with a strange delight at
> the thought of my own death. I felt as
> if I owned the whole world.
> YUKIO MISHIMA, *Confessions of a Mask.*

1

Kimitaké's main interests at fifteen were schoolwork and literature.
He was still very much a 'puny, pale' boy, as Bojo had described him
at thirteen, and he suffered from anaemia—an illness which he privately
attributed to his 'bad habit'; but his health had improved immeasur-
ably since his days in the junior school, and his concentration was
good. He was almost at the top of his class of sixty boys, and he was
proficient in all subjects. But he stayed apart from his contemporaries; they had little to offer him, for his precocious intelligence put
him in a different class from them. And his parents, who, pleading
his ill health, insisted that he not spend the regulation two years
boarding at the *Gakushuin* dormitory, encouraged his tendency to
remain apart. Just as he had done when he first entered middle school,
he sought the company of older boys and teachers. Takashi Azuma,
who was three years older, was already a close friend, and Fumio
Shimizu, his *kokugo* (Japanese) teacher, encouraged him in both
schoolwork and composition. Shimizu, who had come to the *Gakushuin* from Seijo Gakuen School in 1938, was his best teacher, and
the boy visited him at lunch-time and in the evenings when he had
free time.

The boy's taste in literature had developed. He was reading the
work of Junichiro Tanizaki, a leading Japanese novelist, and Rainer
Maria Rilke, Raymond Radiguet and Oscar Wilde. He hoped one day
to emulate Radiguet, and Wilde's decadence—the play *Salome* was a
favourite of his—intrigued him. Kimitaké's aesthetic—the beauty of
death (the handsome youth who dies at his physical prime, as did Radi-

guet at twenty) and the beauty of blood (the severed head of St John the Baptist, kissed by Salome)—was firmly established. And in the angels of Rainer Maria Rilke he found his 'night'. His 'heart's leaning toward Death and Night and Blood' would not be denied.

His literary taste was extraordinary for a boy in Japan at that time; but then he was an exceptional schoolboy at an untypical school. No one at the *Gakushuin* forbade him to read Wilde or Radiguet because they were authors of inferior races (the official creed at that time was that the Japanese were inherently superior to all other peoples and were destined to rule them). Tanizaki, of whom the militarists disapproved because he was interested in 'bourgeois' life, was not criticized at the *Gakushuin*. Kimitaké also took instruction outside the school. His mother had obtained an introduction for him to a renowned romantic poet, Ryuko Kawaji, and the boy called on him regularly to show him his compositions; he was still writing mostly poetry. He liked working with Kawaji, for, as he mentions in his book *Shi wo Kaku Shonen* ('The Boy Who Wrote Poetry', 1956), 'I had feelings of rapture, of rich loneliness, of pure intoxication and of the fraternity of the external and inner worlds.'[1] Most of his poems were cheerful little works in which the boy celebrated his enjoyment of a sensuous world of imagination. An exception was *Magagoto* ('Evil Things'), an evocation of 'night':

> Standing by my window
> I waited each evening
> For strange events.
> I watched for evil omens
> A sandstorm surging across the street
> A rainbow at night.[2]

After his death, a critic, Jun Eto, maintained that this nihilistic work 'held the clue to all Mishima's literature.'

Kimitaké, it seems, remained passively homosexual. He had admired Omi from afar, and as he did not board at the school, his opportunities were much more limited than those of other boys. There was a good deal of adolescent homosexuality at the *Gakushuin*, as at any boys' boarding school; but the main interest was heterosexuality, as Mishima made clear in *Confessions of a Mask*: 'The period called adolescence—I had my full share of it so far as burning curiosity was concerned—seemed to have come to pay us a sick visit. Having attained puberty, the boys seemed to do nothing but always think immoderately about women, exude pimples, and write sugary verses out of heads that were in a constant dizzy reel.'[3] He realized that he was different from other boys; they seemed to derive unusual excitement from the mere word 'woman'. 'I, on the other hand, received no more sensual impression from "woman" than from "pencil".'[4] But he did not appreciate *how* different he was: 'In short, I knew absolutely nothing about other boys. I did not know that each night all boys but me had dreams in which women–women barely glimpsed yesterday on a street corner–were stripped of their clothing and set one by one parading before the dreamers' eyes. I did not know that in the boys' dreams the breasts of a woman would float up like beautiful jelly-fish rising from the sea of night.'[5] Kimitaké was uneasy about his own sexual feelings. He became 'obsessed with the idea of the kiss',[6] and to delude himself that this desire was animal passion, he had to undertake an elaborate disguise of his true self. An unconscious feeling of guilt stubbornly insisted that he play 'a conscious and false role'.

Schoolwork, literature and adolescent passions–he maintained an emotional correspondence with Azuma–preoccupied Kimitaké at fifteen. Internationally, the world situation was rapidly deteriorating; Japan was moving swiftly towards war with Britain and America. In July 1940, numerous British residents in Japan were imprisoned as 'spies', and in the autumn Japan entered into the Tripartite Pact with Germany and Italy. This was followed by a neutrality treaty with Russia, which was concluded in April 1941. There had been two conflicting views in the Japanese military establishment during the 1930s. One side believed that the main threat to Japan was from the Soviet Union, and they advocated a strike north; but they had been virtually eliminated after the *Ni Ni Roku* Incident of February 1936. Their opponents, who favoured a strike south against Britain, Holland and France, gained control of the government. After the success of Nazi Germany in 1940, the strike-south party found events playing into their hands; their strategy seemed correct. America, however, was a problem. To inflict a military defeat on the United States was impossible. The Japanese hoped that the Roosevelt Administration would settle for a stalemate in the Pacific, that Britain would be crushed by Hitler, and Japanese forces would penetrate as far as Australia and India to complete the destruction of the British Empire. With this aim in mind, the armed forces, which had dominated all governments after 1930, planned to deliver an initial crushing blow against the US Navy by making a surprise attack on Pearl Harbor.

The enemy was to be put off-guard by diplomatic negotiations right up to the eve of the attack. Following the appointment in October 1941 of General Tojo as Prime Minister, Home Minister, and Defence Minister, the stage was set for war.

At this moment Kimitaké, aged sixteen, was publishing his first work, *Hanazakari no Mori* ('The Forest in Full Bloom'), in instalments in a literary magazine, *Bungei Bunka*, which his teacher, Shimizu, helped to edit. *Hanazakari no Mori* was the first flowering of Kimitaké's talent: he displayed a gift for language—he wrote a rich, romantic Japanese—which astounded his elders. Zenmei Hasuda, a schoolteacher friend of Shimizu, commented in the September 1941 edition of *Bungei Bunka*: 'The author of *Hanazakari no Mori* is a very young man. We want to keep his identity secret for a while . . . This young writer is the blessed child of Ancient History.'[7] *Hanazakari no Mori*, praised by Hasuda in this Hegelian manner, is a remarkable work. Its theme is ancestry; it consists of five parts, in which Mishima describes the lives of 'ancestors' of aristocratic lineage from widely separated historical periods. One section, for example, relates the experiences of a duchess of the Meiji period (the late nineteenth century), who divorces her husband and spends the ensuing forty years of her life in retirement. Another part describes the religious experiences of a lady of the court who has visions of God. What appealed to Hasuda, a vehement nationalist, was Mishima's evocation of a historical Japan totally different in character from the crude modern age, in which the philistinism of the military leaders of Japan was sweeping all before it. The beauty of his language—full of nostalgia for the past—was the more striking in view of Kimitaké's youth. His Japanese was more distinguished than that of his elders—and all his life Mishima was to display a love of rare characters which distinguished him from his contemporaries.

Hanazakari no Mori was not merely Mishima's first published work and one which contained the seeds of all his writing; it also marked the evolution of his mature thinking, which was pessimistic. At the end of the book, an old acquaintance comes to visit an aged friend, a woman of aristocratic family who lives alone in her retirement. The visitor attempts to revive their common memories of the past, but the aged woman will have none of it. 'It's strange,' she remarks, 'but it's all gone away somewhere.' The scene is very similar to that at the end of Mishima's last work, *The Decay of the Angel*, written almost thirty years later.

For this book, Kimitaké· adopted the *nom de plume* he was to use for the rest of his life: Yukio Mishima. The decision was taken at Shimizu's house in Mejiro, at a meeting in the late summer of 1941. Shimizu proposed that the boy use a pen name, as he was still so young. He suggested the name Mishima: the view of the snowy summit of Mt Fuji is best seen from the town of Mishima, which lies directly between Mt Fuji and the sea to the south. Shimizu derived the first name, Yukio, from the Japanese for snow—*yuki*. The two then discussed which characters they should use to write the name; there is a considerable choice. 'Mishima' was easy; they chose the characters used in the place name: * . 'Yukio' was more difficult. Kimitaké proposed ** . And Shimizu suggested a literary flourish: changing the third character to †. His idea was to give the pen name a romantic flavour; and † had been selected by a romantic poet, Sachio Ito, as the last syllable of his first name. (Mishima's hostile father later said that his son had selected the pen name by flicking through a telephone directory and making a stab with a pencil. He was wrong.)

In the month in which the last instalment of *Hanazakari no Mori* was published, the war started. The root causes of the Pacific War, which began on 8 December, 1941, when carrier-borne aircraft attacked the American fleet in Pearl Harbor, remains a matter for debate. Mishima once told me: 'We were forced to go to war.' This is a view with which many Japanese would agree, though at the time that Mishima said it—early 1966—it was still hard to find a Japanese who spoke openly about the war, such was the trauma of the defeat of 1945, following the first and only use of nuclear weapons in battle. Many Japanese believe that the attack on Pearl Harbour was a 'defensive measure' intended to break the siege of the ABCD alliance (America, Britain, China and the Dutch). President Roosevelt had announced that he would cut off Japan's oil, and the response was a 'defensive' assault on Hawaii and on British colonies in the Far East. Whatever the causes of the war, its effect on the career and the suicide of Yukio Mishima was profound. As Bunzo Hashikawa, a contemporary of Mishima's and a historian, remarked: 'The easiest way to explain Mishima's suicide is by reference to his experiences during the war, when he was in his teens.' The war brought no immediate change in the boy's situation, but Kimitaké and the other students at the *Gakushuin* lived in the belief that conscription and almost certain death awaited them at the end of their school years.

* 三島　　** 由紀雄　　† 夫

2

The Nippon Roman-ha ('Japanese Romanticists') (1942–44)

The war at first made little difference to the Hiraoka family. Azusa Hiraoka was forty-seven, too old to be drafted, and when he resigned from his ministry job in March 1942–he had risen in rank as far as he could–he began a small law practice. His father, Jotaro, aged eighty, died in August, and this was the most important event in the Hiraoka family that year. Kimitaké, who was seventeen, moved up from the middle to the senior school at the *Gakushuin* in March 1942. His record had been excellent academically. For three years he had ranked second out of sixty boys in his year; he had top grades in all subjects but physics, in which he had dropped a grade in a single term. Only in sports was he low down the class, failing to get good marks in *taiso* (physical education), *kyoren* (drill), and *budo* (martial arts). His record of attendance was good, by comparison with that of his early years in the school. Ill-health rarely kept him from his studies any more.

He experienced a disappointment when he entered the senior school in April 1942. 'With the beginning of the war'–he remembered in *Confessions of a Mask*–'a wave of hypocritical stoicism swept the entire country. Even the higher schools did not escape: all during middle school we had longed for that happy day of graduation to higher school when we could let our hair grow long, but now, when the day arrived, we were no longer allowed to gratify our ambition– we still had to shave our heads.'[8] Kimitaké, however, was treated as a star pupil by his senior teacher, Ryozo Niizeki, under whose direction he began German studies (literature and law). He was made a member of the committee of the *Bungei-Bu* (the literary club), and was soon to be its chairman; he was also to be a monitor. The exemplary student published patriotic poems, *tanka* (thirty-one syllable poems), in the school magazine. In *Omikotonori* ('Imperial Edict'), which appeared in April, Kimitaké dedicated himself to the Sun Goddess and to service of the Emperor. His interest in the classics increased. He studied the *Kojiki* ('The Record of Ancient Matters'), and he read the *Manyoshu* ('Journal of a Myriad Leaves'), the eighth-century poetry anthology, for which there was a vogue in wartime. In the summer he published a study of the *Kokinshu*, the tenth-century anthology whose reflective, melancholy poems were more to his taste than the robust *Manyoshu* lyrics. Also, Kimitaké and Takashi Azuma started a little magazine of their own, *Akae* ('Red Picture'), in which they published their own works.

Meanwhile, the war was developing—in the Emperor's famous words —'not necessarily to Japan's advantage'.[9] The first American bombers appeared over Tokyo in April 1942: the raid was a small one, but it was clear that the homeland would be threatened if Japanese military momentum was lost. In June the sea battle of Midway took place. By good fortune, the US Navy sank four Japanese aircraft carriers, destroying a large fighter force in the process; this was a blow from which the Japanese Navy did not recover. Plans for advancing across New Guinea and invading northern Australia were aborted; after Midway, in effect, the war was lost. It continued for another three years, with immense loss of life and destruction of property, but after the Guadalcanal campaign of late 1942 the Japanese were on the defensive in the Pacific.

Mishima associated at this time with a group of writers who believed that the war was holy. Hasuda, the leading spirit in the *Bungei Bunka* group, and twenty-one years Mishima's senior, encouraged the boy to believe in the ideal of death in the service of the Emperor. A scholar with an exceptional capacity for interpreting the Japanese classics in contemporary terms, Hasuda wrote a study of Otsu-no-Miko, a tragic prince of the seventh century. The moral was, in Hasuda's words: 'I believe one should die young in this age. To die young, I am sure, is the culture of my country.'[10] Hasuda had a great regard for the young Mishima; a friend, Masaharu Fuji, recorded this impression of Hasuda saying good-bye to the boy: 'When we visited Hasuda he went out to see Mishima off at the station, and he stared after the departing train for a long time. His attachment to the boy was obvious; he regarded Mishima the prodigy as his own precious jewel.'[11]

Hasuda was a slim, tense schoolteacher from Kyushu, the traditional home of priests in Japan. He had served in China and been invalided back to Japan, but in 1943 he was to be drafted again—to Malaya, where he shot himself to death following the Japanese surrender in 1945. In 1970 Mishima wrote a preface for a biography of Hasuda in which he remarked: 'His enemies [in Japan] had not tried to understand nor wanted to know the source of Hasuda's fierce anger and uncompromising conduct. They were the pure product of his stern tenderness. . . . I received Hasuda's tenderness and affection when I was a boy. I saw the grand spectacle of his anger, suddenly coming and then evaporating. . . . For me Hasuda was a poet who had a scholarly knowledge of Japanese literature. He loved classical lyrical poetry and injected the quality of the classics into his own work. I could not understand his anger. . . . Hasuda placed his confidence in me when he was drafted for the second time [in 1943] and set out on his journey to *shishi* [death granted by the favour of the Emperor], but, naive as I was, I could not understand his feeling even after I heard of his death. . . .'[12] Though as a schoolboy Mishima did not fully understand Hasuda, he did sympathize deeply with his ideals.

The *Bungei Bunka* was a small, little-known band of literary nationalists. Hasuda encouraged Kimitaké to get in touch with the leading intellectuals, who believed in the holiness of the war their country had embarked on. They had formed a movement known as the *Nippon Roman-ha* ('Japanese Romanticists'), led by Yojuro Yasuda, a critic with a rhetorical gift, a highbrow agitator for the 'sacred' war. In 1942 Kimitaké collected *Roman-ha* works, including the poetry of Shizuo Ito, the best artist in the *Roman-ha*, with whom he corresponded. Ito's work was more to his taste than Yasuda's, but this did not keep him from visiting Yasuda in 1943. Yasuda's ideas, however, were too extreme for the young Mishima and his language obscure–a characteristic of *Roman-ha* writers with the exception of Ito. Jun Eto, a scholar with an interest in the *Roman-ha*, summed up the ideals of the movement as follows: 'They believed in the value of destruction and ultimately in self-destruction. They valued "purity of sentiment", though they never defined this; and they called for "preservation of the nation" by purging selfish party politicians and *zaibatsu* (business) leaders. They believed that self-destruction would be followed by reincarnation, linked mysteriously with the benevolence of the Emperor. The Japanese, they considered, were superior to all other peoples.'[13]

The young Mishima was intrigued by the *Roman-ha*. The movement, which derived its name from *Nippon Roman*, a magazine edited by Yasuda from 1935 to 1938, took its ideas from the nineteenth-century German romantic movement. (Hence *Roman*; '*ha*' in Japanese means 'group'.) It had great influence in Japan during the war, incorporating elements of the traditional *kokugaku* (the nationalistic thought of the great eighteenth-century writer, Norinaga Motoori), and also Marxism; it was eclectic, in a peculiarly Japanese way. The *Roman-ha* was encouraged by the military leaders of Japan, and Yasuda gave the movement an inspired leadership. His statements now seem unintelligible, however, and even at the time his notion of irony, a key *Roman-ha* concept, was vague. His well-known 'ironic', pre-war comments include: 'I am saying this purely as an observer. I think it would be more *interesting* if Germany were to win the war, I want her to win. I look at culture from a historical point of view, and it seems to me that the Gods seek to make history more interesting and amusing as one epoch succeeds another.'[14] Another of his remarks was this: 'Even if this war [the Sino-Japanese war] should end with defeat, Japan will have succeeded in accomplishing the greatest step forward in world history. From an ideological point of view, to imagine defeat is the greatest romance.'[15] Yasuda held that historical reality was unimportant and that the emotion aroused by events was more 'interesting' than the events themselves. He argued that it was irrelevant whether a hero was righteous or not. The 'enlightened' man would not commit himself. For such a being, there could be neither decisive defeat nor complete victory; he would be both winner and loser in any game.

Kimitaké was attracted by the *Roman-ha* emphasis on death and destruction. The conclusion of 'irony' was that 'death'–the world's destruction–was the ultimate value. His own fantasies had run on similar lines since childhood. However, he was not influenced solely by the *Roman-ha* in his thinking. He had a highly rational side–and an ideology tailor-made for a nation plunging towards catastrophe was insufficient for him. He was attracted at this time not only by the *Roman-ha* but also by a stoic moral tradition, that of the early-twentieth-century Japanese writer, Ogai Mori. Mishima imitated Ogai Mori as a man and as a writer, especially after 1950, as he recounted in his essay *Sun and Steel*. This long essay was finished in 1968, and Mishima, discussing his literary style, then clarified his debt to Mori: 'In my style, as hardly needs pointing out, I progressively turned my back on the preferences of the age. Abounding in antitheses, clothed in an old-fashioned weighty solemnity, it did not lack nobility of a kind; but it maintained the same ceremonial, grave pace wherever it went, marching through other people's bedrooms with precisely the same tread as elsewhere. Like some military gentleman, it went about with chest out and shoulders back, despising other men's styles for the way they stooped, sagged at the knees, even–heaven forbid!–swayed at the hips.'[16]

That the young Mishima had an inclination towards the *Roman-ha* is suggested by some passages in *Confessions of a Mask*: 'During this time [the early war years] I learned to smoke and drink. That is to say, I learned to make a pretence at smoking and drinking. The war had produced a strangely sentimental maturity in us. It arose from our thinking of life as something that would end abruptly in our twenties; we never even considered the possibility of there being anything beyond those few remaining years.'[17] This was a state of affairs with which Kimitaké was perfectly happy: 'My journey into life was postponed day after day, and the war years were going by without the slightest sign of my departure. Was this not a unique period of happiness for me? Though I still felt an uneasiness, it was only faint; still having hope, I looked forward to the unknown blue skies of each tomorrow. Fanciful dreams of the journey to come . . . the mental picture of the somebody I would one day become in the world and of the lovely bride I had not yet seen, my hopes of fame. . . .'[18] And he thoroughly approved of the war, from the safety of the *Gakushuin*: 'I found childish delight in war, and despite the presence of death and destruction all around me, there was no abatement of the daydream in which I believed myself beyond the reach of harm by any bullet. I even shuddered with a strange delight at the thought of my own death. I felt as though I owned the whole world.'[19]

Kimitaké's 'hopes of fame' depended on publication of *Hanazakari no Mori*. He sought out literary men. From Shizuo Ito, the poet of the *Roman-ha*, he obtained an introduction to a literary editor, Masaharu Fuji of Shichijo Shoin, a small but influential publishing house in Tokyo. Fuji later recalled their meeting in 1943: 'Mishima was a very polite young man with dead pale skin. He had a large head and dark eyebrows. I introduced him to Fujima Hayashi [a poet] and Hayashi took an instant liking to him when Mishima rejected his offer of a beer in a polite but stiff way.'[20] Kimitaké hoped that Fuji would publish his book; but this proved impossible. Censorship, which was handled by the military authorities, was not the problem—though many leading Japanese writers were running into trouble at that time; Mishima had backing from the establishment. The difficulty was shortage of paper. All resources were devoted to the war effort and there was no paper to be found for *Hanazakari no Mori*.

In October 1943 Kimitaké had bad news. His close friend, Azuma, with whom he was publishing the little magazine *Akae*, had died. He closed the magazine and published an obituary in the *Gakushuin* quarterly. His own future was unpredictable; the authorities were drafting university students and he had only a year left at the *Gakushuin*. At nineteen, he remained a romantic. However his fantasies had become more grandiose and narcissistic. As Hashikawa later remarked: 'He thought of himself as a genius, he believed that he could become whatever he liked–the Emperor of Japan, a literary genius, even the *kamikaze* of beauty. He thought his potential unlimited.'[21] The reality was somewhat different, however. Kimitaké was a frail youth, 'ashamed of my thin chest, of my bony, pallid arms', and he only just passed his army medical in May 1944. He was still at the *Gakushuin* at the time and took his medical at Shikata, the hometown of Jotaro, where the Hiraokas had retained a *honseki* (a registered place of residence), although they no longer owned land there. The army doctors laughed when Kimitaké failed to lift a hay bale in a test of strength. The local farm boys easily lifted it above their heads any number of times.

But they classified him 2(b), just qualifying him for service. He would eventually be drafted into a rough local regiment and serve in the ranks. (Had he volunteered in Tokyo, he would have become an officer in a unit there, but Azusa hoped, by registering the boy at Shikata, to delay the time when he would be called to active military service. With luck the war would be over before Kimitaké was drafted.) In July, the boy went with the rest of his class to a naval engineering school at Maizuru on the Japan Sea, to train for a fortnight. This was his first experience of military life, and in the next month he was mobilized again for thirty days, to serve at a naval dockyard at Numazu near Tokyo. The Japanese were steadying themselves for a final assault against the Allies, and every schoolboy had duties. The resignation of the Tojo Cabinet in July 1944 signalled that the leaders of Japan, including the Emperor, believed the war was lost; but there was no thought of surrender. In June, proposals had been put forward for *kamikaze* attacks on US naval vessels; these proposals were secretly being considered in the late summer of 1944.

Mishima's outstanding ability was recognized at the end of his years at the *Gakushuin*. He passed out of the school in September 1944 at the top of his class and was awarded a silver watch by the Emperor. Accompanied by the principal of the school, 'a cheerless old man with mucous clotted in the corners of his eyes,' Kimitaké went by limousine to the palace to receive the prize. Years later he remarked about this meeting with the Emperor: 'I watched the Emperor sitting there without moving for three hours. This was at my graduation ceremony. I received a watch from him. My personal experience was that the image of the Emperor is fundamental. I cannot set this aside. The Emperor is the absolute.'[22] After the presentation ceremony at the palace, Kimitaké returned home to celebrate. Photographs taken with his family show him with a shaven head, the rule for schoolboys and students during wartime. His appearance had changed in the war years; he was no longer the cheeky boy of fifteen with shining eyes, heavy black eyebrows, and pallid face, but a mature-looking youth with a thickened and rounded jaw and a look of assurance.

The rest of the family sat beside Kimitaké for the photograph. Chiyuki, his younger brother, dressed in shorts, was at fourteen in the early stages of adolescence, a spotty child. Next to him sat Mitsuko, sixteen; she had a strong face and broad cheeks—not a beauty. Azusa was the most handsome member of the family. His hair, cut short in the military style, had turned silver. Shizué had aged greatly. At thirty-nine she was a thin matron with a sharp expression. The main worries of the family—including the provision of food, which had become difficult at this stage of the war—were hers. She bore the family burdens, while Azusa enjoyed his retirement.

Kimitaké's father had a special reason for looking pleased with himself. He had won a victory. For the first time in his life he had compelled the young Mishima to do something against his will; he had obliged the boy to enlist in the law department at Tokyo Imperial University, where he was to study German law. Kimitaké had wanted to study literature, but Azusa insisted that for his career it was essential that he read law; his father wanted Kimitaké to join the civil service. Mishima later commented: 'The only thing I have to be grateful to my father for is that he compelled me to study law at the university.' Azusa's choice had been correct, Mishima considered, not for the reasons he thought but because law was intellectually stimulating.

University uniforms were in short supply, and following a custom of the time, Kimitaké borrowed a uniform from a senior student, promising to return it. The university was in danger of disruption, however; 'The air raids were becoming more frequent. I was uncommonly afraid of them, and yet at the same time I somehow looked forward to death impatiently, with a sweet expectation.'[23] Kimitaké 'sensuously accepted the creed of death that was popular during the war' but with reservations: 'I thought that if by any chance I should attain "glorious death in battle" (how ill it would have become me!), this would be a truly ironical end for my life, and I could laugh sarcastically at it forever from the grave. . . . And when the sirens sounded, that same me would dash for the air-raid shelters faster than anyone.'[24]

The university was the best in the land. The *Gakushuin* had not been a first-class school academically. It had been chosen by Jotaro because it was attended by children of the aristocracy, to which Mishima's grandparents aspired to belong; but the Tokyo Kaisei school, which Shizué's father ran, would have been a better choice, academically. So too would the Tokyo First School, another secondary school with high academic standards. To pass out of the *Gakushuin* into *Todai* (Tokyo University) was an achievement. Since its establishment in the late nineteenth century, *Todai* had produced a majority of the leaders of the nation; its prestige had been enhanced by its being named an Imperial University in 1886 under an ordinance, Article I of which had stated that the function of the university was 'to master the secrets of and to teach the arts and sciences in accordance with the needs of the state.' *Todai* was a state university and a passport to the civil service and thence to politics or the upper reaches of the world of business. It had drawbacks as an institution of higher education, however. Close links with the state prevented *Todai* from serving as a centre of the arts and of liberal thought; *Todai* had led the way in the early twentieth century in terminating the practice of employing professors from overseas. Despite these drawbacks, it was the leading university in Japan, and other universities, including private ones, were mostly smaller versions of *Todai*.

Mishima started at *Todai* in October 1944. Normally he would have left the *Gakushuin* in March the following year and entered the university in April, but the war had disrupted university administration. The war also interrupted Mishima's university career. As soon as he entered *Todai*, he was drafted to work in an aircraft factory in the Tokyo region, the Koizumi plant of Nakajima Aircraft Company. The plant was situated in Gumma prefecture, fifty miles north of the capital. Mishima had been drafted twice before, while at the *Gakushuin*. These had been brief assignments, however, and the posting to Nakajima Aircraft Company was for an indefinite period of time. Like other universities, *Todai* had virtually ceased to function in deference to the government's demand that everyone should participate in the war effort.

Mishima described the factory at Koizumi, which manufactured *kamikaze* planes—the *kamikaze* strategy, a last desperate move, had been initiated in October—in *Confessions of a Mask*. The factory was a strange one. The management might have been *Roman-ha* purists: 'This great factory worked on a mysterious system of production costs: taking no account of the economic dictum that capital investment should produce a return, it was dedicated to a monstrous nothingness. No wonder then that each morning the workers had to recite a mystic oath.' This was a vow to the Emperor. 'I have never seen such a strange factory. In it all the techniques of modern science and management, together with the exact and rational thinking of many superior brains, were dedicated to a single end—Death. Producing the Zero-model combat plane used by the suicide squadrons, this great factory resembled a secret cult that operated thunderously—groaning, shrieking, roaring.'[25] The factory was a possible target for American bombers, and when the air-raid sirens sounded everyone would rush to the shelters in a nearby pine grove. As he hurried with the others, Kimitaké clutched a manuscript. He was working on a new book, *Chusei* ('The Middle Ages'). He had finally succeeded in having *Hanazakari no Mori*, his first book, published. It was brought out in October 1944 by Shichijo Shoin, the publishing house for which his friend Fuji worked. Four thousand copies were printed, with an elegant cover showing a fan with blossoms, and the first edition had sold out in a week. A party had been held at a restaurant in Ueno (Tokyo) to celebrate publication. To have published a book in the last year of the war was a phenomenal achievement, and Yukio Mishima won fame among his contemporaries.

In his autobiographical work, *Watakushi no Henreki Jidai* ('My Wandering Years', 1964)—like so many of his books, it remains untranslated—Mishima said that he expected to be drafted and not to live very long thereafter; he wanted to have a book published as a 'memorial' to himself. 'I admit', he said, referring to criticism made against him, 'that I was an opportunist then and I feel disgusted when I see the opportunism of the introduction of my first publication.' *Hanazakari no Mori* sold rapidly: this meant that 'I could die at any moment.' Mishima's narcissism carried him so far that he identified himself with the fifteenth-century ruler Yoshihisa: 'I decided to write a very last novel–I might be drafted at any moment';[26] this was *Chusei*. His choice of Yoshihisa (1456–1489) as the subject of his 'very last' book was intriguing; Yoshihisa was the son of a ruler of Japan, the Shogun Yoshimasa, who built the Silver Pavilion at Kyoto –and ignored problems of government, bequeathing countless problems to his successors. Yoshihisa attempted to seize power from his uncle, an appointee of his father, but the *coup* misfired and he was killed in battle at the age of twenty-four. The civil wars which followed, the Onin Wars, were the most destructive in the history of warfare in Japan. Kyoto was razed to the ground in the course of what was the Japanese version of the Hundred Years War in Europe. It was typical of Mishima that he chose to write about an earlier period of Japanese history in which the capital had been reduced to ashes, at a time when the process was being repeated in Tokyo; he had an eye for striking parallels.

Mishima felt that a disaster comparable to the Onin Wars was about to overtake Japan once more. Whether he received his *akagami*, the 'red paper', or conscription summons, or not, he felt sure that disaster–*ichiokugyokusai* ('Death to the hundred million! No surrender!'), as the wartime slogan had it–awaited the entire nation. 'The reason I now feel that total nuclear warfare is certain,' he wrote in *Watakushi no Henreki Jidai*, 'probably goes back to the emotional experiences I had at that time. Now, seventeen years after the end of the war, I cannot be sure of reality; it is temporary and fleeting. Perhaps I have an inherent inclination to think that way, but it may be that the war, during which things were there one day and gone the next, influenced me a great deal.'[27] Mishima's way of dealing with the situation was 'to cling to my sensitivity'; in retrospect, he could see that he had been foolish, but at the time it had been *shikataganai*–unavoidable.

From the factory Mishima wrote a card to Fumio Shimizu. He was hard at work translating a one-act play by Yeats, he said, and was rendering it into a No play. But he gave up the project; his English was not up to the task of translating *At The Hawk's Well*, the Yeats play in question. 'It is not easy to relate Yeats to the end of the war period,' he wrote. 'Now I would say that I was not trying to relate these two things. I wanted to put reality aside and wrap myself up in my own world, the world of my tiny, lonely, aesthetic hobby.'

3

The End of the War (1945)

Early in 1945, the fighting crept closer to Japan. American naval forces bombarded Leyte in the Philippines and a landing was effected; the US armed forces overran the country. The Emperor's advisers made secret preparations for surrender, while the Imperial armies struggled on against overwhelming Allied forces, suffering heavy casualties. Waiting for his draft call, Mishima continued working at the *kamikaze* factory in Gumma prefecture, and he continued writing. In February 1945 he published part of *Chusei* in a magazine. 'I was probably happy at that time,' he wrote in *Watakushi no Henreki Jidai*; he had no worries about examinations or employment. 'I had a little food—not much—and no responsibilities. I was happy in my daily life and in my writing. I had neither critics nor competitors to contend with. . . . I felt no slightest responsibility for myself. I was in an anti-gravity environment.'[28]

Late in the evening of 15 February, 1945, when Mishima was visiting his parents in Tokyo—he was on leave from the factory—his *akagami* (the 'red paper') arrived. He was to report for duty at Shikata, and prepared to leave the following morning. He composed a traditional *isho*, a farewell note for his family:

> Father, Mother, Mr Shimizu, and my other teachers at the *Gakushuin* and at Tokyo Imperial University, who were so kind to me, I thank you for your blessings bestowed upon me.
>   Also, I shall never forget the friendship of my classmates and seniors at the *Gakushuin*. May you have a bright future!
>   You, my younger sister Mitsuko and younger brother Chiyuki, must discharge your duties to our parents in my place. Above all, Chiyuki, follow me and join the Imperial Army as soon as possible. Serve the Emperor!
>   *Tenno Heika Banzai!*

When he left the next morning, his mother wept bitterly at the gate of their home as she saw him off. 'Even my father seemed no little dejected,' Mishima wrote.[29] The youth boarded a train for the Kansai (the Osaka-Kobe area), and during the long ride, three hundred miles, a cold he had caught at the factory became much worse. By the time he reached the home of close family friends in the village of Shikata, their legal residence, he had such a high fever that he was 'unable to stand.'[30] After a night's rest, dosed with medicine, he made his way to the barracks the following morning. 'My fever, which had only been checked by the medicines, now returned. During the physical examination that preceded final enlistment I had to stand around waiting stark naked, like a wild beast, and I sneezed constantly. The stripling of an army doctor who examined me mistook the wheezing of my bronchial tubes for a chest rattle, and then my haphazard answers concerning my medical history further confirmed him in his error. Hence I was given a blood test, the results of which, influenced by the high fever of my cold, led to a mistaken diagnosis of incipient tuberculosis. I was ordered home the same day as unfit for service.'[31] Once beyond the barrack gates, he 'broke into a run down the bleak and wintry slope that descended to the village.'[32]

Mishima paid a short visit to Shizuo Ito, the poet who had helped him achieve publication of *Hanazakari no Mori*, who lived in Osaka; and that night he got on a train for Tokyo. He recorded this journey in *Confessions*: 'Shrinking from the wind that blew in through a broken window glass, I suffered with fever chills and a headache. Where shall I go now? I asked myself. Thanks to my father's inherent inability to make a final decision about anything, my family still remained unevacuated from our Tokyo house. Shall I go there, to that house where everyone is cowering with suspense? To that city hemming the house in with its dark uneasiness? Into the midst of those crowds where all the people have eyes like cattle and seem always to be wanting to ask each other: "Are you all right? Are you all right?" '[33] Mishima also reflected on his medical: 'What I wanted was to die among strangers, untroubled, beneath a cloudless sky. . . . If such were the case wasn't the army ideal for my purpose? Why had I looked so frank as I lied to the army doctor? Why had I said that I'd been having a slight fever for over half a year, that my shoulder was painfully stiff, that I spit blood, that even last night I had been soaked by a night sweat? . . . Why had I run so when I was through the barracks gate?'[34]

Mishima's statement that he lied to the army doctor is crucial to his whole career. By doing so, he avoided military service; yet, had he served in the army, even for a short while, his view of life in the ranks would have been less romantic, later in life. His own comments on his action at the army medical were clear; a voice within Mishima announced that he would 'never attain heights of glory sufficient to justify my having escaped death in the army.' A second inner voice held that he 'had never once truly wanted to die'; he had been looking forward to army service because 'I had been secretly hoping that the army would provide me at last with an opportunity for gratifying those strange sensual desires of mine. . . . I alone could never die.'[35] A third voice: 'I much preferred to think of myself instead as a person who had been forsaken even by Death. . . . I delighted in picturing the curious agonies of a person who wanted to die but had been refused Death. The degree of mental pleasure I thus obtained seemed almost immoral.'[36]

The end of the war approached swiftly. The Hiraokas, Azusa having finally made up his mind to evacuate, moved out of their Shibuya house to stay with cousins at Gotokuji, beyond Shinjuku, comparatively far from the centre of the city. The air raids had been getting worse and the devastating raid of 9 March, in which over a hundred thousand people died, had persuaded Azusa to move. The spring was a dry one and the main hazard–the American B-29s dropped incendiaries–was fire. The wooden houses of Tokyo, packed closely together, went up in flames like kindling. Mishima described the scene in Tokyo after the giant raid: 'The passageway over the railway tracks was filled with victims of the raid. They were wrapped up in blankets until one could see nothing but their eyes or, better said, nothing but their eyeballs, for they were eyes that saw nothing and thought nothing. . . . Something caught fire within me. I was emboldened and strengthened by the parade of misery passing before my eyes. I was experiencing the same excitement that a revolution causes. In the fire these miserable ones had witnessed the total destruction of every evidence that they existed as human beings. Before their eyes they had seen human relationships, loves and hatreds, reason, property, all go up in flame. And at the time it had not been the flames against which they fought, but against human relationships, against loves and hatreds, against reason, against property. . . . In their faces I saw traces of that exhaustion which comes from witnessing a spectacular drama. . . . They were loud and boastful as they related to each other the dangers they had undergone. In the true sense of the word, this was a rebellious mob; it was a mob that harboured a radiant discontent, an overflowing, triumphant, high-spirited dissatisfaction.'[37]

Mishima had little to do. University classes had ceased and students no longer worked at the *kamikaze* factory. He stayed at home with his family, reading *No* plays, the dramas of Chikamatsu, the mysterious tales of Kyoka Izumi and Akinari Ueda, even the *Kojiki* and its ancient myths. 'How dearly indeed I loved my pit, my dusky room, the place round my desk with its piles of books.'[38] He believed that he would die in the final cataclysm at the end of the war. On 1 April the Americans invaded Okinawa, the large island to the south-west of the main islands of Japan. *Kamikaze* attacks inflicted great damage on the fleet off Okinawa, and the fighting went slowly; but there was no doubt who would win. At the last moment the Japanese commanders committed *hara-kiri* and many officers jumped to their deaths from the cliff where they made a last stand. Mishima, who had been mobilized once more and sent to a naval dockyard at Koza near Tokyo, heard rumours that invasion of the mainland was imminent. 'I was free. Everyday life had become a thing of unspeakable happiness. There was a rumour that the enemy would probably make a landing soon in S Bay and that the region in which the arsenal stood would be overwhelmed. And again, even more than before, I found myself deeply immersed in a desire for death. It was in death that I had discovered my real "life's aim".'[39]

From an air-raid shelter on the outskirts of Tokyo, Mishima watched one of the greatest air attacks of the war, on the night of 24 May. 'The sky over Tokyo turned crimson. From time to time something would explode and suddenly between the clouds we could see an eerie blue sky, as though it were midday. The futile searchlights were more like beacons welcoming the enemy planes. The B-29s reached the skies over Tokyo in comfort.'[40] Mishima saw other men, who had been watching from the caves where they had taken shelter, applaud when a plane was hit and fell, without knowing whether it was American or Japanese. 'The young workmen were particularly vociferous. The sound of hand-clapping and cheering rang out from the mouths of the scattered tunnels as though in a theatre. . . . It seemed to make no essential difference whether the falling plane was ours or the enemy's. Such is the nature of war. . . .'[41]

At the dockyard camp Mishima worked on a new manuscript, *Misaki nite no Monogatari* ('Story at a Cape'), a tale based on a childhood visit to the sea. In June, *Bungei*, a leading literary magazine, published another story of his, and in that month he received his first magazine fee. He wanted to find more allies in the *Bundan*, the literary establishment, and he met older writers whenever he had leave from the camp. Two new acquaintances were the novelists Junzo Shono and Toshio Shimao.

In July the Japanese government made overtures of peace, secretly, via the Moscow embassy, hoping that Stalin would serve as intermediary with America. The Potsdam Conference was about to take place, following the collapse of Germany; it was attended by Stalin, Truman and Churchill and was an opportunity to end the war. The Japanese initiative, however, was ignored by Stalin, who had plans of his own: an attack on the Japanese positions in Manchuria and elsewhere in the Far East. He was about to end the neutrality treaty the two powers had signed in 1941. The Japanese would not make a direct approach to the United States, and the war dragged on. Following the Potsdam meeting, a communiqué was issued which repeated the Allied demands for the unconditional surrender of Japan. The communiqué gave no assurances about the Emperor's future, and the Japanese could not respond without them.

The summer was unusually hot. Mishima wrote in *Sun and Steel*: 'My first–unconscious–encounter with the sun was in the summer of the defeat, in the year 1945. A relentless sun blazed down on the lush grass of that summer that lay on the borderline between the war and the post-war period–a borderline, in fact, that was nothing more than a line of barbed wire entanglements, half broken-down, half buried in the summer weeds, tilting in all directions.'[42]

On 6 August, Mishima learned that Hiroshima had been obliterated by a monstrous bomb. A second atom bomb destroyed part of Nagasaki three days later. 'It was our last chance. People were saying that Tokyo would be next. Wearing white shirt and shorts, I walked about the streets. The people had reached the limits of desperation and were now going about their affairs with cheerful faces. From one moment to the next, nothing happened. Everywhere there was an air of cheerful excitement. It was just as though one was continuing to blow up an already bulging toy balloon, wondering: "Will it burst now? Will it burst now?"'[43]

Nothing happened for almost another week. 'If it had gone on any longer there would have been nothing to do but go mad,' Mishima wrote. Then, on 14 August, US aircraft appeared over Tokyo and dropped leaflets outlining the surrender proposals of the Allies, including a small concession on the status of the Emperor, who would be subordinate to the Supreme Commander of the Allied Powers (SCAP)–General Douglas MacArthur–but would remain on the throne.

Tokyo lay in ruins and there was no possibility of repelling an Allied invasion of the main islands. The terms were accepted by the Japanese government.

Mishima was in bed with a fever at his relatives' house at Goto-kuji when he heard the news of the surrender. 'For me–for me alone –it meant that fearful days were beginning. It meant that, whether I would or no, and despite everything that had deceived me into believing such a day would never come to pass, the very next day I must begin life as an ordinary member of society. How the mere words made me tremble!'[44]

The Emperor's surrender broadcast was made at noon on 15 August. It could not be heard clearly; the squeaky voice of the monarch was partly drowned by static. In his first-ever radio address, the Emperor said: 'We declared war on America and Britain out of Our sincere desire to ensure Japan's self-preservation and the stabilization of East Asia, it being far from Our thought either to infringe upon the sovereignty of other nations or to embark upon territorial aggrandise-ment. But now the war has lasted for nearly four years. Despite the best that has been done by everyone . . . the war situation had developed not necessarily to Japan's advantage . . . Moreover, the enemy has begun to employ a new and most cruel bomb.'[45]

Five hundred military officers, including General Anami, the Minister of War, committed suicide at the surrender, to 'take responsi-bility' for the defeat and to 'apologize to the Emperor.' Anami com-mitted *hara-kiri* alone in his residence in Tokyo, refusing the offer of a *coup de grace*; he bled slowly to death. Many officers overseas took their lives; among them was Zenmei Hasuda, Mishima's friend, who murdered his commanding officer for criticizing the Emperor and then put into effect his principle, 'To die young, I am aware, is the culture of my nation,' by blowing out his brains. A handful of civilians also took their lives, including a dozen members of a fanatical right-wing organization, the *Daitokuju*, who disembowelled themselves in Tokyo; two of the group acted as *kaishaku-nin*, be-heading their comrades with swords.

Mishima began his 'life as an ordinary member of society': 'I passed the next year with vague and optimistic feelings. There were my law studies, perfunctorily performed, and my automatic goings and comings between university and home. . . . I was not paying atten-tion to anything nor was anything paying attention to me. I had acquired a worldly-wise smile like that of a young priest. I had the

1 The group of five who took part in the action at Ichigaya on 25 November, 1970. Standing, from left to right: Morita, Furu-Koga, Ogawa, Chibi-Koga. Mishima is seated.

Mishima addressing *Jieitai* members from the balcony at Eastern Army headquarters. (*Photo WWP*)

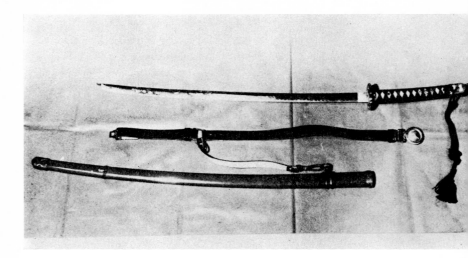

3 Mishima's sixteenth-century *samurai* sword. (*Photo Kyoto*)

4 Chibi-Koga leads the way out of General Mashita's office, carrying Mishima's sword. Ogawa (left) and Furu-Koga escort Mashita. (*Photo WWP*)

feeling of being neither alive nor dead.'[46] His former desire for the
'natural and spontaneous suicide of death in war' had been completely
eradicated and forgotten. The twenty-year-old boy was in a state of
shock. 'True pain can only come gradually. It is exactly like tuberculosis in that the disease has already progressed to a critical stage
before the patient becomes aware of its symptoms.'[47] Later Mishima
would often refer to the experience of living through the end of the
war. 'My life was cut in two,' he said. 'Misfortune attacked me.' The
death sentence on Mishima and his contemporaries had been lifted,
but their whole system of values had been shattered. For Mishima
the experience was even more traumatic. During the war he had
been made to feel a genius, the representative spirit of his age;
after the war he was merely a student. In Hashikawa's words : 'When
the pressure of war was eliminated, he lost his balance.'

Mishima was in utter misery, and his agony was increased by the
death of his younger sister, whom he loved. Mitsuko died in October
1945 of typhoid contracted from well water. Mishima looked after
her in the hospital; he would stay by her bedside for hours, reading
his lawbooks. 'I shall never forget the way she said, "Thank you,
brother," when I gave her water,' Mishima told his mother. Mitsuko,
a student at the Sacred Heart School in Tokyo, died at the age of
seventeen. A family friend remarked to me : 'It was a shame for
Kimitaké that she died. She gave him a different idea of women to
that which he derived from his grandmother and his doting mama.
She was tomboyish and critical. He would say of her: "Can she really
be a woman at all?" He could not understand a normal woman.'

Mishima withdrew into himself and ignored the chaotic world
about him. 'I would see no evil, hear no evil, speak no evil.' He paid
no attention to the important changes in government. Although he was
a law student, he did not interest himself in the 'five reforms', General
MacArthur's programmes for industrial, land, election, union and
educational law reform, which were to lay the foundations for *demokurashi* in Japan. Nor did Mishima concern himself with social problems, although he was surrounded by them. The plight of the people
of Tokyo, whose homes had been destroyed and who had little food,
was acute; a roaring black market rose up and profiteers flourished.
The suffering of ordinary people was immense; suicide by drinking
methylated spirits was common. Mishima clung to his own little
world–his 'castle', he sometimes called it, his 'dark cave'. He paid
little heed to the outside world, ignoring even developments that

D

affected the Emperor, whom General MacArthur had decreed should remain on the throne and should not be put on trial with the 'war criminals'; as a condition, however, the Emperor had to make a statement disavowing the wartime ideology. The *ningen sengen* (human declaration)—with its implication that the Emperor was a mere mortal—was delivered on New Year's Day 1946 and contained this key passage: 'The ties between Us and Our people have always stood on mutual trust and affection. They do not depend on mere legends and myths. They are not predicated upon the false concept that the Emperor is divine and that the Japanese people are superior to other races and fated to rule the world.'[48]

Mishima picked up the threads of his literary career. He took his manuscripts to the editors of the monthly magazines. Utaro Noda, the editor of *Bungei*, later recalled in the magazine: 'He brought to me the manuscript of *Chusei*. Reading it through, I felt that he was brilliant, but that I could not praise him one hundred per cent. He struck me as like a strange plant which had skipped the natural process of maturing and had bloomed straightaway with no more than a couple of leaves on its stem.'[49] Noda criticized Mishima's 'evil narcissism'. Naoya Shiga, one of the best-known writers of the day, was also approached by Mishima, and shared Noda's critical opinion of the youth: 'Shiga remembered Mishima as a boy who had been at school with his daughter for a while. He said that Mishima had often slipped manuscripts and letters into his post box. But he criticized Mishima's works: "His stories are all dreams. They have no reality. They are no good." '[50] Noda passed on these criticisms to Mishima and encouraged him to write still more romantic tales, hoping that the boy would cure himself of his romanticism through an overdose: 'He wrote two romantic short stories and brought the manuscripts to me one day when Tokyo was covered with fresh snow. I remember his seriousness that snowy day.'

But Noda was disappointed by Mishima's next manuscripts. The young man had brought him *Misaki nite no Monogatari*, the story he had written at the Koza naval dockyard just before the surrender. 'It was merely a clever professional work. I told Mishima this and he answered that he had much confidence in the story. I asked, then, if he wanted to be an original novelist or a well-known popular writer, and he replied categorically that it would be the latter.'[51] The literary editor expressed his disappointment and Mishima then began to look for another sponsor. He wanted to break through quickly into the post-war literary world, and he needed the help of an older man with an established reputation as a writer. By himself he would not be able to attain his ambition immediately. From Noda, Mishima obtained an introduction to Yasunari Kawabata, one of the foremost writers in Japan.

Noda remembered. 'After his work had appeared in *Bungei* . . . he came to see me only once. That was when he wanted my introduction to Kawabata.'[52] Mishima had a way of dropping people who were no longer useful to him, and in Noda he made an enemy. 'After the war he became a popular novelist, just as he had hoped that he would do, but the fresh, serious, young Mishima vanished. I felt that Mishima lived only in his pen-name and not as Kimitaké Hiraoka. That pen-name became a narcissistic shadow of the real man, something like Hong Kong flowers.'[53] 'Hong Kong flowers' were the cheap, plastic flowers which used to flood into Japan, much as Japanese goods flooded America, and were regarded as imitations–as 'shadows' of the real thing.

4

Riding the Post-War Wave (1946–9)

Yasunari Kawabata, the first Japanese writer to win the Nobel Prize (in 1968), was forty-six when he first met Mishima. Born in 1899, Kawabata had first wanted to become a painter and then had established his reputation in Japan in the 1920s as a young writer with a classical background and modern tastes. He was one of the handful of eminent literati who came through the Pacific War with their names unblemished by association with the militarists. A man of independent means, married and living at Kamakura, where he did his writing–he is best known in the West for his novels, *Snow Country* and *A Thousand Cranes*–Kawabata was generous by nature and was disposed to help young writers whose work he liked. When Mishima, an almost unknown law student, brought him some manuscripts during the New Year holiday in 1946, he liked a short story about homosexual relationships at the *Gakushuin* well enough to recommend it to a magazine editor. *Tabako* ('Tobacco') was published in *Ningen* magazine that summer, introducing the young Mishima to the post-war literary world.

Mishima was overjoyed by Kawabata's decision to sponsor him, and rightly so. In the inbred world of the Japanese *Bundan*, a young writer needed the backing of an older man, and no one could have been better suited for this role than Kawabata, who instinctively understood the formal, sensitive Mishima. But the young man's dreams of becoming famous overnight were not fulfilled. The publication of *Tabako* caused no sensation. The lack of reaction, even among the other writers he knew, gravely disappointed him, and he decided that his father was right and that he should not concentrate on a literary career.[54]

He made plans to sit for the civil-service examination, the *Kobun*, and to start his working life as a government official. Obviously a writer had to be better known in the *Bundan* before he could hope for any real success. But, while he pursued his studies, he also tried to further his literary associations. He continued to meet Kawabata, and the older writer made him a member of the *Kamakura Bunko*, an exclusive lending library Kawabata had founded with his literary friends. He also tried to meet as many of the other established writers as he could, with the aim of shifting eventually from government service to a literary career.

One of the writers he met in the early post-war years was Osamu Dazai, and his single encounter with this famous romantic writer made a deep impression. The meeting took place in 1947 when a friend of Mishima's, another young man with literary aspirations, who knew Dazai and his circle personally, took him along one evening to meet the writer at a party in the Ginza. Dazai, who was only thirty-eight, was at that time the most popular novelist with the younger generation in Japan. In his best-selling novels he portrayed a mood of hopelessness they responded to, and this reflected a quality in his work as a whole, for it was often dark and depressing, and had something in common with Mishima's own writing.

Mishima, however, was unnerved by the similarities between Dazai and himself, which were at that time personal, and not obviously literary. Both men were snobs; both desired to create sensation and be heroes of the general public; and both were obsessed with suicide. Mishima, in advance of the meeting with Dazai, made up his mind to be aggressive, to be a 'literary assassin', as he once said. When he and his friend joined them, Dazai and his group of admirers were sitting in an upstairs room in their Ginza restaurant. It was a squalid room with dirty *tatami* (rice-straw mats), just the kind of place Mishima disliked, and the company was drinking low quality *saké*, the only alcohol that could be obtained in Japan then, unless one bought imported liquor at black-market prices. Mishima did not drink in those days; and he sat a little apart from Dazai and his disciples, listening tensely to their conversation–waiting for an opportunity to pounce. When there was a brief silence, Mishima broke in. 'Mr Dazai,' he said, 'I hate your work.' The novelist paused for a moment before replying, seemingly surprised (not unnaturally). Then he remarked to those sitting close by: 'I know he loves me, though; otherwise he wouldn't have come here.' The remark stung Mishima, presumably because it had an element of truth; and he remembered the taunt for the rest of his life. He would often tell his 'Dazai story'; twenty years later he was still obsessed with the memory of the remark: 'I know he loves me though. . . .' Dazai was one of the very few men who 'put down' Mishima, and he never had an opportunity to retaliate, as Dazai committed suicide in 1948; he drowned himself in a river in Tokyo with his mistress.

It is interesting to contrast Mishima's relationship with Dazai and with Kawabata. He met Dazai only once and had a very strong reaction to him; the long-haired, pale-faced writer could have been close to Mishima had he lived; even his suicide seems to stress an element they had in common. Mishima's friendship with Kawabata, though it lasted for almost twenty-five years, was far less intense. Mishima kept his distance from everyone and made no exception for Kawabata; they had, in a sense, a literary alliance, based on mutual understanding and appreciation rather than friendship. Kawabata was much less tense than Mishima–or Dazai–and seemed unlikely ever to contemplate suicide (in fact, he gassed himself eighteen months after Mishima's death).

Although his interest was in literature, Mishima read his law books with a whole-hearted concentration typical of him. He studied hard, displaying stoic virtue. In the spring of 1947, 'the time for preparing for the civil service examination was at hand and I had to devote all my energies to dry-as-dust study.' Mishima described in *Confessions of a Mask* how 'spring came and a frantic nervousness built up behind my façade of tranquillity.' At odd moments he would go out for a walk to exercise his body a little, and 'often I became aware that people were looking questioningly at my bloodshot eyes.'[55] He was exceedingly self-conscious.

He wrote at length in *Confessions of a Mask* of an abortive love affair with a girl named Sonoko, but Sonoko was a composite charac-

ter drawn from the experiences of Mishima's friends and several young
women in upper-middle-class families he knew. The law student
went occasionally to a party, but found it impossible to relax with
other young people. Going home alone–he was still living with
his parents, who had returned to their house in Tokyo immediately
after the war–he would play at mental self-torture. 'You're not human.
You're a being who is incapable of social intercourse. You're nothing
but a creature, non-human and somehow strangely pathetic.'[56] Was
he also incapable of sexual love? It is almost certain that he had
no real relationship with a woman until his early thirties. His Japanese biographer, Takeo Okuno, speaks of having received a call late
one night, at about 2 a.m., in which Mishima enthusiastically reported that he had succeeded in bed with a girl (this was 1957, many
years later). His instincts were homosexual, as is clear from *Confessions of a Mask*. Yet he certainly *attempted* to have relationships with
women as well as men, in the early post-war years; he even made
marriage proposals, at least twice. But he was an uncertain prospect,
not least because of his closeness to his mother, to judge by the
comments that one of the women to whom he proposed made to
me: 'I couldn't see myself marrying him, because he was too close to
his mother. She was very nice to me and there was nothing wrong,
but I feared that I would come between mother and son if we were
married. Besides, I wasn't sure that I felt a passion for him.'

Mishima took his *kobun* examination in the autumn of 1947 and
was accepted by the Ministry of Finance, much to his father's delight
(this ministry is the power centre of the Japanese bureaucracy). He
worked hard in the Banking Bureau of the ministry during the day
and then would sit up half the night writing short stories. He was
beginning to get more of his work published. A colleague remembers
him as 'a stylish official who tried his utmost to combine literary
work with his labours in the office'. In the ministry he had a reputation for literary knowledge, joined the group which edited the ministry
magazine, *Zaisei*, and gave lectures to his colleagues on classical
literature. 'Once,' according to his fellow civil servant, Minoru Nagaoka, 'he made a speech to junior officials on the subject of "Women
in the Literature of the Heian Period." ' Mishima was naturally gifted
as a bureaucrat and could have risen to the top of the ministry
had he chosen. He had powers of organization of a rare order and was
an amusing colleague who attracted attention. 'He wrote a witty
speech for the Minister, and his *kacho* [section chief] had to cut out

a great deal of it, as it was far too funny for the Ministry of Finance.'[57] But Mishima did not fancy a career in government. He continued to devote himself to short-story work at home, often staying up until 2 a.m. or later, to fulfil the growing stream of requests from magazine editors. A writer establishes himself in Japan by writing short stories and then goes on to novels or plays. Mishima's output was formidable, as one may see from this representative list of his publications during 1948, up to September:

JANUARY	*Sakasu*	*Shinro* magazine
	Somon no Genryu	*Nihon Tanka* magazine
FEBRUARY	The preface of *Tozoku*	*Gozen* magazine
MARCH	*Jushosha no Kyoki*	*Ningen* magazine
	Ch. Five of *Tozoku*	*Shinbungaku* magazine
APRIL	*Junkyo*	*Tancho* magazine
	Kazoku Awase	*Bungaku Kikan* magazine
MAY	A commentary on Radiguet	*Sekai Bungaku* magazine
	Ayame	*Fujin Bunko* magazine
JUNE	*Kashira Moji*	*Bungaku Kai* magazine
	Jizen	*Kaizo* magazine
	Hoseki Baibai	*Bungei* magazine
JULY	*Koshoku*	*Shosetsukai* magazine
	Tsumibito	*Fujin* magazine
SEPTEMBER	Resigned from the Ministry of Finance[58]	

As the titles of his works suggest—*Koshoku* means 'Sensuality'; *Junkyo* is 'Martyrdom'; and *Hoseki Baibai* is 'Traffic in Precious Stones'—Mishima's writing was sensational. It was also clear and attractive and he was highly popular with editors for his punctuality.

Mishima was now doing well enough as a writer to resign from the ministry. Azusa was enraged by his decision, but he no longer had the power to control his son. Mishima was earning a good income from his writing and could certainly support himself for several years, especially as he was saving money living with his parents. Shizué naturally took Mishima's side in the family quarrel over his resignation, and Azusa was no match for mother and son, so gave in with a typical remark: 'All right, if you absolutely insist, you may go ahead and leave the ministry. But you'd better make yourself the best writer in the land, do you hear?'

Mishima was often melancholy. He wrote in his diary: 'What does it matter to me if A-bombs rain down on us again? All I desire is beauty.' When he embarked on *Confessions of a Mask*, on 25 November 1948, his intention was to analyse his 'aesthetic nihilism'; also, to purge himself of a 'monster' within.

Almost half of *Confessions of a Mask* is taken up with a description of the relationship between the narrator and the young girl Sonoko, whom I have mentioned. These Sonoko scenes are not reliable as autobiography, but they are nevertheless revealing. At one point the narrator goes to his mother–just before the end of the war–and asks whether he should marry Sonoko, for the girl has concluded from his fumbling approaches that he has matrimony in mind. It seems somehow natural that the narrator of *Confessions*, when faced with this decision, should consult his mother and accept her verdict (which is *not* to marry). The scene is greatly in character with what one knows of Mishima himself; he depended on his mother for protection.

The second passage, probably the most well-known scene in the book, is the encounter between Sonoko and the narrator, with which *Confessions of a Mask* ends. It is a sweltering summer day in Tokyo and the pair have entered a cheap dance hall to while away time. The narrator sees a group of *yakuza* (gangsters) who are seated close by, and he is hypnotized by the sight of a young man among them. 'He was a youth of twenty-one or -two, with coarse but regular and swarthy features. He had taken off his shirt and stood there half-naked, rewinding a bellyband about his middle. . . . The hot mass of his smooth torso was being severely and tightly imprisoned by each succeeding turn of the soiled cotton bellyband. His bare, suntanned shoulders gleamed as though covered with oil. And black tufts stuck out from the cracks of his armpits. . . .'[59] At this sight, 'above all at the sight of the peony tattooed on his hard chest,' the narrator is beset by sexual desire. He forgets Sonoko's existence: 'I was thinking of but one thing; of his going out onto the streets of high summer just as he was, half-naked, and getting into a fight with a rival gang. Of a sharp dagger cutting through the bellyband, piercing that torso. Of that soiled bellyband beautifully dyed with blood. . . .'[60] The book closes on a note characteristic of Mishima's writing: 'It was time [to leave]. . . . The group [of thugs] had apparently gone to dance, and the chairs stood empty in the blazing sunshine. Some sort of beverage had been spilled on the table top and was throwing back glittering, threatening reflections.'[61]

Confessions of a Mask was hailed by the critics as the work of a genius. The book established Yukio Mishima, as he was known there-after, as one of the foremost writers of the younger generation. Few of the critics, however, sensed the existence of the profound conflict within the personality of Yukio Mishima, and the nature of his struggle against weakness—a struggle out of which *Confessions of a Mask* was born.

Among the many comments on Mishima's work, one searches in vain for a criticism with the accuracy of Yasunari Kawabata's in his introduction to an earlier, unsuccessful novel by Mishima, *Tozoku* ('Robbers', 1948). 'I am dazzled by Mishima's mature talent,' Kawabata wrote. 'And at the same time I am disturbed by it. His novelty is not easy to understand. Some may think that Mishima is invulner-able, to judge from this work. Others will see that he has deep wounds.' Kawabata had seen into the young writer's being; he knew how vulnerable his protegé was. In this he was almost alone among Mishima's associates and friends. No wonder, then, that when Mishima put an end to his life twenty years later, Kawabata felt an overwhelming responsibility for his death. Who knows, though, whether it was within his power to have helped Mishima to avoid disaster? The wounds were so deep and the end had been so well rehearsed.

Confessions of a Mask had another revealing aspect: Mishima had nothing to say in it about political events that had influenced his life. He made no attempt to analyse the crucial event of his youth—his experience during the war and the collapse of Japanese imperialism in 1945. He was regarded as apolitical by his contemporaries, al-though an emissary from the Japanese Communist Party, Hajime Odagiri, did once make an attempt to persuade him to join the party. It was not until the 1960s that Mishima tried to write about the Emperor and the defeat of 1945. His long silence on these great national topics may be interpreted as a sign that he was not politically involved or as evidence of his depth of feeling. I believe that both theories are tenable: Mishima felt no involvement in politics in a mundane day-to-day sense; but his experiences during the war—and perhaps also the teaching of the *Nippon Roman-ha*—made a deep impres-sion on him. He *was* an imperialist of a kind.

PART TWO

The Four Rivers (1950-70)

Prologue

I want to make a poem of my life.
YUKIO MISHIMA[1]
Suicide is something planned in the
silence of the heart like a work of art.
ALBERT CAMUS

Shortly before he killed himself, Mishima organized an exhibition devoted to his life. It was held at the Tobu department store at Ikebukuro in Tokyo between 12 and 19 November, 1970. In an introduction to the catalogue of the exhibition he wrote:

> Just as I was about to complete my tetralogy, *The Sea of Fertility*, after six years of work, the Tobu department store asked me for permission to do a retrospective exhibition on my literary life. I have been writing for nearly a quarter of a century and should like to re-examine the paths I have trod. A writer, once he begins looking back on his past works, drives himself into a dead end, but what is wrong with letting others arrange his past?
> I made only one suggestion: that was to divide my forty-five years of life–a life so full of contradictions–into Four Rivers, 'Writing', 'Theatre', 'Body' and 'Action', all finally flowing into *The Sea of Fertility*.

The exhibition was a great success. There were one hundred thousand visitors, the great majority of whom were men. 'It seems that I am not popular with the ladies,' Mishima wrote in a letter to his old teacher from the *Gakushuin*, Fumio Shimizu. Among the visitors was Shizué Hiraoka. She was astonished to see so many materials on display which Mishima had not previously shown to the public–pictures, for example, of Shizué herself, as a young woman. She was also surprised by the appearance of the exhibition as a whole; the hall was hung with black curtains.

'What does it mean?' asked Shizué when she saw her son at home. 'Why are all the pictures surrounded by black?'

'It's just so that you can see them properly, to provide contrast,' he replied.

The exhibition was Mishima's farewell to the general public. Placed in a prominent position was the sword made by Seki no Magoroku, the two-handed, three-foot-long weapon with which Masakatsu Morita was to cut off Mishima's head on 25 November. In the black bound catalogue Mishima wrote: 'The visitor will be able to choose just those Rivers that interest him and avoid being swept away into a River that he dislikes. I shall be grateful to those who follow all four Rivers of my life but I cannot believe there will be many such visitors.' I have followed all four Rivers and, like Mishima, I have chosen to include in the River of Writing much information about his private life.

IV

The River of Writing

This River helps me to cultivate my fields with the mercy of its waters, supports my living and at times floods and nearly drowns me in its prolific streams. The River also demands from me infinite patience and daily hard labour through the changing seasons and passing time. How alike are writing and farming! One's spirit must be on guard at every moment against storms and frosts. After such a long and vigilant watch over my field of writing, and after such endless toil of imagination and poetry, can I ever be sure of a rich harvest? What I have written departs from me, never nourishing my void, and becomes nothing but a relentless whip lashing me on. How many struggling nights, how many desperate hours, had to be spent on those writings! If I were to add up and record my memories of such nights I would surely go mad. Yet I still have no way to survive but to keep on writing one line, one more line, one more line. . . .

YUKIO MISHIMA—*the catalogue to the Tobu Exhibition*

1

1950–4

Towards the end of his life Mishima was in a deep depression about his writing. In his essay *Sun and Steel* he stated that he feared that he was 'on the verge of non-communication'; and in a letter to me he wrote of 'my failure as a novelist' as an accomplished fact. Both comments were made in 1968.

Mishima had embarked on his literary career twenty years earlier in a fairly optimistic mood: 'I am not the kind of writer who can "rush ahead with a work on inspiration". I give the impression of liveliness, as a man, and I attract attention; but I am in general a writer who is like a banker in his method of work. Imagine a bank with a large, cheerful display in the window. . . . The work of Thomas Mann, who remarked that "writers should look like bankers", came to be my ideal at this time [1950]. His Teutonic stubbornness

111

and unnecessary meticulousness are far from my original character. But I was captured by the dramatic quality of his writing, by the unique character of tragedy in German literature and by a combination of the highest artistic quality and a sense of discrimination akin to snobbery.'[2] On publication of *Confessions of a Mask* Mishima became famous. He was regarded as a prodigy, and he was summoned to give lectures to literary audiences. The former Ministry of Finance official appeared at these occasions clad in three-piece suits, looking very much like an *oshare* (smart) young man from Mitsui.

And yet he was not at peace with himself. 'In 1950 I went up and down, from a peak of happiness down to the pit of melancholy.' At this time, and up until his departure on his first world trip at the end of 1951, he was 'emotionally more unstable than at any other time of my life.' The smart young Mishima was 'constantly lonely' and 'jealous of the mediocre youth of others'; he thought of himself as 'a *hen na* [peculiar] grinning old man of twenty-five.'[3] And he was ill. He had taken up riding after leaving the ministry, but the exercise had not restored his health. 'I was continually troubled by stomach aches.' He decided that he must at all costs get out of Japan and tried to book a passage on an Antarctic whaler, but without success. The degree of his nervousness is evident from *Watakushi no Henreki Jidai*: 'I decided to divide my energy between two worlds: my work and my everyday life. I would no longer trouble with the intermediate existence, "association with others".'[4] He came to hate 'others'.

Early in the autumn of 1950, as he was standing outside a large bookshop in Tokyo inspecting a poster for an exhibition of mummies from the Chuson temple, it suddenly seemed to him that the people going in and out of the shop were themselves mummies. 'I detested their ugliness. How unattractive intellectuals are!' Out of this experience came a bold resolution. Spurred by uncontrollable hate', he decided that he must travel to Greece, 'the land of my dreams'. 'My aspiration . . . was, of course, a kind of self-hatred,' he wrote later. 'I felt a keen passion for harmony and a deep antipathy against disharmony and exaggeration; and these reactions must have been born in my internal crisis.'[5] Later, with the benefit of hindsight, he changed his self-diagnosis: 'I was probably mistaken. My antipathy for intellectuals was a reaction against my own enormous, monster-like sensitivity. That is why I wanted to become a classicist.' 'Travel,' he said, not without self-contradiction once more, for he was ignorant of nature, 'consoled me and I experienced a sensual attraction towards scenery. . . . Descriptions of nature have an importance in my literature similar to that of love scenes in the work of other men.'[6]

Mishima, who was Western in many respects, was encountering in his mid-twenties the difficulties of many young romantic writers of the same age in the West. It was a crisis period that affected his work. During 1950–1 he wrote a novel that he described as a failure: *Mashin Reihai* ('Worship of Evil'). 'I also wrote *Ao no Jidai* ['Blue Period'], a novel whose construction and style were miserable. And I finished *Forbidden Colours*, an unnecessarily confused work, and also some peculiar short stories. Others thought that I wrote well, but in fact the pace of my work was disturbed. I don't like to write like that.'[7] His successful novel of this time was *Thirst for Love*, a novel which, according to Mishima, was written under the influence of François Mauriac, whose work he considered, had a unique attraction for Japanese writers. 'Surely there can be no foreign author as much to Japanese taste as Mauriac,' he said. According to Donald Keene, the American scholar: 'He explained this in terms of a Japanese fascination for details—the expression on a woman's face when, on the point of weeping, she holds back her tears; just how far back one can see in a woman's mouth when she smiles; the pattern the wrinkles make in her dress when a woman turns around. Mauriac is a master of such details, but, according to Mishima, American novels afford little pleasure of this nature and therefore have never had much appeal for the Japanese. *Thirst for Love* abounds in such details; they suggest not only Mishima's indebtedness to Mauriac but his place in the tradition of Japanese literature.'[8]

The central character of *Thirst for Love* is Etsuko, a woman in her early thirties, who has gone to live with the family of her husband in the country near Osaka, after his death. The novel is set in the immediate post-war period, a time of great social upheaval. Mishima describes Etsuko thus, in a scene at the beginning of the book: 'Etsuko passed her hand through the handle of her shopping bag. The curving bamboo scraped down across her forearm as she lifted her hands to her face. Her cheeks were very warm. That was a common occurrence with her. There wasn't any reason for it; of course, it wasn't a symptom of any illness—it was just that suddenly her cheeks would start to burn. Her hands, delicate though they were, were calloused and tanned, and because of that very delicacy seemed rougher. They scratched her cheeks and intensified the burning.'[9] She comes from a middle-class family in Tokyo and does not like the rural life about her. As she walks home from a shopping expedition: 'Lights were burning in the rows of government housing. There were hundreds of units—of the same style, the same life, the same smallness, the same poverty. The road through this squalid community afforded a short-cut that she never took.'[10] (In this description, Mishima's own feelings about post-war *demokurashi* are evident.)

Etsuko is secretly in love with a farm boy, Saburo, who also lives with the family. And in the autumn there is a festival which gives her a chance to come physically close to him after months of longing. Saburo and the other village youths, wearing only *fundoshi* (loin-cloths), dash about in front of the village Shinto shrine, in pursuit of a lion's head borne on a standard. For this, Etsuko prepares herself as if she were going to chic reception in Tokyo. On the way to the festival she tears her jacket, but does not notice. Her thoughts are on the fiery scene ahead. Arriving at the shrine and witnessing the young men dancing round the lion's head, struggling back and forth while bamboo crackers explode, Etsuko suddenly rushes towards them having recognized Saburo in their midst: 'Etsuko stumbled forward, pushed by the throng, and collided with a bare back, warm as fire, coming from the opposite direction. She reached out her hands and held it off. It was Saburo's back. She savoured the touch of his flesh. She savoured the majestic warmth of him. The mob pushed again from behind her, causing her fingernails to gouge into Saburo's back. He did not even feel it. In all the mad pushing and shoving he had no idea what woman was pressing against his back. Etsuko felt the blood dripping between her fingers.'[11]

Thirst for Love ends with another scene in the genre of the 'murder theatre', in which Etsuko drives a mattock through the neck of Saburo. Her love for him turns into panic, when she discovers that Saburo is attracted to her. As Flaubert was Madame Bovary, so Mishima was Etsuko. He, too, felt a compulsion to love and to hurt the object of his love; he, too, was repelled when another responded to his approaches. His thirst, like that of Etsuko, could not be quenched with love; to accept the love of another was the hardest thing that could be required of him.

In his next major work, *Forbidden Colours*, Mishima examined himself more explicitly and much less artfully than in *Thirst for Love*. He wrote of *Forbidden Colours*: 'The basic proposition of the modern novel is, as Dostoevsky said . . . the expression of dia-

metrically opposed attitudes within human beings. Due to the nature
of the Japanese language I intended to give this expression in classical
terms. In *Forbidden Colours* I tried to show the discrepancies and
conflicts within myself, as represented by two "I's".[12] The first 'I'
is Shunsuké, a writer of sixty-five, a celebrated novelist whose
Collected Works are being published for the third time. Shunsuké was
the 'grinning old man' whom Mishima feared to find in himself:
'The new collection of *The Works of Shunsuké Hinoki* would be his
third. The first one was assembled when he was forty-five. At that
point in time, I recall, he thought to himself, that in spite of the
great accumulation of my works, acclaimed by the world as the epi-
tome of stability and unity and, in a sense, having reached the
pinnacle, as many predicted, I was quite given over to foolishness . . .
to a wild ability to handle abstractions, which threatened to make me
misanthropic.'[13] (Thus, twenty years in advance, Mishima predicted
his state of mind in the year of his suicide with considerable accuracy
–'misanthropic' was correct.)

The second 'I' of *Forbidden Colours* is Yuichi, a youth of exquisite
beauty, first seen by Shunsuké as he emerges from the sea after a
swim: 'It was an amazingly beautiful young man. His body surpassed
the sculptures of ancient Greece. It was like the Apollo moulded in
bronze by an artist of the Peloponnesus school. It overflowed with
gentle beauty and carried such a noble column of a neck, such gently
sloping shoulders, such a softly broad chest, such elegantly rounded
wrists, such a rapidly tapering tightly filled trunk, such legs, stoutly
filled out like a heroic sword.' Shunsuké sees Yuichi's face: 'Quick,
narrow eyebrows; deep, sad eyes; rather thick, fresh lips–these made
up the design of his extraordinary profile. The wonderful ridge of his
nose, furthermore, along with his controlled facial expression, gave
to his youthful good looks a certain chaste impression of wildness,
as if he had never known anything but noble thoughts and starva-
tion.'[14] (Mishima probably never wrote less skilfully than when he
described his radiant, non-existent self.)

Yuichi, unlike the protagonist of *Confessions of a Mask,* is an un-
complicated homosexual, who enjoys the act of love. He is, however,
very much more of a narcissist than he is a homosexual–true to
Mishima's own character in this respect. When Yuichi makes his
first appearance at a celebrated gay bar in Tokyo, 'He floated on
desire. The look they gave him was like that a woman feels when she
passes among men and their eyes instantly undress her down to the

last stitch. Practised appraisers' eyes do not usually make mistakes. The gently sloping chest . . . the potential lovely harmony between what one saw and could not see seemed as perfect as a product of the ratio of the golden section.'[15]

This novel–described by Mishima as 'unnecessarily confused'– was strongly misogynic; Shunsuké uses Yuichi to wreak his revenge upon several women whom he hates. In one scene Shunsuké, confronted with the drowned body of his third and last wife, who has committed suicide with her lover, presses a *No* mask onto the swollen face of his dead spouse 'until it buckled like ripe fruit'. The novel was also intensely chauvinistic; the foreigners in the book are all homosexual and odd: one has the custom of shouting *'Tengoku! Tengoku!'* ('Paradise! Paradise!') when he reaches a sexual climax; another makes an assault on Yuichi and, when repulsed by the boy, weeps and kisses the cross which hangs from a chain about his own neck.

Mishima's private life at this time bore a resemblance to that led by Yuichi. 'He knew far more about boys than we did,' remarked one of his literary friends. He patronized the Brunswick, a gay bar in the Ginza; there he met the seventeen-year-old Akihiro Maruyama, who had just begun a golden career in the gay bars–from which he was to graduate to the theatre, where he became the most celebrated female impersonator of his day. The two men danced together some-times but they did not have an affair, according to Maruyama, who 'did not think him handsome, he was not my type.' Mishima had reservations about the gay bars, which are the haunts of scandal-seeking journalists and blackmailers and, like the whole of the Ginza, are under the protection of *yakuza* (gangsters). He particularly dis-liked certain types of effeminate men–his own ideal was a masculine type–as one may sense in this description of a gay bar in *Forbidden Colours*: 'Men dancing together–this uncommon joke. As they danced, the rebellious smiles beaming from their faces said: "We aren't doing this because we are forced to; we are only playing a simple joke." While they danced, they laughed, a spirit-destroying laugh.'[16] Mishima wrote to a friend a little later: 'I am not going to the Brunswick any more.' His friendship with Maruyama, though, lasted all his life.

Like Yuichi in *Forbidden Colours*, Mishima pursued both male and female company. According to one of his girl-friends: 'He liked women with long necks and round faces and he was very particular in some ways. When we went out together, he would specify what I was to wear. For the Comédie Française I had to wear a gown from Paris.' He was, in the Japanese phrase, a 'bearer of two swords'; he certainly enjoyed the company of women, but preferred men. Shizué remained the centre of his life. At night she would set out in the *tatami* room in which her son lived in their new home in Midorigaoka –a fashionable suburb of Tokyo–the things which he needed at night: fresh paper, pen and pencils, tea, fruit, blankets, glasses and so on. Shizué was always the first person to see her son's writing.

The family home was quiet. Chiyuki, Mishima's younger brother– an entirely different kind of man, soft, unassuming and unambitious –had decided to take the entrance examination for the Foreign Ministry. He came and went, travelling between home and Tokyo University. Azusa had closed his legal practice and had become an 'adviser' to one or two businesses run by friends; in retirement he had a comfortable, regular income. Mishima worked quietly, writing at night. It was a peaceful home, though Mishima's parents would quarrel from time to time, out of habit. Azusa, a grumbler rather than a stickler, enjoyed an occasional dispute, and would criticize his eldest son over minor things: 'he would keep a cat on his knees while he worked at his desk,' remarked Azusa, 'that really annoyed me.' The father of the family liked dogs and Mishima cats: 'Your brain must be like a dog's,' the latter would say to his father. 'You can't understand the delicate psychology of cats.' Azusa tried unsuccessfully to throw his son's cats out of the house, while Mishima cut a little door in the wall of his room so that the animals could come and go freely. When he travelled he sent postcards with *rusu mimai* (greetings, usually reserved for human beings) to his cats, and he would urge Azusa to treat them kindly.

With his father's help, late in 1951, Mishima finally engineered an arrangement under which he could travel abroad. Azusa had a friend at the *Asahi Shimbun*, the leading Japanese newspaper; and with his help Mishima obtained an appointment as a special correspondent without reporting duties and yet with an entitlement to an issue of foreign exchange, available from the Ministry of Finance, his old ministry, only under the rarest circumstances (Japan was desperately short of foreign exchange). He left Yokohama on Christmas Day on the *President Wilson*, seen off by his parents, who waved good-bye from the quayside. Mishima had long been looking forward to this chance to travel overseas: 'I felt the strong necessity of travelling abroad. . . . I was in the midst of an emotional crisis, I had to discover a new man within myself.'[17]

On board ship he felt perfectly happy. He mixed with the other passengers, abandoning 'my long-held claims to the solitude of a writer and my contempt for the world'. He attended New Year fancy-dress parties with some Americans, tying a *hachimaki* (head-band) on his head, and during the day he sat on deck, reading.

Sitting in the sun, which he had been unable to do earlier in life, when his lungs had been delicate, opened up a new world to him: 'I found the sun for the first time. I had come out of a dark cave. How long I had suppressed my love of the sun! All day long, sun-bathing on deck, I wondered how I should change myself. What did I have in excess? What did I lack?' He concluded that he had 'quite enough sensitivity. What I lack is an existential awareness of myself and of my body. I know how to despise mere cool intelligence. What I want is intelligence matched by pure physical existence—like a statue. And for this I need the sun, I need to leave my dark, cave-like study.'[18]

Arriving in New York he met Meredith Weatherby, an American friend who was working on a translation of *Confessions of a Mask*. According to Weatherby: 'We spent a whole day going over only two or three points. Mishima showed no sign of irritation. The translation was not published, but I learned a great deal from Mishima on that occasion. Translation of his works is harder than translating classical No. Sometimes it took me three hours to translate a single sentence. He always expressed the most subtle things in the most condensed sentences.'[19] (His translation was eventually published in 1958, after a delay occasioned, in part, by the prudishness of American publishers.)

From America Mishima travelled to Brazil and then on to Paris. From there he set out for Greece. This was an important journey for him. Unlike other Japanese writers, Mishima had long been interested in Greek literature and in the classical tradition of Europe. Four years previously he had written a short story, 'Shishi' ('Lion'), based on Euripides' *Medea*. While his contemporaries in Japan paid little attention to Aeschylus, Sophocles and the Homeric epics, Mishima knew the classical literature well, having read it in translation. His interest in the Greek classics—and, also, in the writers of the *Grand Siècle*, notably Racine—matched his love of the Japanese classics, also a most uncommon taste for one of his generation in Japan.

On his visit to Greece Mishima 'fell in love with the blue seas and vivid skies of that classical land.' He visited the well-known spots—an exception was Cape Sounion–travelling alone and unable to speak Greek; and he was enraptured: 'During my stay in Greece, the country of my dreams, I felt completely intoxicated all day long. In ancient Greece, so I thought, there had been no [Christian] spirituality. There had been, however, an equilibrium between the physical body and intelligence, *soma* and *sophia*. "Spirituality", so I thought, was a grotesque outgrowth of Christianity. In ancient times the Greeks had lost their equilibrium only too easily. Still, the strain and effort of maintaining their balance had helped to create beauty. Tragedy, in which arrogance was always punished, had helped men to understand how to keep their balance . . . in Greece the Gods were forever on the look-out for loss of equilibrium. My interpretation may have been wrong, but that was the Greece of which I stood in need. . . .'[20] Mishima discovered his 'classical inclination' in Greece: 'In other words I discovered an ethical criterion according to which I could produce beautiful works and also make myself beautiful. The ancient Greeks, I thought, had known this secret.'[21] His visit to Greece, he maintained, healed him of 'my self-hatred and liking for solitude.' In their place, he discovered a 'will towards health'–this phrase he adapted from the Nietzschean expression, 'will toward Power'. He returned to Japan 'in good humour, full of confidence in myself, sure that I could no longer be hurt by others.'[22] (He was guilty, so he would discover, of naïveté in this respect.)

Back in Japan in May 1952, Mishima felt that 'one part of my career was coming to an end, and I was entering a new phase of my life.' The transition period lasted for a year; he had a back-log of plays, novels and short stories to write, works which he had already planned in his mind. In the summer he published 'Death in Midsummer', a haunting (but misogynic) story about a woman whose two young children are drowned. And early in 1953 he completed a sequel to *Forbidden Colours*. In the second volume of *Forbidden Colours*–both volumes were later published as one novel–the story of Shunsuké, the ageing author, and Yuichi, the beautiful boy, winds to a conclusion. Shunsuké takes an overdose of drugs after giving Yuichi a long and meaningless lecture. Yuichi remains precisely the same person throughout this long novel: a 'doll' . . . 'Yuichi was a doll.' Asked by his wife to be present at the birth of their first child, he witnesses the Caesarean delivery: ' "I must look. No matter

what, I must look," he told himself, attempting to control his
nausea. "That system of countless, gleaming, wet red jewels; those
soft things under the skin, soaked in blood. . . ." '²³ Yuichi attempts
to persuade himself that the insides of his wife are 'just so much
pottery,' and he fails. For once, he has been moved.

Mishima's 'classical inclination' made itself felt again in 1953,
when he made a first journey to the island of Kamishima, south
from Ise–a small island at the mouth of the bay–which he proposed
to make the setting of a new novel based on the classical love story
of Daphnis and Chlöe. He did not rush at the work; instead, he made
elaborate notes on the life of the island and its small community of
fishermen. Thereafter he returned to Tokyo and set to work methodically. In the summer Shinchosha, his main publishers–he gave his
purely commercial novels to other houses–brought out Mishima's
first *Collected Works*, in six volumes. The publishing house gave a
reception, to which Mishima escorted his mother, and at which
Kawabata was a guest of honour. Standing around at the reception,
in white shirt and Western suit, Mishima–'young Mishima' as he was
known–looked about eighteen, a bright child whom his mother had
brought along for a prize-giving, a boy with a precise, sometimes
pedantic manner and pale face. Mishima was established, at this time,
as one of the major writers of the post-war generation, along with
Kobo Abé, Yoshie Hotta and Shohei Ooka. He was, however, regarded
as a superior writer to them–hence the decision to publish his
Collected Works at so early an age; he was also distinguished from his
contemporaries by his lack of interest in politics (Abé was a Communist Party member and Hotta a socialist) and by his style.

Edward Seidensticker, the translator of Kawabata (and of Mishima's
last novel, *The Decay of the Angel*), has written: 'So decorated as
sometimes to seem mannered and contrived [his language] shows a
concern which the rest of the nation seemed to be abandoning for
the beauties of the Japanese language. A language that lends itself
generously to the uses of mannerism and decoration, it is rather
like English in its way of enriching a native essence with imported
sauces and spices.' Mishima was 'delighted' with the richness of the
Japanese vocabulary: 'Of numbers of writers of Mishima's age and
younger it may be said that the style is difficult . . . only of Mishima
can it be said that the subtlety and richness of vocabulary and phrase
and allusion force even the fairly erudite reader to keep a reference
shelf at hand.' Professor Seidensticker compares Mishima to Joyce:

'He was master of a variety of styles, and was perhaps unique among his peers in being able to use the classical literary language . . . with ease, confidence and indeed elegance. In this respect he might be called Joycean.'[24] Joyce 'could be many different people and so could Mishima.'

In 1954 Mishima's *The Sound of Waves* was published, a novel which indeed revealed a 'different' person. The book was written under the influence of his visit to Greece two years before. It was a classical idyll of love, for which Mishima transported Daphnis and Chlöe to the island of Uta-jima (Kamishima, in reality) and reincarnated them as a simple fisherman and a young girl who dives for abalone. The hero and heroine of the story are almost children. The boy wears the same clothes every day, 'a pair of trousers inherited from his dead father and a cheap jersey'; and the girl works on the beach wearing the cotton-padded jacket and baggy trousers of fishing folk. Jealous rivals keep the lovers apart, but the story ends happily. There is none of the morbid sexuality of *Forbidden Colours* and *Thirst for Love* in *The Sound of Waves*. The book was a best-seller in Japan in 1954 and Shinchosha awarded Mishima a prize for the work; it was also adopted by the Ministry of Education as a standard text and made into a film by Toho, the largest production company, whose team Mishima accompanied to Kamishima on location. The critics paid little attention to the novel, however, and Mishima himself had doubts about the book: 'its success cooled my passion for Greece,' he said. The descriptions of nature in *The Sound of Waves* were somewhat artificial, 'in the style of the Trianon' at Versailles, as he put it. A common criticism of the work was that Mishima did not really know the mood of rustic, simple places. He had difficulty, in fact, in distinguishing the most elementary forms of natural life. He could not remember the names of trees, confusing pines and cedars.

'Classicism' was a major influence on Mishima. Keene has described the 'shift of emphasis in his works to structure, theme and intellectual content, as opposed to the baroque lushness of, say, *Forbidden Colours*. His style had already shifted from the archaisms of the early period and the heavy influence of translated literature, particularly the works of Radiguet and Stendhal, in his first novels, to the leanness of style of Ogai Mori (1862–1922). Ogai's masculine, intellectual diction often suggests a translation from the Chinese; the favoured tense is the historical present, and there is a rigorous insistence on purity of language . . . he followed Ogai in the unhesitant use of rare characters and words when they corresponded exactly with the desired nuance of meaning. . . . The use of the Japanese language for intellectual rather than emotional expression is an aspect of his classicism.'[25] Mishima, however, was never a pure 'classicist'. After completing *The Sound of Waves* he wrote the short story 'Kagi no Kakaru Heya' ('The Room with the Locked Door', 1954). An Okurasho official has a love affair with a married woman, who dies in their bed–he leaves the room, locking the door behind him and meets the nine-year-old daughter of the woman in the passage outside. The two play together for a while, and the man dreams of ripping the frail body of the little girl to shreds, to make himself a 'free inhabitant of this disorderly world'.

Mishima stated the limits to his 'classicism' in his autobiography *Watakushi no Henreki Jidai* ('My Wandering Years,' 1964): 'Looking back on those years [the early 1950s] I notice that there was a drastic social change but that nothing definite emerged. . . . Now I feel like destroying everything, as soon as possible. I don't believe in the classicism for which I had such a passion at the age of 26. It may sound merely clever to say so, but I exploited and used up my sensitivity completely; I know well that my sensitivity dried up. I now think of youth and the period of youth as foolishness. At the same time I feel no attachment towards age and experience. Thus, in a sudden flash, is born within me the idea of Death. This is, for me, the only truly vivid and erotic idea. . . .

'In a sense I may have suffered from an incurable romantic illness since birth.

'I, 26-years-old, I, the classicist, I, the one closest to Life–all of these "I's" may have been fakes.'[26]

2

1955–63

Mishima had great difficulty in building relationships with other people, apart from his mother Shizué. Like Etsuko, the protagonist of *Thirst for Love*, he had a compulsion to love; yet, when he gained the attention of another, he would take flight. One rare exception was his friendship with Utaemon, the *onnagata* (a *Kabuki* actor who takes female roles), of which Mishima gives an account in his short story 'Onnagata', published in 1957. In the story, Mangiku, a famous *onnagata*, falls in love with a young man of the modern theatre. The development of their relationship is observed by a third party, Masuyama, with whose descriptions of Mangiku ('Ten Thousand Chrysanthemums') the story begins: 'Mangiku Sanokawa was a true *onnagata*, a species seldom encountered nowadays. Unlike most contemporary *onnagata*, he was quite incapable of performing successfully in male roles. His stage presence was colourful, but with dark overtones: his every gesture was the essence of delicacy. Mangiku never expressed anything—not even strength, authority, endurance or courage—except through the single medium open to him, feminine expression, but through this medium he could filter every variety of human emotion. That is the way of the true *onnagata*, but in recent years this breed has become rare indeed.'[27]

Mishima had been a visitor to Utaemon's dressing-room at the Kabukiza since 1951 and knew the off-stage persona of the *onnagata*: 'Mangiku faithfully maintained the injunctions of the eighteenth-century *onnagata*'s manual *Ayamegusa*: "An *onnagata*, even in the dressing-room, must preserve the attitudes of an *onnagata*. He should be careful when he eats to face away from other people, so that they cannot see him." Whenever Mangiku was obliged to eat in the presence of visitors, not having the time to leave his dressing-room, he would turn towards his table with a word of apology and race through his meal so skilfully that the visitors could not even guess from behind that he was eating.'[28]

'Mangiku's body, when he removed his costume, was delicate but unmistakably a man's. Masuyama found it rather unnerving when Mangiku, seated at his dressing table, too scantily clad to be anything but a man, directed polite, feminine greetings towards some visitor, all the while applying a heavy coating of powder to his shoulders.'[29] 'The make-believe of his daily life supported the make-believe of his stage performances. This, Masuyama was convinced, marked the true *onnagata*. An *onnagata* is the child born of the illicit union between dream and reality.'[30]

The world of the *onnagata* was totally different from that of women, in Mishima's experience: 'Anyone pushing apart the door curtains dyed with the crest of the Sanokawa family and entering Mangiku's dressing-room was certain to be struck by a strange sensation; this charming sanctuary contained not a single man. Even members of the same troupe felt inside this room that they were in the presence of the opposite sex. Whenever Masuyama went to Mangiku's dressing-room on some errand, he had only to brush aside the door curtains to feel–even before setting foot inside–a curiously vivid, carnal sensation of being a male.

'Sometimes Masuyama had gone on company business to the dressing-rooms of chorus girls backstage at revues. The rooms were filled with an almost suffocating femininity and the rough-skinned girls, sprawled about like animals in the zoo, threw bored glances at him. . . .'[31]

'Onnagata' threw light on Mishima's private life. *The Temple of the Golden Pavilion* (1956), regarded by many as the best of his novels, illuminated his values. *Kinkakuji*–as the book was entitled in Japanese–was the story of a young monk, Mizoguchi, who serves at the renowned Kyoto temple of Kinkakuji (the Golden Pavilion), a fifteenth-century Zen temple. The young acolyte, a chronic stutterer from the home of a poor priest, believes that the whole of Kyoto –its citizens, its 1,500 temples and shrines and all of its other many treasures–will be destroyed at the end of the war. As did Mishima, living in Tokyo in 1945, Mizoguchi regards this wholesale destruction as inevitable and desirable; he has no compunction about dying himself. The novel is a parable; Mizoguchi, unable to accept the continued existence of Kinkakuji, his ideal of beauty, burns the ancient pavilion to the ground one night; so, Mishima, having created his own temple of beauty, his 'Greek' body, was to destroy that temple. Mizoguchi says: 'Beauty, beautiful things, those are now my most deadly enemies;' and he speaks with the voice of Mishima. The destruction of beauty is more beautiful than beauty itself. 'Destruction' is the principal value.

The Temple of the Golden Pavilion contains much philosophical discussion, which Mishima described thus: 'With respect to the conversations in my novels, I believe I have already freed myself to a considerable extent from Japanese fastidiousness. Japanese writers enjoy displaying their delicate skill at revealing in an indirect manner, by means of conversations, the personalities, temperaments and outlook on life of their characters; but conversations that are un-related to the personalities and temperaments of the characters, conversations that are read for their content alone, and, finally, long conversations that fuse into the same tempo with the des-criptive passages, are the special quality of the novels of Goethe, and of the German novel in general.'[32] Mann, he said, had inherited from Goethe 'the epic flow of conversation'; and the style of *The*

Temple of the Golden Pavilion he characterized as 'Ogai plus Mann'.

The long conversations in *The Temple of the Golden Pavilion* are dominated by Kashiwagi, a fellow student of Mizoguchi at a Buddhist seminary, an evil man with club feet.

Kashiwagi harasses Mizoguchi, using the aggressive conversational technique of a Zen priest:

'"Stutter!" he said. "Go ahead and stutter!"

'I listened in sheer amazement to his peculiar way of expressing himself.

'"At last you've come across someone to whom you can stutter at your ease. That's right, isn't it? People are all like that, you know. They are all looking for a yoke fellow. Well, now, are you a virgin?"'[33]

The club-footed fellow follows up this attack on Mizoguchi with a reference to his physical ailment and his use of the deformity to intrigue women and lure them into bed. Mizoguchi, who is a virgin, is hypnotized by Kashiwagi's aphorism: '"The special quality of hell is to see everything clearly down to the last detail. And to see all that in the pitch darkness."'[34]

Kashiwagi gives a demonstration of his technique of seducing women. As the two students walk along a path, Kashiwagi catches sight of a beautiful girl approaching them. At the critical moment he lurches and tumbles with a pitiful cry, attracting the attention of the girl, who helps him to his feet and takes him into her home, near at hand, to bandage his undamaged leg. Thereafter, the two have an affair. Kashiwagi later gets rid of the girl, after teaching her how to disguise the fact that she has lost her virginity from the man whom she is to marry. One day Mizoguchi steals a bunch of irises from the garden at Kinkakuji and brings them to Kashiwagi's lodging as a gift. While the latter makes a flower arrangement on a dish in his room, Mizoguchi questions him about the girl-friend he has just disposed of; Kashiwagi replies:

'"Do you know the famous words in the chapter of Popular Enlightenment in the *Rinsairoku*? 'When ye meet the Buddha, kill the Buddha! When ye meet your ancestor, kill your ancestor! . . .'"

'"When ye meet a disciple of Buddha.'" I continued, "'kill the disciple! When ye meet your father and mother, kill your father and mother! When ye meet your kin, kill your kin! Only thus will ye attain deliverance.'"

"That's right. And that was the situation you see. That girl was a disciple of Buddha."

"And so you delivered yourself?"

"Hm," said Kashiwagi, arranging some of the irises that he had cut and gazing at them, "there's more to killing than that you know." '[35]

Kashiwagi then introduces the Zen *koan* (riddle), 'Nansen Kills a Kitten'. One day a beautiful kitten is found in the neighbourhood of two temples. The monks of the two temples dispute amongst each other as to who should look after it. Nansen ends the dispute by asking the monks to tell him why he should not kill the kitten and, when they cannot reply, he kills it at once. When his chief disciple, Joshu, who has been out at the time, returns to the temple, Nansen tells him of the events; thereupon Joshu takes off his muddy shoes and places them on his head. 'If only you had been here,' says Nansen, 'then the kitten could have been saved!' ' "You see," continued Kashiwagi, "that's what beauty is like. To have killed the kitten seemed just like having extracted a painful decayed tooth, like having gouged out beauty. Yet it was uncertain whether or not this had really been a final solution. The root of the beauty had not been severed, and, even though the kitten was dead, the kitten's beauty might very well still be alive. And so, you see, it was in order to satirize the glibness of this solution that Joshu put those shoes on his head. He knew, so to speak, that there was no possible solution other than enduring the pain of the decayed tooth." '[36]

Mizoguchi is very much frightened by this 'completely original solution' of the *koan*. He asks:

' "So which of the two are you? Father Nansen or Joshu?"

"Well, let's see. As things are now, I am Nansen and you're Joshu. But someday you might become Nansen and I might become Joshu. This problem has a way of changing—like a cat's eyes." '[37]

As Mizoguchi watches Kashiwagi, at work on his arrangement of irises, he has a premonition of approaching disaster: 'There was something cruel about the movement of his hands. They behaved as though they had some gloomy privilege in relation to the plants. Perhaps it was because of this that each time I heard the sound of the scissors and saw the stem of one of the flowers being cut I had the impression that I could detect the dripping of blood.'[38]

The book ends with Mizoguchi's destruction of Kinkakuji—Mishima's story is based on a real event, the burning down of Kinkakuji by a psychopathic monk in the summer of 1950.

The Temple of the Golden Pavilion won high praise. The *Asahi Shimbun* said that Mishima had 'outgrown the smart young writer and has evolved as a mature observer of human nature.' The *Yomiuri* newspaper awarded Mishima a prize; and Kon Ichikawa, one of the best of the post-war directors, filmed the book. Its publication in the translation by Ivan Morris was to seal Mishima's reputation overseas. (Only one criticism was made. Hideo Kobayashi, probably the most powerful critic in post-war Japan, said he doubted if *The Temple of the Golden Pavilion* was a novel; it was a poem, he said, which revealed the author's attitudes too directly. A photograph taken of Kobayashi and Mishima having dinner together in January 1957 shows Mishima with his head uncharacteristically bowed, as he listens to his critic.)

To many writers their public reputation is secondary. To Mishima, however, it was cardinal. With the publication of *The Temple of the Golden Pavilion*, he established himself as the leading writer of his generation in Japan. His claim to this title, as novelist, playwright and critic—an all-rounder—was strong: his style was vastly superior to that of his contemporaries. Mishima was not content with this success; as Keene has remarked, 'He wanted to conquer the world with his books'. By 1956–7 this ambition was within the realms of the possible. There was a boom in the West in Japanese literature —many of the leading authors of the twentieth century were being published in America; this was an essential precondition for Mishima's success. A second factor was that Mishima was in a better position to exploit the surge of interest in Japanese literature than any other writer; his books were 'Western' in structure, unlike those of, for example, Kawabata, in which mood is all-important and which are difficult for a Western reader to appreciate. Finally, Mishima was personable and anxious to communicate with Western audiences, while other Japanese writers were either too elderly to care very much about their standing in the West or—simply—indifferent. His only major problem was that he was not fluent in English.

Early in 1957 he received two invitations which sealed his determination to overcome this one handicap. The first came from Alfred Knopf, his publisher in New York, who asked him to travel to America for the publication of *Five Modern No Plays*, a collection of his 'modern No plays', translated by Keene. In the previous year Knopf had brought out *The Sound of Waves*, which had been successful for a Japanese author–10,000 copies had been sold. The second invitation was to deliver a speech at Michigan University, on the subject of modern Japanese literature. Mishima eagerly accepted these invitations, and settled down to learn English with characteristic determination. A friend recalls how 'he bought tapes and earphones for his taperecorder, and sat down with the machine for hours every day. He went over the same tapes again and again, battering the unfamiliar sounds into his head.'

On 1 July Mishima boarded a plane at Haneda, ready to begin his second world trip.

Anyone who saw him that day would not have taken him for a writer. He had his hair cut short, and he wore a blazer and white shirt and tie; he radiated good health. One might have thought he was a sports coach, with his thick neck and physical flamboyance. Two years previously he had taken up body-building and had transformed his physical appearance. In place of the spindly, white arms of his youth, he had strong, muscular arms and shoulders; he had turned into a healthy, sun-tanned specimen of Japanese manhood–marred only by his being a little short in the leg.

His stay in America lasted for nearly six months. He travelled in the southern states, visiting New Orleans, and then on to the West Indies–in Port-au-Prince he saw a voodoo ceremony–arriving in New York in the late summer. He hoped to see his *No* plays, free adaptations from the classical plays in modern settings, which were exciting interest in many parts of the world, performed in New York. They would provide, he hoped, a vehicle for him, and would make him instantly well-known in America. He stayed in a first-class hotel in New York and waited. Weeks went by, his money began to run out and he received no news. He moved to a third-class Greenwich Village hotel, which he likened to a *yoroin* (old people's home), as it had many elderly, permanent residents. Waiting in vain for performance of his *No* plays and with little money (Japan still had tight foreign exchange controls), Mishima became progressively more gloomy; like many Japanese he was not good at managing abroad, by himself. 'In a foreign country everything is a source of fear. You cannot go to the post office or to the bank as you are frightened of going by yourself. You don't know how to get about, whether by bus or by underground. All around you is a mystery, so much so that you cannot tell one man from another, who is good and who evil.'[39]

In New York at the time was Donald Keene, then an assistant

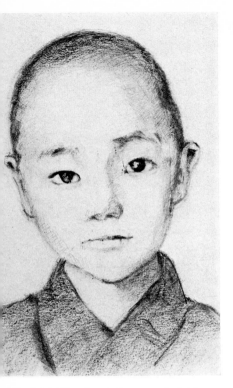

Kimitaké Hiraoka at the age of eight.
(*Pencil drawing after photographs by
A. Sugiyama*)

Natsuko Hiraoka, Mishima's grandmother. (*Pencil drawing after photographs
by A. Sugiyama*)

7 Yukio Mishima on his wedding day,
June 1958.

8 Yoko and Yukio Mishima in New York, 1960. (*Photo WWP*)

professor of Japanese literature at Columbia University: 'I wanted to
see him and to encourage him more often than I did, but I was busy
with lectures and did not invite him out for meals. One day Mishima
came to my apartment, unannounced, and said, proudly, that he had
taken the subway. I was about to go out and told him this. Then, in
a hesitating manner, speaking in a low voice, he asked if I would permit him to stay behind a little longer, alone.'[40] Mishima was weak and
unable to prevent himself from showing his weakness to others.
'This was an incredible scene,' remarked Keene, 'if one considers the
man he was in the 1960s.' In the end there was a private performance
of one *No* play, *Hanjo*, and Mishima left for home, dispirited, at the
end of the year, returning by way of Europe and arriving back in
Japan just before his thirty-third birthday.

In Japan it is rare for a man to remain unmarried. Most people marry
in their twenties, the girls in their early twenties, the men a little
later. Not to marry is considered odd, especially if one comes from
the upper middle class, as did Mishima. That he had not got married
in his twenties was surprising, for he was guided in what he did by a
strong sense of duty, especially duty to his parents, i.e. Shizué. Both
Mishima and his mother, however, had been restrained for years
by their own close relationship. His mother did not press him to get
married and Mishima himself was in no hurry to do so. However,
early in 1958, on his return from abroad, Mishima was told that his
mother had cancer and would probably die. He immediately made
up his mind to get married, in order to fulfil his duty to his mother,
and to give her the pleasure of seeing him married before she died.
Having no particular girl in mind he opted for an arranged marriage,
a common practice in Japan. He attended a series of *omiai*–these are
formal meetings with eligible girls, found by family friends and
acquaintances and the outer circle of their friends and acquaintances,
which commit neither side, and simply provide an occasion for two
young people to get a first impression of one another.

One of Mishima's first *omiai* was with Michiko Shoda, the
beautiful daughter of a flour company president, who subsequently
married Crown Prince Akihito. Possibly, Mishima's precise ideas about
the kind of person he wished to marry were too much for Miss
Shoda and her family. He stipulated that his bride must be neither a
bungaku shojo (a blue-stocking) nor a *yumeibyo kanja* (a celebrity
hunter), and he had five other requirements:

E

(i) His bride must wish to marry Kimitaké Hiraoka, the private citizen, not Yukio Mishima, the writer.

(ii) She should be no taller than her husband, even in high heels.

(iii) She must be *kawaii* (pretty) and have a round face.

(iv) She should be eager to take care of Mishima's parents and capable of running the home efficiently.

(v) She must not disturb Mishima while he worked.

These were the guidelines given to the intermediaries who had the task of finding candidates for *omiai* with Mishima.

His choice settled finally on Yoko Sugiyama, the twenty-one-year-old daughter of a famous traditional painter. Mishima chose her partly because she was the daughter of an artist. And also, 'I could not help choosing one from amongst those who lived in a spot I did not know . . . and who was not interested in my writing.'⁴¹ Yoko was two inches shorter than Mishima—she was just over five feet tall—and she was *kawaii* and round-faced; and, according to the confidential reports that the Hiraoka family received from a marriage counsellor, she was thoroughly competent in daily life. Mishima met Yoko in early April and after two meetings made up his mind to marry her; they were engaged early in May 1958. Mishima asked Kawabata to act as the *baishaku-nin* (the 'go-between'), who officiates at the long dinner party which follows the marriage ceremony, a Shinto service. He wanted to rush ahead with the wedding—'it is not a good idea to delay, while people whisper advice into one's ear'—and would have liked to get married in May. This proved to be impossible, as the couple could not find a *taian* (lucky day) by which Yoko's three wedding dresses would be ready—the bride at a Japanese wedding parades in *kimono*, Western wedding dress and ball dress, in succession. In the end they were married on 1 June. 'An important day,' Mishima said later, 'may be chosen for trivial reasons.'

Mishima, however, need not have been in such a hurry. Shizué had not had cancer at all. She was in poor health, but was to make a steady recovery.

After the wedding the couple left for Hakone, in the mountains near Mt Fuji, spending their first night at the old-fashioned Fujiya Hotel. From the hotel Mishima made phone-calls to his home, to check on Shizué's condition. At the end of their honeymoon Mishima and Yoko came back to Tokyo to live with his parents for a short time. Mishima had bought land in Magome, some miles north of the airport, and was building two houses, one for him and Yoko, and a second for his parents next-door. The expense was considerable and in order to pay for the building he raised a loan from Shinchosha, his publishers, against the royalties on his next novel, *Kyoko no Ie* ('Kyoko's House', 1959).

Most Japanese homes are small and unpretentious, a mixture of Japanese and Western styles; as their houses are small in size, Japanese people do not generally invite friends to their homes, unless they are exceptionally close. There is no tradition of entertaining at home, as there is in the West. Mishima, however, decided to be thoroughly Western. He built as large a home as he could afford, giving it a reception room with a high ceiling, and a rectangular, formal, Western garden. Travelling in the West Indies, he had been attracted by the spectacle of decaying, colonial mansions, and the design of his house was 'colonial'–it had thick, white, painted walls, the antithesis of Japanese traditional taste. It was, Mishima said, an 'anti-Zen house'. The architect had a problem: how to realize his client's idea of a 'colonial' house on a plot of land of a size sufficient only for a house of normal size. To make room for a garage on one side of the house, a drive, and also a garden, he was eventually compelled to cut the house itself down to a modest size. The reception room, with its high ceiling running up to the second floor, was in the end rather cramped.

Mishima's aim–his fundamental aim in life, it might be said–was to shock. He was determined to create an effect with his new house; unable to build on a grand scale he fell back on unusual decor. He decorated the reception room of the new house in Victorian style; and he filled it with copies of nineteenth century furniture. On the walls he put oil paintings with 'classical' themes; and he hung the large window which faced the garden with heavy, ornate curtains. 'This,' he said, 'is my dream–or nightmare–of Victorian opulence.' To a Western eye the effect was a little unusual; to a Japanese eye it was grotesque. In the garden he placed an outsize statue of Apollo on a plinth: 'my despicable symbol of the rational.'

This desire to shock others was fundamental to Mishima's character and was evident in the articles which he wrote for Japanese magazines: 'Now I am a *dannasama* [a family head, a traditional term, here used ironically]. I rule my wife at home, act according to common sense, build a house, am fairly cheerful, love speaking ill of others, rejoice when people remark on my youthful appearance, pursue the latest fashions and favour all manner of things in bad taste. I say nothing serious . . . and do my utmost to live to the age of Methuselah.'[42]

Statements about his family were, however, rare. He divided his life into two distinct compartments: his family life and his public career. In this sense he had something of the Confucian within him, for all his exhibitionism; in certain circumstances, he regarded his duty to his family as his prime consideration. For instance, photographers who came to his home were not allowed to take pictures of Yoko; nor, later, when the Mishimas had children, could they photograph them. Equally, Mishima's parents were kept out of the glare of publicity in which he lived. 'Mishima', the public figure, was always Mishima the novelist, playwright and exhibitionist; he was never Mishima the son, husband and father. In order to make the separation between his public and private lives complete, he never used any other name than 'Mishima'; 'Kimitaké Hiraoka' was a name which appeared only in literary dictionaries. Indeed, I did not know his real name until after his death.

At home, for the benefit of reporters, Mishima assumed a pose of insouciance: 'My ideal life is to live in a house where I sit on a rococo chair, wearing an aloha shirt and blue jeans.'[43] He was also, though, a relentless self-disciplinarian. Early in 1959, six months after his marriage, he began a heroic programme of physical exercise. On Mondays and Fridays he trained at the *kendo* hall, and on Wednesdays, Thursdays and Saturdays he went to the body-building gym. He worked hard at both *kendo* and body-building; these were no graceful exercises. Meanwhile, he kept up his writing programme as before, working each night until dawn and sleeping in the mornings. His intense efforts drove him, sometimes, into a gloomy state of mind: 'I will split my 24-hour day into three parts, hours for sleep, for work and for physical exercise. No more personal associations. This way people will think that I am always busy and I will have 24 hours a day of solitude and leisure.'[44]

Mishima's longing to shock others was as apparent in his literature as well as in his daily life. 'He would never write two novels in the same style,' Keene says. 'He would always try to find something new in order to surprise his readers.' The novel which he wrote shortly after his marriage, *Kyoko no Ie* ('Kyoko's House'), exemplified this urge; he called the book his 'study of nihilism': 'The characters run about in one direction or another as their personalities, their professions and their sexual tendencies command them, but in the

end all roads, no matter how roundabout, flow back into nihilism.'[45]
In this novel Mishima represented himself by four 'I's': 'When I
am developing a single character in one of my novels, I sometimes
feel him quite close to my own thinking, but at other times I drive
the same character away from myself and let him wander into
independent action. The attitudes of the hero change convulsively,
as the course of composition dictates. In *Kyoko no Ie*, in order to
resolve this contradiction which has always appeared in my novels
(and was most extreme in *Forbidden Colours*), I have avoided having
a single hero, but have represented various aspects of myself through
four different heroes.'[46]

The four 'heroes' are these:

Shunkichi, a boxer. His principle is 'to think about nothing.' By
'disorderly' and 'free' anarchism he hopes to destroy the social
order of post-war Japan. He believes in 'Might', which he associates with beauty and death—not with justice and order. He envies
his elder brother who died in the war; his brother had sped
through life 'without fear of boredom and without thinking at all'.
Shunkichi lives in a hateful epoch of 'normality', and in such an
era he cannot maintain his 'purity'. Believing in 'Might' he
sets about to make himself a boxing champion. However, his
career ends after he has suffered a beating at the hands of thugs,
who break the bones of his hands. Shunkichi believes that his
future will be boring and insignificant; he joins an *Uyoku* (rightist)
group 'in order to oppose the future'. In such a group he is 'close
to death, even in this age of normality.' In a street brawl Shunkichi
meets his death.

Osamu, a beautiful, narcissistic actor, who practises body-building. Osamu is racked with anxiety: 'Do I really exist or not?'
He is constantly peering at himself in a mirror. He has a mistress,
an elderly usurer, who has bought Osamu's services. The woman
loves Osamu, and expresses her love by torturing him. The handsome actor wonders whether the shedding of his blood will prove
his existence. He desires to perform in 'a complete drama'. He
and his mistress commit a bloody *shinju* (double love suicide).

Natsuo, a traditional Japanese painter. Natsuo believes that he
is an angel, whose pure and gentle existence is protected by a

special deity. He has no troubles in life. However, on a trip to Mt Fuji he has a vision of the destruction of the world. He reflects on his situation; he is well-known and successful; but he is the subject of jealous gossip amongst his contemporaries. Talking to friends, he suggests that one should kill oneself, while one's body is beautiful, with fine muscles. Natsuo is captured by a strange world of 'reality' and 'nihility'. In the end he has an existential experience: 'what I see and I that see belong to one world.' He is saved.

Seiichiro, a capable businessman. He is a *shoshain*, a trading company executive. The world, he considers, is doomed; total destruction is inevitable. He is, however, outwardly cheerful and competent, and he is successful at work. His motto is to play the role of 'somebody else' and to lead a 'conventional life'. He marries the daughter of a senior director. His company later sends him to New York, where he continues as before. Seiichiro suffers from 'an incurable illness'–'healthiness'.

Kyoko no Ie revealed more about Mishima than any other work of his in the 1950s. Each of the four heroes of the novel suggests aspects of the author's character which had been largely hidden, and which were to emerge clearly in the 1960s. His right-wing inclinations, exemplified in the character of the boxer Shunkichi, became conspicuous after 1965. His notion that one must commit suicide while one still has a beautiful, muscular body was another idea that emerged in Mishima's life in the late 1960s. The same may be said of Osamu's desire to 'prove' his existence by shedding his blood, and his wish to perform in a 'complete drama'. The most interesting feature of *Kyoko no Ie*, however, is the conviction of three of the four heroes that the destruction of the world is inevitable; Mishima's nihilism bore a close resemblance to that of the *Roman-ha*. A literary critic, Jun Eto, has pointed out that Mishima was 'the only possible spokesman for the lost *Roman-ha* cause. *Expectation of the world's destruction*, the theme that has appeared almost obsessively in his post-war works, is one of the most typical ideas of the *Roman-ha* group. This theme is clearly recognized in his novels *Bitoku no Yoromeki* ['Tottering Virtue', 1957], *Kyoko no Ie* and *Utsukushii Hoshi* ['Beautiful Star', 1962].'[47]

Kyoko no Ie was, however, a failure with the public. Mishima himself suggested the reason for its failure: 'The painter represents sensitivity, the boxer action, the actor self-awareness and the business-man knowing how to get along with the world. It is naturally to be expected that the personalities of these characters will become abstract and purified. I have for the time being given up any attempt to create characters as single, co-ordinated, organic entities.'[48] Perhaps it was this intellectual attitude that undermined his 'study of nihilism'—without character, what could he do? Mishima may well have reflected thus, for his next book, *After the Banquet*, was a great triumph of characterization.

Mishima once remarked: 'All my works can be divided into two categories, *pièces roses* and *pièces noires*, as Anouilh used those terms.' *After the Banquet* is the best of his *pièces roses*. Kazu, the proprietress of a fashionable Japanese-style restaurant in Tokyo, the Setsugoan (in real life, the Hannya-en), is the chief protagonist of the novel, which satirizes political life in Japan and the mores of the upper class. Kazu, Angus Wilson has remarked, 'is a woman of Balzacian dimensions and Flaubertian truth.' Mishima describes her thus: 'A streak of rustic simplicity in Kazu's plump, attractive figure, always bursting with energy and enthusiasm, made people with complicated motives who came before her feel ashamed of their complexity. People with drooping spirits, when they saw Kazu, were either considerably heartened or else completely overpowered. Some curious blessing of heaven had joined in one body a man's resolution with a woman's reckless enthusiasm. This combination carried Kazu to heights no man could reach.'[49]

Mishima describes her taking a stroll in the garden of her restau-rant: 'This morning stroll was the poem of Kazu's security. She was over fifty, but no one seeing this carefully groomed woman, whose complexion and sparkling eyes had lost none of their loveli-ness, as she sauntered through the huge garden, could help but be struck and moved to romantic conjectures. But, as Kazu herself realized better than anyone, for her romantic stories were a thing of the past, her poem was dead.'[50] Her conviction is disproved. She falls in love with a politician, Noguchi, and they get married. Noguchi stands for election to the governorship of Tokyo, and Kazu throws all her energy, and, finally, all her money, into the campaign. Noguchi, a liberal candidate, loses the election, however, as the conservatives have far more money than he. Mishima knew a great deal about the functioning of party machines in Tokyo and here he describes party politics to perfection. His knowledge of the nuances of behaviour in upper-class society was also evident in *After the Banquet*. After the elections, Kazu runs into a woman she dislikes, Mrs Tamaki, the widow of a diplomat; the two women meet by chance in a fruit shop, where Kazu discovers Mrs Tamaki rummaging in a bin of Sunkist oranges:

'Mrs Tamaki, after much deliberation, selected three oranges. "Even oranges have become expensive these days. And just think, in America they practically give them away!" Mrs Tamaki, as part of her brave display of inverse snobbery, deliberately ordered the salesgirl to wrap just three oranges. . . .

' "My husband liked oranges," Mrs Tamaki went on. "Sometimes I offer them at the family altar. That's why I bought them today. . . . You know, it suddenly occurred to me that my husband, without realizing it, of course, played the part of cupid for you and Mr Noguchi." ' [By falling ill in Kazu's restaurant, Tamaki had by chance brought together Kazu and Noguchi.]

' "In that case I suppose I'll have to offer him some oranges myself."

' "I didn't mean it that way."

'Kazu did not herself understand why she was behaving so rudely. On a sudden impulse she motioned to the salesgirl with the sandalwood fan she had been using, and ordered her to make up a gift box of two dozen oranges.'[51] Presents must be neither too large nor too small, in Japan. By flouting this convention, while knowing that Mrs Tamaki will not have the courage to refuse the offer of the gift, Kazu crushes her enemy. Her present was far too big for the occasion.

After the Banquet was a brilliant success for Mishima; it is also the work by him which I like most as entertainment (*Confessions of a Mask* is compelling enough, but it is gloomy reading). But he was never satisfied with his successes. He had been put off by the applause for *The Sound of Waves* and the great triumph of his career in the 1950s, *The Temple of the Golden Pavilion*, had also not provided him with lasting satisfaction. What did he want of life? 1960 was without doubt a crucial year in his life. He does not appear to have known what he wanted; once more he was deep in a personal crisis, as he had been in 1950–51, just before his first travels abroad. But in the 'fifties something had changed. Ten years had gone by–his 'classical' period lay behind him–and he seemed, to himself at any rate, to have nothing

to show for that decade. Worst of all, he had failed as a novelist–
with *Kyoko no Ie*. This failure, I believe, made a very deep mark on
Mishima. One has to remember that he had had almost no experience
of failure–and, at the same time, he set an enormous premium on
success. He had thrown everything he had, he said, into *Kyoko no Ie*.
All his accumulated experience–as a man, as a craftsman, and as a
novelist–was contained in that long book, the longest novel of his
career (the two volumes of *Forbidden Colours* excepted). And he had
had the book virtually cast back in his face. The critics were extremely
harsh in their treatment of the novel; scarcely anyone–Takeo Okuno
was an exception–expressed a liking for it. Some reviewers said that
this was Mishima's 'magnificent failure'; he sensed instantly that
beneath the sycophancy was a barely concealed sense of triumph:
the brilliant young Mishima had fallen flat on his face. Under such
circumstances, the success of *After the Banquet* did not console
Mishima. What he wanted, urgently, was to re-establish himself; and,
for the first time in his life, he found that he lacked the thrust, the
energy to do so. As a novelist, Mishima experienced the gravest crisis
in 1960; it was not until 1965 that he attempted another major
work in the field of the novel–when he embarked on his monumental
The Sea of Fertility.

It may be, however, that he felt a still deeper sense of failure at
this time in his life. Not only was he beset with difficulties as a
novelist–they may have acted as a catalyst–but the position in which
he found himself seems to have been far graver than the failure
of *Kyoko no Ie* alone would have justified. I do not know exactly
what was going on in his mind, but judging by his actions, Mishima
was in profound despair. In the autumn of 1959, presumably after
he had learned the bad news about *Kyoko no Ie*, he decided to play a
part in a film. There was nothing extraordinary about this. Why should
he not amuse himself a little? (He said that he would like to be 'a
jazz singer, to be eighteen again'.) But the movie he chose to appear
in was bad. It was an ugly, irresponsible, *yakuza* (gangster) movie
in which Mishima played the part of an insignificant hood who gets
himself murdered–and is, indeed, a nasty little specimen. Had Mishima
chosen to play in a good film, one would not be surprised; this was
his first movie and the experience was plainly one that someone of
his temperament would enjoy. But why *Karakkaze Yaro* ('A Dry
Fellow'), a grubby tale of prison, of betrayed girl-friends and broken
trust, with no redeeming features? It is as if Mishima, at the end of

Confessions of a Mask, in that famous scene with Sonoko in the cheap dance hall, had risen from his seat, leaving his friend at the table, and gone over to the group of *yakuza* standing in the sun winding their belly-bands around their hot torsos, and spent the afternoon carousing with his new friends—having left his girl to find her own way home, without even saying goodbye.

He had, of course, every reason to lead his life in his own way; he was free. But by taking on the part in *Karakkaze Yaro* Mishima alienated people of good sense (of whom Sonoko stands as a symbol in my parable). What had he to gain? His decision to enter the world of the cinema in this fashion was equivalent to an announcement to society that he no longer recognized the conventions. If the critics did not care for his novel *Kyoko no Ie*, so much the worse for them; he didn't heed them. I have no quarrel with Mishima's dislike of the critics; the *Bundan* strikes me as a pitiful society which is inimical to talent. But Mishima was not simply saying 'Boo!' to the critics. He was turning his back on quiet people—friends, family acquaintances, people he had never met but who could have become close to him, people of no great power or influence, whose collective disapproval, however, would go against him in the long run. Ten years before, he could have got away with an action like this (in a sense he did: parts of *Forbidden Colours* are in dreadful taste). At the age of thirty-five, with an enormous critical reputation (despite *Kyoko no Ie*), and a great following among the general public, he could not afford to cut such a caper as his appearance in *Karakkaze Yaro* represented. To be an immature romantic at twenty-five is understandable. At thirty-five? No.

I take Mishima's decision to appear in the *yakuza* movie—he had the leading role—as indicative of his parlous state of mind at this time, as a sign that he was losing control. And it was not the only indication that he was in a serious state. Here let us jump ahead to the summer of 1960. As one instalment after another of *After the Banquet* appeared in a monthly magazine, it became apparent that he was satirizing an extremely well-known public man in his portrayal of Noguchi, the lover of Kazu in the book. His target was a former Foreign Minister, a man of liberal views, Hachiro Arita. I do not imagine that Mishima had a personal grudge against the man, still less that he had any objection to his politics. But he made a complete fool of Arita. *After the Banquet* was a thinly disguised, brilliant, witty account of Arita's affair with a restaurant owner, the proprietress of the *Hannya-en* in Tokyo. Why did Mishima take such a risk? The libel laws in Japan are weak—by Western standards they are a farce—but Mishima was going much too far. Each successive instalment of *After the Banquet* sank another, only too accurate shot into a man who had already virtually failed in public life. What the Arita family thought about this can be imagined; and they found much sympathy among friends, influential people in Tokyo, and even editors and publishers in the city.

In the end Arita was provoked to the point where, discarding normal Japanese rules of behaviour (in cases of libel it is usual for the disputing parties to settle their quarrel through intermediaries who may not even be lawyers), he brought a suit against Mishima. It was an unprecedented case which came to public notice early in 1961; Arita's complaint was that his privacy had been invaded. The libel suit attracted much public interest. *Puraibashii* (or 'privacy' as it is spelled in Japanese too—the word has been adapted directly from English into the Japanese language) instantly became a vogue word and was accepted as a neologism by the Japanese at large. Mishima lost the suit; it took many years, but in the end Arita's lawyers nailed him down. The key factor, I suspect, was that people with influence in Tokyo felt that the novelist had behaved monstrously. In the absence of a precedent, their opinion must have affected the court, which had no specific guide as to the law.

Mishima was succeeding in antagonizing a good number of people at this time. He was, of course, a charming person, when he was on form. He was entertaining, more than a little witty at his own expense, and, above all, intelligent. He had, say what he might about the *Bundan*, very many friends in the literary establishment. About this time in his life, however, he reached a parting of the ways with one particular group of former associates; these were the members of a little literary club called the *Hachi no Ki Kai* ('Potted Cherry Tree Club'). They were a powerful group: Toson Fukuda, a playwright; Mitsuo Nakamura, the *Asahi Shimbun* critic; Shohei Ooka, the novelist; and Ken-Ichi Yoshida, a rare instance of a Japanese man of letters. Mishima had got on well with these people for many years; when they started a magazine, they had printed his work right away. But for the most part the *Hachi no Ki Kai* was a social affair; the members met for dinner, enjoyed drinking together, and indulged in merry gossip at the expense of others. By 1960, however, Mishima's relations with this group had begun to deteriorate. A member of the *Hachi no Ki Kai* once told me of an incident at one of their dinners:

'I had had too much to drink, I expect, and for some reason I was feeling antagonistic and decided to give Mishima a piece of my mind. I don't know what I said exactly but the others told me afterwards that I spoke with unwonted frankness; I suppose I told Mishima he was a snob who took himself too seriously.' Whether it was on this occasion or another that Mishima finally took offence, I do not know; but certainly the time came when he severed his ties with the *Hachi no Ki Kai*, the only literary group with whom he had ever got on well and with whom he sustained a link over many years. He was foolish; he *was* a snob and he *did* take himself too seriously: he should have listened and not taken umbrage.

These were small matters in their way–the gangster movie, the quarrel with Arita and the parting with the *Hachi no Ki Kai*–but it was through such incidents that Mishima found himself increasingly isolated in 1960. And, as luck would have it, this was the year in which political events impinged on his life, for the first time since 1945. Just at a point in his literary career when he was vulnerable, Mishima came under pressure. The story is a complex one. During the late 1940s, terrible years for Japan, Mishima had paid no attention to political matters. After the end of the Occupation, during which momentous decisions had been made about the future of Japanese society, Mishima still did not respond to events on the political scene. Throughout the 1950s he contented himself with his literary pursuits. He was thought by his contemporaries to be vaguely leftist, a man inclined towards acceptance of the popular creed of political neutrality between the Western world and the Communist bloc. By 1960, however, his interest in politics was coming to life. *After the Banquet* is not a political novel, but it shows that Mishima had learned more about politics in Japan than many of his friends and fellow writers. It is a classic description, in its way, of the alliance between money and power in Japanese society.

After the Banquet was the first sign that Mishima was curious about the political world. The second was his interest in the huge demonstrations against the government in May and June of that year–the most spectacular political demonstrations in post-war Japanese history. Mishima went out onto the streets to see the 'demos' and wrote articles for the press about them.

What was at stake, essentially, was the neutralist vision. Intellectuals, students, union leaders–even the opposition parties at last–had finally awakened to a realization that the ruling conservative party, the Liberal Democratic Party, which had governed Japan since 1945, almost without a break, had all along been making a nonsense of the ideals of the Left. While subscribing to 'neutralist' tenets–refusing, for example, to play a direct, military role in the Korean War–the conservatives had given the public the impression that the LDP would keep Japan on the path of neutralism for the indefinite future. By 1960, however, the conservatives, under the leadership of Nobusuké Kishi–a strong reactionary–had made up their minds to challenge the popular assumption that they were, in effect, prisoners of the ideological Left. Kishi and his ministers decided to strengthen the alliance with the United States–enshrined in the US-Japan Security Treaty–by revising that treaty to make the ties between America and Japan closer, above all in the economic field. Mishima was not interested in these issues. However, he was curious about the demonstrations, which became more violent during the early summer; and he reacted very strongly, it seems, to the new political atmosphere. The story 'Patriotism' is evidence of this.

At this point the latent imperialism in him suddenly burst forth. 'Patriotism' describes an act of devotion to the Emperor, the *hara-kiri* of a young army lieutenant at the time of the *Ni Ni Roku* Incident. It is not so much Mishima's imperialism that impresses, however; it is the re-emergence of his old aesthetic, that leaning towards 'Death and Night and Blood' that characterized his adolescence as described in *Confessions of a Mask*. Gone is his 'classical aspiration'. In its place is a sensuous, anti-rational, romantic longing. What the object of that longing might be, no one could know; certainly Mishima had no concrete idea, no notion of what he himself would do. The theoretical ideal was clear enough, however; it was death. Thus Mishima resolved the crisis that he faced in 1960, by a reversion to romanticism.

Curiously, he was subject at this time to the only threats of murder ever made against him. They were issued by *Uyoku* (rightist) extremists, who warned him that they would burn down his house and kill him because he had supported a fellow writer who had published a short story describing a dream in which leftists attacked the Imperial family. For two months Mishima had a bodyguard. The house of the publisher of the story was attacked, and a maid killed, but Mishima was not assaulted.

Suicide, it is clear from Mishima's writing, had been a theoretical option for him for many years. It was still no more than that; he was still fairly young and had many literary projects in mind–particularly in the theatre–and he also had a family. Mishima's second child, his son Ichiro, was born in 1961; like many Japanese parents, the Mishimas would seem to have decided to have no more children.

What was the nature of his relationship with Yoko? She is still alive, of course, and this is one subject on which I cannot write without inhibition. The evidence, however, is that Mishima treated Yoko with a consideration that far exceeded the kindness most Japanese husbands of his generation show their wives. For example, he took Yoko with him on his foreign travels. She had never been abroad, and when Mishima embarked on a long journey round the world in late 1960, he took her with him. They went to New York for the off-Broadway premiere of Mishima's modern *No* plays. Then to Europe, to meet publishers, and to secure the publication of *The Temple of the Golden Pavilion* in France, and finally they returned to Japan by way of Greece, Egypt and Hong Kong. It must have been a refreshing experience for Yoko to travel freely around the world in the company of her husband, leaving the little girl in Tokyo in the care of her family. Life in Tokyo, certainly, was not easy for Yoko; she was very young, just twenty-three on their return from abroad in 1961; but her days were full. She had the house to care for–and Mishima had become very social, giving dinner parties to diplomats, to foreign friends, and to Japanese friends from well-known families. His standards were high and he expected the dinner parties–for which he issued invitations on printed, embossed cards in English–to run smoothly. Yoko also had her child to care for. She was also a kind of secretary to Mishima, taking phone calls, running errands, going out on combined shopping and secretarial missions in the family car (Mishima did not drive). Her life was a busy one. Things were not made easier by her mother-in-law. Shizué had suffered greatly at the hands of Natsuko and having experienced such treatment, was able to dispense not a little herself. Yoko's policy seems to have been to ignore her mother-in-law's jealousy and to continue to run the household as she saw best.

I do not believe that his marriage put Mishima under great strain. His literary career, however, was another matter. His books did not sell well in the 1960s. He continued to write an enormous amount; some of it was trash, intended purely for the commercial market. He also wrote a succession of 'serious' novels: *Utsukushii Hoshi* ('Beautiful Star', 1962), *The Sailor Who Fell from Grace with the Sea* (1963), and *Kino to Meisatsu* ('Silk and Insight', 1964). Sales of these books were poor. They sold only twenty or thirty thousand copies in some cases, as compared with two hundred thousand for his books in the 1950s. At one point he even felt obliged to go to his publishers to make a formal apology. As Mishima's reputation was soaring in the West, he was actually losing ground in Japan, not only in terms of sales but in critical reputation. Any novelist, Mishima not excluded, must have lean years; but he did not see it this way. He was deeply concerned. The tone of his pronouncements over the years became increasingly pessimistic. Mishima, as always, was his own best guide to himself. As he neared the age of forty Mishima pondered his future: 'Within two or three years I shall be forty years old and will have to make a plan for the rest of my life.

'I feel better when I think that I have lived longer than Ryunosuke Akutagawa, but then I'll have to make a great effort to live as long as possible. The average life for men in the Bronze Age was eighteen, and in the Roman era twenty-two. Heaven must then have been filled with beautiful youths. Recently, it must look dreadful. When a man reaches the age of forty, he has no chance to die beautifully. No matter how he tries, he will die in an ugly way. He has to compel himself to live.'[52]

Ryunosuke Akutagawa was the most brilliant of the many Japanese writers who have committed suicide in modern times. The high incidence of suicide amongst Japanese writers may be attributed in part to the extraordinary tension and stress in life in modern Japan, a tension caused by massive social change which has been brought about in turn by the need to modernize a feudal society overnight. The writers include :

Bizan Kawakami	1908	Tamiki Hara	1951
Takeo Arishima	1923	Michio Kato	1953
Akutagawa	1927	Sakae Kubo	1958
Shinichi Makino	1936	Ashihei Hino	1960
Osamu Dazai	1948		

Mishima was toying—no more—with the idea of adding his name to this list. His obsession was 'to make a plan for the rest of my life'.

3

1964–70

Mishima did not discover his 'plan for life' for some time. He had many diversions; in the autumn of 1964, for example, he immersed himself in the task of reporting the Tokyo Olympic Games for the Japanese press and wrote enthusiastic articles about sports 'from my own experience'. He donned a blazer, put on a press armband and watched the many events of the Olympics with child-like enthusiasm; he described in his articles how he had trained at sports and at body-building 'so that today I can move the muscles of my chest in time to music'. Later that year he edited the *Collected Works* of Shintaro Ishihara, a younger and more glamorous novelist friend whose first work, *Taiyo no Kisetsu* ('Season of the Sun', 1955)–a 'shocking' *après-guerre* novel–had made him famous at the age of twenty-three. Mishima admired Ishihara's talent and was at the same time envious of this polished, sophisticated and handsome individual, whom he was to criticize harshly towards the end of his life, as a political oppor-tunist. (Ishihara later went into politics, winning a seat in the Upper House as an LDP member, after gaining the largest number of votes ever won by a candidate for parliament.) Early in 1965 Mishima accepted an invitation from the British Council to visit England. It was his only long stay in England and he did not find a great deal to please him–although he liked the Brighton Pavilion. Amongst those whom he met during his stay were Margot Fonteyn, Edna O'Brien, Ivan Morris, Angus Wilson and Peter Owen.

Back in Tokyo he and Yoko busied themselves with alterations to their house in Magome. They added a top floor which gave both husband and wife comfortable sitting-rooms where each could receive their friends privately. Mishima also amused himself by designing book jackets; he had always been interested in the covers of his books, especially in the *genteibon* (luxury edition) covers. He designed two jackets with the help of experts, one for *St Sebastian no Junkyo* ('The Martyrdom of St Sebastian'), a translation of the work by Gabriele D'Annunzio which Mishima had supervised, and one for *Kurotokage* ('Black Lizard'), a play. For the latter he chose a design which incorporated frontal views of male nudes. Early in 1965 Mishima published one of his strangest short stories, 'Kujaku' ('Peacocks'), the story of a man who beats a flock of peacocks to death. He also filmed his short story 'Patriotism', acting as producer, director, *metteur en scène,* and chief star–he played the part of an army lieutenant who commits *hara-kiri.* In his customary whirl of activity Mishima found time to produce one of his short 'modern *No* plays', *Yuya,* in which his friend Utaemon took the lead.

In the summer of 1965 Mishima implemented one of the major decisions of his literary career–to begin a long novel, in four volumes, a work which he expected would take him about six years, into the early 1970s. This was the biggest project of his career. The novel would cover a span of sixty years of modern Japan, beginning in the early Taisho period, about 1912. Each volume would have a protagonist who would be a reincarnation of the hero of the previous book, starting with Kiyoaki, a peerlessly handsome boy from an aristocratic family. Kiyoaki would be the main character of the first volume and his closest friend would be Honda, a fellow student at the *Gakushuin* school. Only one character, Honda, the friend of the protagonists of all four volumes, would know the secret of their reincarnations; a physical feature common to all four would be a group of three moles under the left arm; by these moles Honda would recognize the reincarnations of the handsome Kiyoaki. The lives of Honda's four friends would also be linked by dreams. Through chance remarks and by diary entries Honda would be informed of the dreams and would thereby obtain additional clues to the future existences of Kiyoaki. All the protagonists of the first three volumes of the novel would die young, at the age of twenty. This was, of course, entirely characteristic of Mishima, who romanticized early death in many of his works.

For the design of his new, long novel Mishima drew on a Heian romance of the eleventh century, the *Hamamatsu Chunagon Monogatari* ('The Tale of Hamamatsu'), a not very well-known work, in which the Buddhist idea of reincarnation is used and in which there also appear prophetic dreams. As a religious background to the novel, Mishima used the teaching of the small Buddhist sect known as *Hosso,* whose *yuishiki ron* or 'theory of consciousness only' affirms that all experience is subjective and that existence cannot be verified. Mishima gave a twist of his own to the teaching of this ancient Buddhist sect, which came to Japan in the seventh century and lost most of its hold in the succeeding five hundred years. As only consciousness existed, there was no telling reality from illusion.

Mishima, who published most of his novels by instalments in magazines before they appeared in book form, gave the first part of the first volume (*Spring Snow*) of his long novel to *Shincho* magazine in the late summer of 1965. In the early autumn, following reports from Stockholm that he was a candidate for the Nobel Prize that year, he set off on a world trip with Yoko, travelling to Cambodia, where he visited Angkor Wat–he was to write a play about the temple of Bayon at Angkor–and thereafter on to western Europe. Following the death of the elderly novelist Junichiro Tanizaki, in June 1965, Mishima was considered the leading Japanese contender for the Nobel Prize, and agency despatches stated that he was amongst about ninety candidates for the prize. He regarded himself, rightly, as an outsider–the winner in 1965 was to be the Russian, Sholokhov–as he was still comparatively young (he was forty). But he had faith that he would eventually win the prize and wanted to gauge how soon his chances would become serious. He made delicate inquiries at Japanese embassies in Europe, to find out if anyone had an inkling when the Swedish Academy would eventually turn to Japan. His conclusion was that it could not be many years before the Nobel Prize for literature would go to a Japanese for the first time. Unwisely he shared this information with friends in Japan and he was mentioned repeatedly in the press thereafter as a candidate for the prize. Mishima's concern was in part an indication of his excessive self-regard; but it was also a reflection of the extraordinary interest taken by the Japanese, as a people, in international distinctions, particularly Nobel Prizes.

On his return to Japan he made a journey to the nunnery of Enshoji, close to Nara. He had decided to use this small, isolated nunnery in a later section of *Spring Snow*. Enshoji was a *Rinzai* sect Zen temple, but he converted it in the book to a *Hosso* sect temple and gave it a different name, Gesshuji. In the autumn of the following year, 1966, Mishima completed *Spring Snow*. It is a love story whose heroine, Satoko, exemplifies what he called *tawoyameburi*–' "the way of the graceful young maiden", an archaic term referring to the traditional beauty and charm of the Japanese girl' (Keene). Satoko and Kiyoaki, her lover, are the children of aristocratic, powerful families in Tokyo. Their passion is inflamed after the betrothal of Satoko to a member of the Imperial family (some Japanese saw in this tale an evocation of Mishima's relationship with Michiko Shoda before her marriage to the Crown Prince; a romantic, but slightly far-fetched idea). Satoko is the daughter of a very old family with a long tradition of service at Court, where Kiyoaki has also been brought up, having been despatched to the household of the Ayakuras, Satoko's parents, by a proud father who wishes his only son to learn the manners of the aristocracy. Keene has written: 'Mishima's long association with the aristocracy, ever since his childhood days at the Peers' School, had led him repeatedly to choose for his characters members of this tiny fraction of Japanese society, and he wrote with a unique knowledge of their speech and attitudes. His account in *Spring Snow* of the aristocrats who built the Victorian mansions still standing here and there in Tokyo is curiously affecting. . . . The billiard room, the well-stocked wine cellar, the racks of suits tailored in London, the cut-glass chandeliers and the freshly starched tablecloths obviously attracted Mishima himself, but he did not neglect to describe the Japanese aspects of their lives as well—the spacious garden with its pond and artificial hill, the servants in kimonos eternally dusting and, above all, the elaborate etiquette that revealed itself most conspicuously in the distinctive language.'[53]

Kiyoaki is in two minds about Satoko, who is in love with him. When he compares her charms to those of merely beautiful women, however, as in a scene in which he scrutinizes a crowd of *geisha* in his father's park, on the occasion of a party given for an Imperial prince, he is sure that Satoko is greatly superior to the professional beauties: 'He wondered how these women could laugh and play as happily as if they were bathing in water warmed to their liking. He observed them closely—the way they gestured as they told stories, the way they all nodded alike, as though each had a finely wrought gold hinge in her smooth white neck . . . and of all these many devices, the one that interested him most was their manner of letting their eyes rove incessantly. Kiyoaki found them tasteless.'[54]

Satoko and Kiyoaki quarrel on the occasion of this garden party and during the long period which ensues before their next meeting, Kiyoaki will not respond to a series of letters and calls from Satoko; the girl becomes engaged to a young prince. The arranged marriage is not one she would have chosen, and she finds means of meeting Kiyoaki secretly. These encounters lead to a love affair which is connived at and arranged by a scheming lady companion of Satoko's.

Satoko becomes pregnant by Kiyoaki shortly before her marriage is due to take place, and the parents of the two lovers desperately hustle her off to Osaka for an abortion. The operation is performed, but Satoko, instead of returning to Tokyo, as had been planned by the parents, takes refuge in a nunnery close to Nara, Gesshuji. Kiyoaki goes to see her and is refused admittance by the Abbess. He makes repeated journeys to the nunnery in cold weather, when spring snow is on the ground, and his health begins to suffer. Honda comes down from Tokyo, too, and pleads with the Abbess to allow Kiyoaki to see Satoko: ' "It's a frightening thing to say, but I somehow feel that he's not going to recover. So I am really giving you his dying request. Would letting him see Satoko for just a moment or two be quite outside the scope of the Lord Buddha's compassion? Won't you please permit it? . . ." At that moment he thought he heard something. . . . It sounded like a muffled laugh, as faint as the opening of plum blossom. But then after a moment's reflection, he was sure that unless his ears had deceived him, the sound that had carried to him through the chill convent atmosphere on this spring morning was not a muffled laugh, as he had thought, but a young woman's stifled sob.'[55] The Abbess remains firm in her refusal to let Kiyoaki see Satoko. To Honda she gives a lecture on the precepts of the *Hosso* sect: 'The Abbess referred to the net of Indra. Indra was an Indian God, and once he cast his net, every man, every living thing without exception was inextricably caught in its meshes. And so it was that all creatures in existence were inescapably bound by it. Indra's net symbolised the Chain of Causation or, in Sanskrit, *pratitya-samutpada*. *Yuishiki* (*Vijnaptimatrata* or Consciousness) the fundamental doctrine of the Hosso Sect, to which Gesshuji belonged, was celebrated in *The Thirty Verses of Yuishiki*, the canonical text attributed to Vasubandhu, whom the sect regarded as its founder. According to the Verses, *Alaya* is the origin of the Chain of Causation. This was a Sanskrit word that denoted a storehouse. For within the *Alaya* were contained the karmic "seeds" that held the consequential effects of all deeds, both good and evil.'[56] After the lecture—only a section of which is given above—Honda returns to the inn where Kiyoaki is staying and then accompanies his friend, now desperately ill, back to Tokyo. In the train Kiyoaki tells Honda a snatch of a dream: 'Just now I had a dream. I'll see you again. I know it. Beneath the falls.' Two days later Kiyoaki dies and the volume ends at this point.

Spring Snow is beautifully written; the romantic lovers—and the lackeys who surround them—are marvellously described. Once the love affair has begun, however, the interest of the book declines and its ending—the death of Kiyoaki—is not especially moving; perhaps this is because his character is static, like that of Yuichi in *Forbidden Colours*. The second difficulty with *Spring Snow* is Mishima's description of religion. He was not a religious man and his description

of *Hosso* teaching reads like part of a doctoral thesis; yet the theme
of reincarnation is central to the whole novel, in Mishima's scheme.
Here was a major problem for the writer: how to make an idea con-
vincing when he did not believe it himself. In later volumes of his
novel Mishima was forced to confront this problem.

There is not space in these pages to describe all of Mishima's private
and literary activities (I have already chosen to bypass several of his
novels written in the early 1960s). He was perpetually in motion; in
addition to his activities with his family and an enormous amount of
entertaining, he continued to train at gymnasia several times a week,
and his workouts were strenuous. He was in excellent health and at
the height of his physical and intellectual powers in his late thirties
and early forties. A brief account of his most conspicuous activities
in a single year should give an indication of his unbounded energy.
In 1966, the year in which he wrote most of *Spring Snow*, a four hundred page volume, Mishima recorded the following activities and
achievements. In January he was awarded a prize by the Ministry of
Education for his play, *Madame de Sade*. In the same month he was
made a member of the committee which awards the Akutagawa prize
for young novelists—an illustrious award and an important position
demanding a good deal of effort on the part of a committee which
must read many manuscripts. In April Mishima's short film *Yukoku*,
which had won a prize at Tours film festival, was released in Japan
and it was an instant success. In July Mishima appeared at a cabaret
performance organized by Akihiro Maruyama and sang a ballad of his
own composition, *The Sailor Who Was Killed By Paper Roses*. In the
following month he went on a *shuzai*, or fact-finding trip, to Kyoto,
Omiwa, Hiroshima and Kumamoto, gathering material for *Runaway
Horses*, the second volume of his long novel; and in the autumn
Mishima succeeded finally in obtaining a reconciliation with the family
of Hachiro Arita, the former Foreign Minister whom he had defamed
in *After the Banquet*. He was also invited to the autumn garden
party at the Palace that year and was formally presented to the
Emperor.

In the midst of these activities he completed a dozen minor literary
works; these are listed below together with the months in which he
published them—or began to do so, in the case of serial works:

January: *Fukuzatsu no Kare* ('A Complex Man'), *Josei Seven* until
    July.

February: *Kiken na Geijutsuka* ('Dangerous Artist'), *Bungakukai*.
> *Owari no Bigaku* ('The Aesthetic of the End'), *Josei Jishin* until August.

March: *Hanteijo Daigaku* ('Against Faithful Women'), *Shinchosha*.
April: *Yukoku* ('Patriotism'), *Shinchosha*.
May: *Eigatekki Nikutairon* ('On the Body in Films'), *Eiga Geijutsu*.
June: *Eirei no Koe* ('The Voices of the Heroic Dead'), *Bungei* and *Kawade Shobo*.
July: *Watashi no Isho* ('My Final Word'), *Bungakukai*.
> *Narcissism Ron* ('Essay on Narcissism'), *Fujin Koron*.

August: *Mishima Yukio Hyoronzenshu* ('Collected Criticism'), *Shinchosha*.
September: *Danzo, Geido, Saigunbi* ('Danzo, Art and Rearmament'), *Niju Seiki*.
> *Yakaifuku* ('Ball Costume'), *Mademoiselle* until August 1967.
> *Mishima Letter Kyoshitsu* ('Mishima Letter School'), *Josei Jishin*.

October: *Koya Yori* ('From the Wilderness'), *Gunzo*.
> *Taiwa Nihonjinron* ('On the Japanese'), with Fusao Hayashi, *Bancho Shobo*.

December: *Ito Shizuo no Shi* ('The Poetry of Shizuo Ito'), *Shincho*.

Two of these works, *Eirei no Koe* and *Taiwa Nihonjinron*, belong to Mishima's 'committed' literature and will be mentioned later. A great many of the pieces were for women's magazines (*Josei Jishin, Fujin Koron, Josei Seven, Mademoiselle*), publications which paid well and demanded light fare. In this year alone, however, Shinchosha, Mishima's main publishers—who took only his serious work—brought out three volumes and also published an essay in the house magazine, *Shincho*. The above list excludes new and luxury editions of Mishima's works. This was the pace which he kept up throughout the 1960s.

Most men would have collapsed after a few weeks of living under this pressure, yet he barely looked tired. As luck would have it, the only occasion on which I saw him that year—also the first time I set eyes on him, at the dinner at the Foreign Correspondents' Club at which he was guest speaker—he looked distinctly wan. Usually he had a deep suntan, but on that particular evening he appeared pale and a little nervous. But that was an exception. Normally, when he was in public, he affected high spirits and immediately dominated any gathering in which he took part: gesturing, joking and laughing the raucous, rather ugly laugh which he is said to have been taught by his overbearing grandmother. His 'mask' was firmly in place; a stranger might have classified him as a former amateur boxing champion turned night-club owner or band leader. For there was something coarse about his 'mask'; he projected an air of deliberate vulgarity which deceived all but those who knew him well. What is truly remarkable is that he was able to go through with this act—for that is what it was—although he was under the most terrible strain. As evidence of this one may rely on his writing; for example, the autobiographical essay, *Sun and Steel*, which he began late in 1965, publishing the work regularly over a period of three years in a small magazine, *Hihyo* ('Criticism'), founded by a right-wing friend, the critic Takeshi Muramatsu, and supported, among others, by Mishima himself. *Sun and Steel* is a work which he classified as 'confidential criticism', and it afforded glimpses into the inner man of a far more intimate nature than those who knew him only superficially were able to obtain by meeting him and talking to him.

The key to this work—which is central to an understanding of his suicide—is the author's definition of 'tragedy'. From this definition springs the whole of the remainder of *Sun and Steel*, an essay of eighty pages: 'According to my definition of tragedy, the tragic *pathos* is born when the perfectly average sensibility momentarily takes unto itself a privileged nobility that keeps others at a distance, and not when a special type of sensibility vaunts its own special claims. It follows that he who dabbles in words can create tragedy, but cannot participate in it. It is necessary, moreover, that the 'privileged nobility' finds its basis strictly in a kind of physical courage. The elements of intoxication and superhuman clarity in the tragic are born when the average sensibility, endowed with a given physical strength, encounters that type of privileged moment especially designed for it. Tragedy calls for an anti-tragic vitality and ignorance, and above all for a certain 'inappropriateness'. If a person is at times to draw close to the divine, then under normal conditions he must be neither divine nor anything approaching it.'[57] There is much to criticize in this statement. Mishima's notion of a 'privileged nobility' is repulsive; his idea that he must abandon his keen sensibility and settle for a 'perfectly average sensibility' is absurd. What matters most, however, is that Mishima yearned to be a hero; so much is clear from his definition of tragedy. He also believed that he must abandon his role as a writer, one 'who dabbles in words', in order to become a tragic hero.

In his essay, Mishima describes a scene in which he becomes convinced of his aspiration to be a tragic figure: 'One summer day, heated by training, I was cooling my muscles in the breeze coming through an open window. The sweat vanished as though by magic, and coolness passed over the surface of the muscles like a touch of menthol. The next instant, I was rid of the sense of the muscles' existence, and—in the same way that words, by their abstract functioning, can grind up the concrete world so that the words themselves seem never to have existed—my muscles at that moment crushed something within my being, so that it was as though the muscles themselves had similarly never existed. . . . I was enveloped in a sense of power as transparent as light. It is scarcely to be wondered at that in this pure sense of power that no amount of books or intellectual analysis could ever capture, I should discover a true antithesis of words. And indeed it was this that by gradual stages was to become the focus of my whole thinking.'[58] From this point it is not a long step to the conclusion that it is death that he desires. With the aid of 'sun and steel'—by sun-bathing and weight-lifting—Mishima had discovered his body and created his muscles. Thereafter, he 'glimpsed from time to time another sun quite different from that by which I had been so long blessed, a sun full of the fierce dark flames of feeling, a sun of death that would never burn the skin yet gave forth a still stranger glow.' Mishima's conclusion, as he described it towards the end of 1966, was this: 'The goal of my life was to acquire all the various attributes of the warrior.' It was thus that he arrived at the romantic idea of death as a '*samurai*'. If *Sun and Steel* is to be trusted, Mishima cared nothing for ideology; his was to be strictly a non-political action. And the essay is in fact persuasive, more so than Mishima's 'political' writing, as will be seen.

Mishima was well versed in Nietzsche, as one sees from the internal evidence of the passage quoted above. The model which he chose for his life-style at this point in his life—and which he faithfully followed for the last four years of his existence—was, however, a Japanese one, which Mishima adapted from feudal times. The ideal *samurai* pursued his life (and death) according to the ancient practice of *Bunburyodo*, the dual way of literature (*Bun*) and the Sword (*Bu*); he was expected to cultivate the literary and the martial arts in roughly equal proportions. In practice very few of the ancient knights of Japan lived up to this demanding standard. Nonetheless, it was the ideal and was encouraged by the authorities from the seventeenth century onwards, when peace had finally settled upon Japan and it was desirable that the *samurai* class should no longer unsheathe their weapons at the slightest pretext. Mishima had long been intrigued by the feudal idea of *Bunburyodo*–'*ryodo*' may be translated as 'dual way'–as he recounts in *Sun and Steel*: 'During the post-war period, when all accepted values were upset, I often thought and remarked to others that now if ever was the time for reviving the old Japanese ideal of a combination of letters and the martial arts, of art and action. For a while after that, my interest strayed from that particular ideal; then, as I gradually learned from the sun and the steel the secret of how to pursue words with the body (and not merely pursue the body with words), the two poles within me began to maintain a balance, and the generator of my mind, so to speak, switched from a direct to an alternating current. . . . [These two poles] gave the appearance of inducing an ever wider split in the personality, yet in practice created at each moment a living balance that was constantly being destroyed and brought back to life again. The embracing of a dual polarity within the self and the acceptance of contradiction and collision–such was my own blend of "art and action." '[59]

It is at this point in his essay that Mishima begins to describe the stress under which he lived–the strain which he so faithfully hid behind his 'mask'. 'Why' he asks, 'should a man be associated with beauty only through a heroic, violent death?' His answer is that 'such is the beauty of the suicide squad, which is recognized as beauty not only in the spiritual sense but, by men in general, in an ultra-erotic sense also.' He does not argue the point. He states it as a fact of his consciousness (certainly not of 'men in general'). Thereafter, he veers out of control–there was indeed 'an ever wider split in the personality': 'The most appropriate type of daily life for me was a day-by-day world destruction; peace was the most difficult and abnormal state to live in. . . . No moment is so dazzling as when everyday imaginings concerning death and danger and world destruction are transformed into duty. . . . To keep death in mind from day to day, to focus each moment upon inevitable death, to make sure one's worst forebodings coincided with one's dreams of glory . . . the beautiful death that had earlier eluded me [in the war] had also become possible. . . . I was beginning to dream of my capabilities as a fighting man.'[60]

His reaction to loss of control was to discipline himself still more rigorously than before. *Bunburyodo* then became more than simply a life-style for Mishima, it became the 'plan of life' for which he had been so anxiously casting about for almost five years. And it had very specific objectives in the two fields of art and action. His long novel was naturally his main endeavour in art; and in action his aim became nothing less than 'the beautiful death . . . as a fighting man.' The greater the stress upon him, the more furiously Mishima fought to control himself. *Bunburyodo* came to mean for him that every time he completed a stage of his novel, a new volume, he must simultaneously commit himself one further step on the road to martial action–and death. As he completed *Spring Snow*, in the autumn of 1966, he submitted an application to the *Jieitai* for permission to train at army camps.

Not inappropriately, the second volume of Mishima's long novel, which he began early in 1967, depicts what Mishima called *masuraoburi*, the way of the warrior. Its hero, Isao, is a right-wing terrorist, who commits *hara-kiri* after stabbing an aged businessman to death. The action of this book, entitled *Runaway Horses*, takes place in the early 1930s, twenty years after the death of Kiyoaki; Isao dies, also, at twenty years of age. The young man, who is nineteen at the outset, is a brilliant swordsman and *kendo* performer, who already holds the rank of 3-*dan*; he is a student at Kokugakuin University in Tokyo–an institution at which many nationalists have been trained– and is the son of Kiyoaki's former tutor, Iinuma, a cunning, corrupt rightist. Isao, a sturdy youth, quite unlike Kiyoaki in appearance, has sharp, furious eyes and firm-set lips; he is keen and 'pure'–his father, however, takes money from tainted sources (i.e., business). Honda, who is now a judge at an Osaka court, attends a *kendo* match in which Isao appears; he knows nothing of the boy, apart from the fact that he is the son of Iinuma. After the match, which Isao wins, Honda climbs a nearby hill with a priest; the latter persuades him to bathe in a waterfall on the way down. Isao, too, is bathing there, and seeing him under the falls, Honda suddenly notices, as he raises his arms above his head, that the boy has three moles on the left hand side of his chest. The youth laughs as he tumbles in the water but Honda is terrified by what he sees, remembering the last words of Kiyoaki: 'I'll see you again. I know it. Under the falls.' Isao, then, must be Kiyoaki's reincarnation. Honda feels that his way of life, his dry-as-dust rationalism, is threatened.

Isao is at this time reading a book which impresses him deeply, *Shinpuren Shiwa* ('The History of Shinpuren') by Koki Yamao; it describes the Shinpuren Incident of 1877, one of the last occasions in Japanese history on which *samurai* appeared in action. A summary follows:

One summer day in 1874 four men of middle age, seekers after divine guidance, gathered to pray at Shingai close to Kumamoto castle, led by Tomo Otaguro, the son-in-law of an old priest, Oen Hayashi, who has already died. The four men were Harukata Kaya, 38, Kengo Ueno, over 60, Kyuzaburo Saito and Masamoto Aiko—both the latter were over 50. All had swords with them. They were all pure believers in *Sonno Joi* ['Revere the Emperor and Expel the Barbarians'] and they hated Western culture from the bottom of their hearts. After praying they waited for the priest Otaguro to perform the *Ukei* divination ceremony. They wished to put two questions to the Gods. The first was whether they might present a petition to the authorities, calling for *Kamiyo* [the rule of the Emperor] and then commit *hara-kiri*. The second was whether, if their desire to present a petition be not allowed, whether the Gods would permit them to assassinate the villainous retainers, ostensibly acting for the Emperor, in their district. All four men eagerly desired the restoration of *Kamiyo*, the practice of *Kodo* [ancient morality] and the unity of Shrine and State. Their teacher had been Oen Hayashi.

On this occasion both requests of the four men were rejected.

In the next year (1875) the Saga Rebellion occurred. Otaguro thought that this was a chance not to be missed and performed a second *Ukei*. Once again the Gods replied in the negative. The feeling of *Sonno Joi* was strong amongst the group and in that year fifteen followers of the four men were made priests.

In 1877, on 18 March, the Government announced the decree abolishing the wearing of swords. Shortly afterwards came a decree ordering former *samurai* to trim off their topknots from their heads. These two announcements convinced the group to take action. Alone, Kaya decided to present a petition and then to commit *hara-kiri*.

Otaguro performed the *Ukei* ceremony for a third time in May. This time he received an affirmative reply from the Gods. He accordingly prepared a plan for the assassination of government officials in the Kumamoto area; some army officers were also put on the list for assassination. He gathered men together in secret from the neighbourhood.

His plan was this:

(i) One party of thirty men to assassinate the general at the

Kumamoto barracks, and to kill, also, the local governor and the chairman of a local commission in their homes.

(ii) A second party to attack the artillery camp in the barracks. Seventy men.

(iii) A third party to attack the 2,000-man-strong infantry garrison at the camp. Seventy men.

Kaya decided to join the group again three days before their day of action.

The sole preparation made for the event by the attackers was prayer. They would not arm themselves with guns. They hated these abominable Western weapons. (When obliged to walk under electric power lines they covered their heads with white fans.) The men armed themselves with sword, spear and halberd. They had oil, also, to set fire to the camp. Very few of them wore armour. Their treasured possession was a sacred tablet, the *Mitamashiro*. This Otaguro carried on his back.

The decision was taken to attack on 24 October.

The attack began at midnight. The general was killed and the governor and chairman injured. The attack on the barracks, by men without guns, led to the deaths of the majority of the rebels by early morning. The two leaders, Otaguro and Kaya, were shot. Otaguro asked his brother-in-law to give him a *coup de grace* by *kaishaku*. Forty-six survivors of the attack retired to Kinposan, a hill west of the castle. They withdrew after only three hours fighting. There, the survivors decided to disperse and hide. Seven boys were ordered home, and three badly injured men committed *hara-kiri*.

Thereafter the rebels committed *hara-kiri*, some at home, others in the mountains. One was a boy of sixteen. Six men fled by ship to Konoura and waited there for news. After receiving a report of the defeat they climbed Omidake mountain early in the morning. There they made a circle with rope and with pendant papers, on a flat spot. All the men committed perfect *hara-kiri*.

Almost all the men committed *hara-kiri* or were burnt to death. One man, Kotaro Ogata, surrendered. Arrested and in prison, he puzzled over the failure of men whose will had been sincere. He wrote a last statement: '*Ikade taoyame no gotoki furumai aran* [How could we have behaved like graceful women?]'. These words well expressed the uncontrollable impulse which fired the rebels to action.[61]

Isao worships the 'purity' of the men who sacrificed their lives in the Shinpuren Incident. Paying a visit to a lieutenant of a regiment stationed in Azabu in central Tokyo, he reveals his wish to commit *hara-kiri* 'on a cliff . . . just at sunrise . . . under a pine tree . . . looking down at the shining sea'. At a second meeting, the lieutenant introduces Isao to a member of the Imperial family, a prince, and

Isao gives him his copy of the book about the Shinpuren Incident. Toin no Miya, the prince, has been told in advance of Isao's idea of sacrificing himself for the Emperor and he asks: 'Supposing the Emperor turns down your idea, what would you do?' Isao replies that he would commit *hara-kiri*. Loyalty, says Isao, using a parable, is to prepare hot *nigirimeshi* (rice balls) for the Emperor as a present. If the Emperor refuses the food for whatever reason, Isao would commit *hara-kiri*. Equally, if he accepted the dish, Isao would commit *hara-kiri* for it is a grave sin for a *somo* (humble subject) to make *nigirimeshi* for the Emperor. One kind of loyalty would be to make the food and then not to present it, but this would be loyalty without bravery. Real loyalty would be to present the *nigirimeshi* without regard to one's life. Prince Toin is greatly moved by the speech and comments: 'With such young men we can have hope for the future.' He gives Isao a cake upon which his crest has been pressed.

Isao, thus encouraged, plans, with a group of friends, to assassinate government and business leaders; they will also blow up the Bank of Japan. His father, however, who is receiving money from Kurahara, one of the tycoons Isao plans to murder, informs the police of the plot; the boy is arrested and put in prison. (Honda, meanwhile, has been meditating on his discovery of Isao; he has become greatly disturbed and his thoughts have drifted towards romanticism. When he hears that Isao is to be put on trial, Honda gives up his judgeship. He makes his way to Tokyo and offers himself as defence counsel for Isao, whom he defends with help from Prince Toin.) In prison Isao reads *Nihon Yomeigaku no Tetsugaku* ('The Philosophy of *Yomeigaku* in Japan') by Tetsujiro Inoue, a description of the teaching of the neo-Confucian school whose maxim is: 'to know and not to act is not yet to know'. He is attracted by a chapter on Heihachiro Oshio, a nineteenth-century hero who sacrificed his life in an attack on the great merchant houses in Osaka, who were hoarding rice at a time of famine. Oshio had said:: 'I do not fear the death of my body, but I fear the death of my soul.'

At his trial, under examination by the judge, Isao gives an account of the two sources of his inspiration. One has been *Yomeigaku*, the teaching of the Chinese Wang Yang-ming, a soldier philosopher who broke the hold of Confucianism on China in the sixteenth century. Isao says: ' "Yes. I wanted to carry out the principle of the unity of knowledge and action, the main principle of the school of Wang Yang-ming.

'To know and not act is not yet to know.' Knowing of the corruption around us, of the dark clouds that close off the future of Japan, the poverty of farm villages and the sufferings of the poor; knowing that the origins of it all are in corrupt government and in an irresponsible moneyed class whose interests are served by the corruption; knowing that these are the roots of the growth that cuts off the light of His Revered and Benevolent Majesty: knowing all this, I find it evident that to know is to act." '[62] His second inspiration has been the Shinpuren Incident: ' "I have believed that the dark clouds which mask heaven must one day be swept away, that a clear and radiant Japan must one day emerge. But waiting does no good. The longer we wait the darker are the clouds. . . . And who then will take upon himself the responsibility for the grand mission, go up and speak to heaven with his own death? . . . *A pure and resolute act is necessary to bring heaven and earth together*." '[63] He concludes: ' "Loyalty is to throw one's life away and seek to be in accord with the great heart [the Emperor]. It is to rend the clouds and ascend to the centre of the sun, of the great heart. This is the whole of the vow which my fellows and I made to ourselves." '[64]

Shortly afterwards the judge lets Isao go free. Following his release, he hears a report that Kurahara, the business leader who finances his father, has committed an impiety at the Ise Shrine—the shrine of the Sun Goddess. He had visited the shrine, accompanied by the governor of Mie prefecture, as an honoured guest. While listening to the recital of *norito* (prayers) Kurahara had put down his sprig of *tamagushi* (a sacred leaf) onto his chair, in order to have a hand free to scratch his back. Then he had sat down on the *tamagushi* by mistake, failing to realize what he had done. The right-wing press make much of the incident. Kurahara had unknowingly profaned the most holy shrine in the country.

Isao is unimpressed by the story when he first hears it. Later, however, when drinking with his father and Honda, he learns the secret of his father's tie with Kurahara and is told that his father had informed on him. He weeps: ' "I have been living on illusions and have been punished for them. I should have been born a woman. Women don't need to run after illusions." ' Honda helps the boy to bed and watches over him as he sleeps. He hears him say, as he dreams: ' "Far from here . . . a place in the south, much hotter . . . in the rosy sunshine of the tropics." ' Two days later Isao evades his father's assistant, buys a short sword and a knife in the

Ginza, and takes a train to Atami, where Kurahara is reported to be.

He reaches the cottage where Kurahara is staying at about ten at night. Crossing an orchard he looks into a lighted room, furnished in the Western style, in which a fat, stern-looking old man is sitting on a sofa. Waiting until a maid has left the room Isao dashes in with his sword. Kurahara stands up but does not cry out.

'Who are you?'

'Be punished for profaning the Ise Shrine,' replies Isao calmly.

'What?' says Kurahara, unable to remember anything.

The old man looks very frightened. He makes a movement of his body and Isao jumps at him. Holding the businessman to him he thrusts the sword through his heart. Kurahara's eyes open wide and his false teeth fall out. Isao pulls out his sword and dashes from the room, brushing the maid aside.

He heads for the sea close by, looking for a cliff. At last, he finds the high cliff he seeks. Making his way towards its top he pauses to pluck a *mikan* (tangerine). He eats the fruit and rests, getting his breath back. He has run and is out of training after months in prison. Isao takes off his jacket and gets out his knife. He has lost the sword. A cold wind blows from the sea.

'It's far from sunrise,' he thinks, 'but I can't wait. I can see neither the rising sun nor the sacred shadow of the pine trees nor the bright surface of the sea.'

Isao takes off his shirt and unbuttons his trousers.

Far away there are voices: 'He might have made for the sea . . . a ship.'

Runaway Horses concludes thus: 'Isao took a deep breath and rubbed his abdomen with his left hand. Then, closing his eyes, he brought the point of the dagger against it with his right hand, gave direction with the fingers of his left hand and pressed with all the strength of his right arm. At the moment the dagger entered, the sun rose glowing red behind his eyelids.'[65]

The book contains a brilliant picture of the manner in which right-wing terrorism functioned in Japan in the 1930s; it is a unique portrayal of the mechanism of the *Uyoku* (the Right) in the days of greatest power of this small minority. The involvement of a member of the Imperial Family in Isao's plotting of a *coup d'état*, although Toin no Miya is not himself a party to the affair, is especially intriguing (the roles of the Imperial princes in the numerous fracas of the 1930s are still a mystery). *Runaway Horses*, however, has a kind of coldness about it, the murder by Isao of a man totally unknown to him, with whom he has no personal quarrel, is brilliantly done, but the boy's preoccupation with the act of *hara-kiri* reflects Mishima's own obsession with the subject, so it seems, rather than appearing as one aspect of a credible terrorist personality. Isao has a woman-friend, Makiko, and he faces two alternatives: one is to have an affair with Makiko and be corrupted; the other is to commit *hara-kiri*–when and where does not seem to matter ultimately. Thus, the act of *hara-kiri* acquires a sexual meaning which rings true with the character of Mishima but not with that of Isao. The author's interest in *hara-kiri* –about which no other Japanese novelist of repute has ever written– lends a morbid air to *Runaway Horses*. When he analysed his aesthetic of 'Blood' directly, as in *Confessions of a Mask*, Mishima wrote better.

At the same time that he completed *Runaway Horses* Mishima also finished *Sun and Steel*. In the later passages of that essay he confirms the points which he had made in the sections which I have already analysed; 'tragedy' remains the core of the work. Of his training with the *Jieitai*, Mishima wrote: 'My life with the army could be finally endorsed only by death.' The essay is imbued with a sense of the gradual weakening and ageing of his body. 'I, however, had already lost the morning face that belongs to youth alone'; 'My age pursued me, murmuring behind my back "How long will it last?" ' What he is seeking is the 'tragedy that I had once let slip.' 'More accurately, what had eluded me was the tragedy of the group or tragedy as a member of the group . . . the group was concerned with all those things that could never emerge from words–sweat, and tears, and cries of joy or pain. If one probed deeper still, it was concerned with the blood that words could never cause to flow . . . only through the group, I realized –through sharing the suffering of the group–could the body reach that height of existence that the individual alone could never attain. . . . The group must be open to death–which meant, of course, that it must be a community of warriors. . . . We were united in seeking death and glory; it was not merely my personal quest. . . . I had a vision where something that, if I were alone, would have resolved back into muscles and words, was held fast by the power of the group and led me away to a far land, whence there would be no return.'[66]

In an epilogue to the essay, in which Mishima described a test flight in an F104 jet fighter, he fell back on sexual metaphor to describe his attitude to the experience which he felt awaited him: 'Erect-angled,

the F104, a sharp silver phallus, pointed into the sky. Solitary, sperma-
tozoon-like, I was installed within. Soon, I should know how the
spermatozoon felt at the instant of ejaculation.'

Such was the mood in which Mishima created his *Tatenokai* in the
autumn of 1968. That his inspiration was fundamentally personal and
aesthetic (and not political) is suggested by *Sun and Steel* and also by
the manner in which he described the *Tatenokai* in an essay written
a year after its formation in October 1968: 'The words I value are to
be found only in the pure realm of fiction. For I support the tradition
of *yuga* in Japanese literature [*Yuga*: a type of refined elegance having
its origins in Courtly aesthetics during the period before the *samurai*
rose to power]. Words used for political action are soiled words. To
revive the traditions of the *samurai* and the way of the warrior
(*Bushido*), which are so vital in Japanese culture, I have chosen a way
without words, a way of silence. . . . My aim is to revive the soul of
the *samurai* within myself. . . . I should like to describe an episode
that may typify the soul of the *Tatenokai*. Last summer I took a group
of about thirty members to the foot of Mt Fuji. It was a mercilessly hot
day and under a broiling sun all of us worked hard in combat exercises.
After a bath and supper several of the young men gathered in my
room. There was the sound of thunder in the distance; from time to time
lightning flashed across the deep purple fields; directly outside our
window we could hear the first autumn crickets. After a long talk
about how to command the attack squad, one of our members, a young
man from Kyoto, brought out a flute in a beautiful damask bag. It was
the type of flute used for Court music ever since the ninth century,
and only very few people can play it nowadays. This lad had been
studying it for about a year. . . . Now he began playing for us. It was
a beautiful and moving melody that reminded me of the heavily
bedewed autumn fields and of the Shining Prince Genji who had danced
to this very music. As I listened in sheer rapture, it crossed my mind
that for the first time in the post-war years the two Japanese traditions had come happily together, if only for a fleeting moment—the
tradition of elegance and that of the *samurai*. It was this union that I
had sought in the depth of my heart.'[67]

By the autumn of 1968 the tone of Mishima's *oeuvre* had changed
drastically. In place of the light articles that he had been writing for
women's magazines two years before, he had switched to a different
type of light literature. For the magazine *Eiga Geijutsu* he wrote a
piece entitled 'Samurai'; Japanese *Playboy* serialized *Inochi Urimasu*

F

('I Will Sell My Life'); and for the publisher Pocket Punch Oh he wrote a long series entitled *Wakaki Samurai no tame no Seishinkowa* ('A Lecture in Psychology for Young *Samurai*'). He also wrote an ironical work with the mispelt title of *Alle Japanese Are Perverse* and completed the play *My Friend Hitler*. His chief preoccupation, however, was the third volume of his long novel. *The Temple of Dawn*, as he called the book, was quite unlike its two predecessors, *Runaway Horses* and *Spring Snow*; the two latter volumes had contained lengthy stories, full of drama. *The Temple of Dawn* is primarily a description of religion, both Buddhism and Hinduism. In the previous year Mishima, accompanied by his wife, had visited India at the invitation of the government; and he had then conducted research for his book, visiting Calcutta, Benares and Ajanta as does Honda in *The Temple of Dawn*.

Just after the appearance of the first instalment of the book in *Shincho*, Mishima heard that, once again, he was being considered for the Nobel Prize; the previous year the rumour that he might get the prize had also been strong. A friend recalls that Mishima was returning from an overseas trip in 1967, and had timed his arrival back in Tokyo for the day on which the announcement of the Nobel Prize was to be made in Stockholm. He had fancied a hero's welcome: 'He had taken a VIP room at Haneda. When the plane landed he came out first from the first-class compartment, laughing and smiling. But no one was there to greet him, apart from a few of us; the VIP room was empty; there were no reporters. I have never seen him so depressed.'

A Guatemalan novelist, Miguel Angel Asturias, had won the prize the previous year, and in 1968 it was once again Mishima's turn to be disappointed. He very nearly was awarded the Nobel Prize, according to Swedish journalists' hearsay, but at the last moment the committee veered in favour of an older man, on the theory that Mishima would have his turn later. Their choice was Yasunari Kawabata, Mishima's former sponsor and good friend. Mishima, when he heard the news, rushed down to Kamakura to be the first to be seen congratulating Kawabata; photographs were taken of the two men sitting together and smiling. Mishima was disappointed: 'If Hammarskjold had lived I would have won,' he said afterwards; the diplomat had been reputed to have been an admirer of his work. But this failure to win the Nobel may not have been the turning point in his life, as some have said. The slow creep of age and his doubts about his literature were probably the dominant considerations for Mishima. Not for nothing had he remarked in *Sun and Steel* that he feared he was 'on the verge of non-communication' as a writer. To all appearances he remained unchallenged in Japan as the leading novelist of his generation. But, as he himself well knew, his reputation with the critics was not high.

The extent to which Mishima had fallen out of favour with the critics was apparent in early 1969, when *Spring Snow* and *Runaway Horses* came out in book form. The first volume sold 200,000 copies in two months, and rights were bought by television and the theatre as a matter of course. *Runaway Horses* sold less well, but this had been predicted on account of its grisly subject matter. Mishima had announced by this time that his tetralogy was to be called *The Sea of Fertility*, after a region of the moon (close to the Sea of Tranquillity). He had made this choice, he said in a letter to Keene, for this reason: 'The title *The Sea of Fertility* is intended to suggest the arid sea of the moon that belies its name. Or, I might go so far as to say that it superimposes the image of cosmic nihilism with that of the fertile sea.' Mishima's novel, however, though its first volumes sold well, and despite its challenging theme–it might be argued that this was the most ambitious literary project so far conceived in Japan in the twentieth century–received scarcely a single notice in the press. Mishima had associated himself with the Right in politics since 1966 and had alienated the *Bundan*, a literary establishment which is inclined to the Left; his work had become taboo. The only man to speak out strongly in favour of *The Sea of Fertility* was Yasunari Kawabata. Kawabata told a foreign interviewer, Philip Shabecoff of *The New York Times*, that 'a writer of Mishima's calibre appears only once every two or three hundred years in our history' and, he added, *The Sea of Fertility* was Mishima's masterpiece. With the exception of this lone voice, no one of importance praised the work. Mishima found himself in a peculiarly Japanese situation; he had alienated the *Bundan* but there was not one hostile squeak from the critics, just silence–a characteristic Japanese method of criticism.

Mishima had always been at odds with the critics, and at this point in his career he became hysterically hostile towards many of them– rather like a foreign businessman who has been surrounded and outwitted by unseen competitors in Japan. In his preface to the biography of Zenmei Hasuda, he wrote: 'When I got close to the age of forty, at which age Hasuda killed himself, I gradually understood the man better. Above all, I recognized the source of his anger; his fury was directed at Japanese intellectuals, the strongest enemy within the nation. It is astonishing how little the character of modern intellectuals in Japan has changed, i.e. their cowardice, sneering, 'objectivity', rootlessness, dishonesty, flunkeyism, mock gestures of resistance, self-importance, inactivity, talkativeness and readiness to eat their words. . . . Hasuda's anger has become my own.'[68]

Personally, he remained on good terms with some of the best-known critics. He also had many friends–fellow writers and theatre people –on whom he could have fallen back at this time of crisis in his career and, much more so, in his private life. It required no special powers of observation to realize that Mishima was in grave trouble; his pranks and capers had gradually assumed a more and more grotesque form, culminating in the *Tatenokai*. Mishima's difficulty, however, was that he had no truly close friends to warn him of the dangers into which he was running. He had no *kokoro no tomo* or real intimates; he was too self-controlled a man to have encouraged close friendship. Among those he met regularly during a period of many years were a number of individuals of sterling character, full of common sense; amongst his fellow novelists I think of Kobo Abé; in the world of the theatre, Takeo Matsuura. But Mishima had never trusted others with his innermost thoughts. Neither Abé nor Matsuura nor anyone else close to him fully understood what was on his mind. The odd thing is that they might easily have done so had they read his writing, for example *Sun and Steel*. But no one–or scarcely anyone–took the essay seriously. Mishima suffered from a peculiar misunderstanding which he had described long before in *Confessions of a Mask*: 'What people regarded as a pose on my part was actually an expression of my need to assert my true nature, and . . . what people regarded as my true self was a masquerade.' In other words, the *Tatenokai*, while it appeared to be part of Mishima's masquerade, was in fact a reflection of his need 'to assert my true nature'. Those who had known Mishima for a long time had become so accustomed to his clowning and his endless talk of death and suicide that they did not take him seriously any more. Only those who came to know him for the first time at this stage in his life, or those who relied upon a knowledge of his writing, could see what sort of man he was. Mishima's plight was thus ignored by those friends who were his contemporaries. Equally, his family was not able to do much for him; his mother was far too uncritical to chide her son for anything that he did, and Azusa had had no influence upon him for decades. Yoko, in fact, was in a better position than anyone else to chide and tease her husband back to common sense. When I saw them together I felt that she was doing this all the time, but Mishima was too closed up in himself to respond.

Meanwhile, Mishima associated with people whose politics were to the Right, a minority of critics and intellectuals in Japan. Among them were Takeshi Muramatsu and Toshiro Mayuzumi, both Francophiles with right-wing inclinations; Kinemaro Izawa, an educationalist and an exact contemporary of Mishima, who was perhaps the only person who retained his confidence to the very last; Fusao Hayashi, who had a record of opportunistic alternation between the extreme Left and the extreme Right; Kei Wakaizumi, an establishment intellectual who was closely associated with Prime Minister Sato during the latter's long tenure of office; and Seiji Tsutsumi, a poet and businessman, almost the only *zaikai*–man of high finance–with whom Mishima had much patience. There were others, but these men were probably those people whom Mishima saw the most of during the last years of his life. One might add to the list two politicians, Shintaro Ishihara and Wataru Hiraizumi, younger men of the Right in the LDP–the first a brilliant showman, the second a man of aristocratic family and of immense wealth, a member of the upper class to which Mishima aspired, not without success, to belong. The collective influence of these individuals upon Mishima, whom they all tended to regard in a patronizing manner–with the notable exception of Izawa, a humble man–cannot be said to have been good.

The Temple of Dawn, which Mishima began in the late summer of 1968, took him almost two years to complete, and is the most difficult of the four books of *The Sea of Fertility*. In this respect it is quite unlike anything that Mishima, who favoured lucidity and clarity of exposition, had ever written before. What makes *The Temple of Dawn* difficult to understand is Mishima's extensive treatment of religion; he incorporated his study of Hinduism and of Buddhism in the volume, however, for specific and good reasons. He was afraid that the Buddhist theme running through his long novel–the idea of reincarnation–would fail. Specifically, he thought that if the reader did not believe that he was serious about reincarnation then he would regard the entire novel as a kind of fairy story. In *The Temple of Dawn* Mishima set out to emphasize that the idea of reincarnation was fundamental to his novel, and was to be regarded as a fact. This, at any rate, is true of the first half of the book.

At the outset Honda, who is by this time a successful lawyer of forty-seven–a man with a desperately nihilistic outlook but nonchalant outward appearance–pays a visit to Bangkok. The year is 1941 and he has been sent there by a big trading company to take care of a complicated lawsuit. Mishima describes the city of Bangkok, the history of the Thai royal family and also the Hinayana Buddhism of the country. Honda's companion in the city is Hishikawa, a Japanese who acts as his interpreter–a strange-looking, perpetually exhausted man who has been supplied by the trading company. Honda has brought with him the diary of Kiyoaki–the dream diary–and he tries to see someone connected with two Thai princes, who had studied with him and Kiyoaki at the *Gakushuin* many years before.

Honda also remembers how, before his death, Isao had spoken during a dream of a place 'down south, very hot, in the rose-coloured light of some country in the south. . . .' The lawyer is steadfastly pursuing his notion of the reincarnation of Kiyoaki into Isao and then of Isao into a third person, whom he feels intuitively may be in this part of the world. With the help of Hishikawa, Honda obtains an audience with a mad, seven-year-old princess, the daughter of one of two princes he had known at the *Gakushuin*, a little girl who lives in a 'Rose Palace'. During this meeting the girl suddenly jumps up and flings herself at Honda, insisting that she is a Japanese who had died eight years previously (Isao had killed himself in 1933). She answers Honda's questions about the dates of the deaths of Kiyoaki and Isao correctly and he concludes that in this little princess, Ying Chan ('Moonlight') by name, he has probably found the reincarnation of Isao –though he is unable to discover whether Ying Chan has three moles on her body. After a short while Honda is offered a trip to India by his trading company client and he sets off for the sub-continent, planning to return to Bangkok. In Calcutta he witnesses the Durga Festival and watches the sacrifice of the goats. A headless kid kicks its back legs in the air as if it is having a terrible nightmare; the youth who beheads the kids has a shirt spotted with blood and Honda reflects that the sublime and the dirty go hand-in-hand in India (they are poles apart in Japan). Thereafter the lawyer travels to Benares, a city where 'holiness and defilement reached an extreme'. He walks down a tiny street passing the booth of a clairvoyant and goes out onto a stone-paved square facing the river. Lepers crouch there; they have come on pilgrimages from all over the country, intending to die on the banks of the Ganges. Flies cluster on the wounds of deformed creatures; they shine a golden green.

Honda takes a boat on the Ganges and sails towards the funeral *ghats*. He observes the burning of corpses; a blackened arm appears from the fire and a corpse bends itself backwards, as if a man were turning his back during his sleep. A sound of boiling comes to Honda across the water. At the end, the skulls remain and a man with a bamboo stick walks about the fire cracking the skulls. His muscles shine in the fire as he works and the sound of cracking bones echoes off the walls of the temple close by. It is not a sad spectacle, at all. What appears to be heartlessness is joy. Karma is a plain and natural pheno-menon like fruit on a tree or rice growing in paddies. Honda believes that at Benares he has seen the ultimate truths of this world.

From Benares, Honda travels to Ajanta, where he views a beautiful waterfall, two streams dashing over a cliff-face. One runs down between rocks, while the second falls like a silver rope; both are narrow, steep falls. Honda watches one of the falls, dropping down towards the Wagola River, slipping over a rock wall of yellow-green, giving an echo from the mountains around. Behind the fall is a dark, empty, stone cave; otherwise bright green surrounds it. Trees and vermilion flowers spread about the fall. The water gives off a shining light in which floats a rainbow. As Honda watches the stream, he sees several yellow butterflies, precisely in a line between him and the fall. And looking farther up, he is astonished by the dazzling height from which the water tumbles. It is so high that a world of a different dimension seems to manifest itself above. The rock wall is green, with dark moss and ferns. At the top a light yellow is visible. The grass above is so bright in colour, it seems to be not of this world. A single black kid is feeding on the grass there. High above float clouds and light at a dizzy height in the blue sky. . . . As he watches Honda remembers the words of Kiyoaki, which remain like a single drop of water in his mind: 'I'll see you again. I know it. Under the falls.' This must be the fall of which Kiyoaki spoke, not the fall under which Honda had once found Isao, after all.

Returning to Bangkok once again, Honda is forced to mingle with Japanese businessmen, seekers after gold who have nothing in common with the beautiful Kiyoaki and the stern Isao (Mishima's descriptions of the Japanese business community might be translated to the present day without a line being changed). One day Honda comes across a little book of poems written by an unsuccessful revolutionary in Thailand in 1932. He takes comfort in the poetry which would, he believes, console the spirit of Isao; he gives the book to Ying Chan, believing that Isao has been reborn in the little girl. India, Honda has concluded, showed him that his life's work must be the observation of karma. Since his childhood, he has firmly believed that history cannot be altered by human will, but he acknowledges that the core of human will is precisely a ceaseless endeavour to influence history. He pays a last visit to Ying Chan and has to tear himself away from her, as she clings to him, weeping desperately, and asking to be taken back to Japan, as she is really Japanese. After his return home, war breaks out and Honda spends most of his spare time in the study of karma. Here Mishima explains in great detail the various ancient theories of karma, of Greece, Rome, India and Thailand. There is a long discourse on Mahayana Buddhism: at the core of karma is *arayashiki*, the fundamental *raison d'être* of existence itself. Everything in this world is to be attributed to *arayashiki*, and this is mysteriously connected with reincarnation. The first part of *The Temple of Dawn* concludes with a description of an air raid in Tokyo during the war. By chance, Honda runs into Tadeshina, the aged servant of Satoko (in *Spring Snow*); from this aged woman he receives the present of a book of sutras.

In the second half of the book the mood changes. There is a sense of collapse and of failure; this is seen in Honda who has undergone a decline. It is 1952 and Honda, fifty-eight-years-old, has built a country villa for himself at Gotemba; he is rich and visits the place at week-ends. Between the study and a guest bedroom next-door Honda has had a secret peep-hole constructed, so that he can peer into the bedroom at his leisure. Honda has turned into a peeping-tom; he is no longer the observer of karma. In the house next-door lives an ageing lesbian, Keiko Hisamatsu, a former countess who has become the mistress of a US army colonel. Ying Chan, who is eighteen by this time, is studying in Japan. One evening Honda invites her to a party at his house; Keiko is invited as well. Honda conceives a desire to see Ying Chan without her clothes on; he contrives that a playboy nephew of Keiko shall seduce Ying Chan in the bedroom next to Honda's study. As he watches through his peep-hole Honda observes Ying Chan's body. Suddenly, however, the girl leaps up and pushes the young Japanese boy aside; she flees from the room and takes refuge in Keiko's house next-door, declining to meet Honda whom she has identified as the author of an unsuccessful plan to seduce her. Honda, desperate to confirm that Ying Chan has the three moles on her body, casts about for a way of proving the fact; he hits on the idea of building a swimming pool at his home and inviting a swimming party. But at the swimming party Honda is unable to see whether Ying Chan really has the tell-tale moles. He puts her and Keiko in the guest-room that evening and takes up watch at his spy-hole. Through the hole he sees the two women embracing and making love, and he verifies, at last, that Ying Chan's body bears the three moles.

That night a fire breaks out in Honda's home and the house is burned to the ground. The book ends with a short meeting between Honda and the twin sister of Ying Chan, in 1967, almost fifteen years after the fire at Honda's home. Honda learns that Ying Chan died at the age of twenty in Thailand, from the bite of a cobra (Isao had had a dream of being bitten to death by a 'green snake', much, we assume, as Ying Chan was killed).

A judgement of *The Temple of Dawn* must rest on the passages in the first part of the book in which Mishima describes Honda's study of karma and reincarnation. But only someone truly knowledgeable on the subject can gauge Mishima's familiarity with Buddhist theology. This is, however, a telling criticism of the book. The great majority of Japanese readers are certainly not able to understand the religious passages of *The Temple of Dawn*. (Finding a translator for the book proved a headache to the US publisher, largely on account of the section on Buddhism.) By and large, Mishima must be deemed to have failed in his great effort to convince the reader that he takes reincarnation seriously; sheer weight of doctrinal study will not do the job for him. The fact is that Mishima was not a religious man and was not deeply interested in religion. The sense of let-down which the concluding part of *The Temple of Dawn* gives is, however, a warning of what is to come in the fourth and final volume of *The Sea of Fertility, The Decay of the Angel*–a much more striking book which Mishima wrote in its entirety after his decision to kill himself and which was published after his death.

In conclusion, I summarize the four stages of Mishima's *Bunburyodo*, his dual way of Art and Action. This may be done in a table:

Date	Art	Action
Late autumn 1966	Finishes *Spring Snow*.	Applies for *Jieitai* training.
Summer 1968	Completes *Runaway Horses*.	Forms *Tatenokai*.
Spring 1970	Ends *The Temple of Dawn*.	Plans 'coup d'état'.
25 November 1970	*The Sea of Fertility* finished.	*Hara-kiri*.

Rarely can a suicide have been more elaborately orchestrated than this. Such was Mishima's 'plan for life'.

V

The River of Theatre

Once the theatre was like a jolly party I enjoyed attending after a hard day's work. There I could find another world–a world of glittering lights and colours, where the characters of my own creation, clad in alluring costumes, stood in front of a handsome set, laughed, screamed, wept and danced. And to think that I, as a playwright, governed and manipulated all these theatrical worlds from behind the scenes!

Yet such delights gradually turned bitter. The magic of the theatre– to give people the illusion of life's noblest moments and the apparition of beauty on earth–began to corrupt my heart. Or was it that I grudged being an alienated playwright? Theatre, where a false blood runs in the floodlights, can perhaps move and enrich people with much more forceful and profound experiences than anything in real life. As in music and architecture, I find the beauty of the theatre in its abstract and theoretical structure, and this particular beauty never ceases to be the very image of what I have always held in the depth of my heart as Ideal in Art.

YUKIO MISHIMA–*the catalogue to the Tobu Exhibition*

Yukio Mishima was a brilliant playwright, perhaps the best playwright of the post-war era in Japan. His dialogue is superb and the structure of the plays excellent. Some critics maintain that Mishima was a better playwright than a novelist. Had he lived–according to Seidensticker–he might have been one of the greatest playwrights in Japanese history, a master to be compared with the authors of the classical *No*. I think differently. Mishima's plays are, in a positive sense, parochial. They are admirable from the point of view of the *Shingeki* –the modern theatre in Japan. However, they may never reach a larger audience, outside Japan, because they are hard for a non-Japanese to follow. Only one of Mishima's long plays has been translated–*Madame de Sade*–and the reason for the comparative lack of translations of his plays (by contrast seven of his novels have been translated and *The Sea of Fertility* is also being published in its entirety in English) is that they are generally judged to be lacking in appeal to a Western audience.

Mishima might indeed have become a playwright of international stature; but that is a hypothesis which he ensured would not be tested.

Mishima as a playwright contented himself with the comparatively modest task of writing for the *Shingeki* (literally, the 'new theatre' in Japan). The challenge was no small one, but it was within his powers. By contrast, his determination to become known throughout the world as a novelist–his desire 'to conquer the world with his books'– imposed a heavy burden on him. One of those who worked with Mishima in the theatre, Takeo Matsuura, who produced most of his plays for the *Shingeki*, told me: 'He was much more free as a playwright than as a novelist. He used foreign settings, for example, in his plays; he had no difficulty with them at all. In his novels he rarely wrote about life overseas at all; and his foreign characters, in fiction, tend to be stiff and unconvincing portrayals.' Matsuura is right. Mishima was much more free in his use of foreign settings in his plays–perhaps because he was straining less at the leash; as a playwright he was writing well within his powers. A better explanation of Mishima's success as a playwright, however, may be that in certain ways the form of the modern, Western-style play suited him better than the form of the novel. He had the cast of mind of a playwright, finding in drama 'the very image of what I have always held in the depth of my heart as Ideal in Art'. To say that he was 'a better playwright than a novelist'–as the critic Jun Eto remarked to me–is nonetheless a puzzling verdict. How, in his case, would one put the two–his novels and his plays–in the balance? Certainly, Mishima worked harder at his novels than at his plays and he himself regarded the former as his chief works. I prefer to treat the two separately as different fields of artistic endeavour.

The modern theatre had a slow start in Japan. Whereas Japanese writers were attracted to the Western novel in the decades which followed the Meiji Restoration of 1868, and the first 'modern' novels were written in Japan in the late nineteenth century, Western-style theatre did not really become established until after the Pacific War. Valiant attempts were made by small groups of actors and actresses to create a modern theatre in Japan long before the war–the beginning of *Shingeki* is customarily traced to 1906, when a society for the promotion of the arts, the *Bungei Kyokai*, which specialized in drama, was founded. But the theatre suffered from censorship and, after a brief flowering in the 1920s, virtually succumbed to government control. There were always small, politically radical groups ready to brave the authorities' disapproval, but few permanent achievements were made before the onset of the Pacific War. (An exception is the foundation of the *Bungakuza*–'Literary Theatre'–in 1938. It survived through the war, taking as its slogan 'art for art's sake'.) One other reason for the failure of the modern theatre to establish itself in the early twentieth century was the strength of the competition from the traditional Japanese theatre, the *Kabuki*, a form established in the seventeenth and eighteenth centuries. A third factor was the success of a low-brow theatre known as *Shinpa*, which had none of the intellectual appeal of *Shingeki* (*Shingeki* groups were putting on dramas by Ibsen and Chekhov as well as new works by Japanese dramatists) and which drew large audiences, catering to a popular taste for Western-style, sentimental drawing-room drama.

After the war, *Shingeki* benefited from a relaxation of censorship. The radical character of modern theatre in Japan was apparent in the choice of plays produced by the leading theatrical groups: works by Ibsen, Gogol, Tolstoy, Chekhov and a number of Japanese authors who drew on the Russian tradition. The prestige of Western writers was great. Among the most popular *Shingeki* performances in the 1950s were *A Streetcar Named Desire* and *Look Back in Anger*; the Western classical repertoire was also drawn upon–in 1955 the *Bungakuza* played *Hamlet* with great success. For the first time, good translations of the plays of Shakespeare were available and Shakespeare was for a time the height of fashion; veteran *Kabuki* actors vied for the honour of playing *Hamlet*. Few Japanese writers of the older generation rose to the challenge of the *Shingeki* in the late 1940s. It was left to young men–among them Yukio Mishima and Kobo Abé–to respond to the situation. Abé did so in a manner consonant with the tradition of *Shingeki*, in which radical, proletarian protest had played so large a part before the war. In one of his early plays, *Dorei Gari* ('Slave Hunt', 1952), he satirized the business world in Japan–describing a particularly bizarre form of post-war commerce (a trade in the mortal remains of the war dead). Mishima, by contrast, showed no taste for ideology; his forte was style. These two young playwrights, the most successful newcomers to *Shingeki* after the war, were poles apart in politics–a fact which was equally apparent in their novels and in the translations of their works (Abé was taken up by the Soviet literary world, Mishima was translated exclusively in the West). Mishima showed a taste for the Western classical tradition–he was to write plays modelled on works by Racine and Euripides; Abé had a taste for Brecht.

Mishima's first work for the *Shingeki* was the one-act play *Kataku*

('Fire House', 1949). This was performed by the *Haiyuza*, one of the two leading *Shingeki* groups, and he was gratified to hear well-known actors and actresses speaking his lines. His first major success came the following year, in a genre which he made his own, the modern *No* play. Since its establishment in the fifteenth century as the theatrical form of the feudal aristocracy and the Imperial Court, *No* has attracted many writers, even in modern times. According to Donald Keene : 'Some have fashioned pastiches on the traditional themes, others have tried to fit modern conceptions into the old forms. The hysteria of wartime propaganda even led to the composition of a *No* play about life on a submarine. Some modern works have enjoyed temporary popularity, but they were essentially curiosities, having neither the beauty of language and mood of the old plays, nor the complexity of character delineation we expect of a modern work. The first genuinely successful modern *No* plays have been those by Yukio Mishima.'[1] As an example of Mishima's success, Keene takes *Kantan*, the first of his modern *No* plays, written in 1950; he compares the classical original with Mishima's work. In the classical *No*, 'a traveller naps on a magic pillow, and during the brief time that it takes his hostess at the inn to cook a bowl of gruel, he dreams of a glorious life as Emperor of China. He awakens to the realization that life is but a dream. In Mishima's play, instead of a traveller, we have a spoiled young man of today who sleeps on the magic pillow while his old nurse prepares the breakfast. His dreams are not of ancient China but of riches and power as a financial tycoon and a dictator.'[2]

Thereafter Mishima wrote many modern *No* plays. The second of his books to be translated was a collection of these plays, translated by Keene, and published under the title *Five Modern No Plays* in America in 1957. The plays had a great success overseas, they were performed in many European countries and in Australia and Mexico as well as in North America, eventually receiving an off-Broadway production late in 1960 which ran for two months and had good notices. It was partly through these short plays—all are one-act dramas—that Mishima first acquired a measure of fame in the West; the dialogue is taut and the playwright retains sufficient of the ghostly quality of the classical *No* to give his works a unique character. Their appeal was considerable in Japan itself. The plays were produced by *Shingeki* companies and also appeared on the classical *No* stage; one of the plays, *The Lady Aoi*, was sung as a Western-style opera. Translations of the classical *No* plays were long ago done by Arthur Waley, but they can scarcely be performed without the settings of the genuine *No*—the uniquely-shaped stage, the gorgeous costumes and masks and the musicians and chorus —often compared to classical Greek drama. Mishima's modern *No* plays gave the West a taste for *No* some time before it was possible for *No* companies to travel to foreign cities to perform the superb repertoire of the classical Japanese theatre.

Mishima also wrote plays for the *Kabuki* theatre in the early 1950s— before he had established himself as a *Shingeki* playwright. He had a unique advantage over his contemporaries in this field; he alone had mastered classical Japanese and knew sufficient of the difficult language used in *Kabuki* to write plays in this genre. Mishima loved the *Kabuki*; the baroque blood-letting and fierce swordplay appealed to his instincts; so, too, did the theme of many a *Kabuki* play—that true love may end in a *shinju*, or double suicide. His attitude towards the *No* was reverent and a little constricted, even ridiculous; his admiration for *Kabuki* was unrestrained. Many of the great actors of the day were his friends and he spent long hours backstage conversing with them. Mishima's *Kabuki* plays are of no great importance; during his life, however, they attracted much attention. In some ways the most successful was his last work for the theatre, *Chinsetsu Yumiharizuki*, a work with an untranslatable title, which he wrote in 1969 and himself produced at the National Theatre. It includes one scene which marked this as a Mishima production: snow is falling steadily on a mountain lodge, on the steps of which a kimonoed beauty tortures her naked male captive to death by drilling holes in his body with an awl. Mishima was a good mimic and an able *Kabuki* actor and after this production he made a record of the play in which he took all forty parts.

Mishima defined his approach to *Shingeki*, for which he wrote most of his forty plays, in these terms in 1951: 'The modern play is far, far removed from the chaotic world of the novel, as I see it. It must look like a paper cathedral floating in the sky. No matter how naturalistic a play may be the theme which makes for dramatic tension is such that it never suits the novel form. Strong emotion bears down upon the details and marches forward treading the details underfoot.'[3]

His first successful long play was *Shiro Ari no Su* ('The Nest of the White Ant', 1955), set on a Brazilian coffee plantation where an aristocratic Japanese couple have taken refuge with two servants—a chauffeur and his wife—after the war. The construction of the play, a tale of adultery and suicide attempts, is excellent and *Shiro Ari no Su* —the hollow nest of a white ant colony is a symbol of the empty lives of the Japanese emigrés—established Mishima's reputation as a *Shingeki* dramatist. Not long after completing this work, for which he won a dramatic award, Mishima declared : 'My ideal life would be to write one long novel a year and no short stories at all. Or, if I have to, then nothing longer than twenty pages. Otherwise I would devote my time to plays.'⁴ And on the relationship between his novels and his plays he commented: 'Plays awaken a different part of my desire, that part which is unsatisfied by writing novels. Now, when I write a novel, I want to write a play next. Plays occupy one of the two magnetic poles of my work.'⁵

Mishima never achieved his ideal. He continued to write two or three novels a year, and some of his most striking works—for example, 'Patriotism', the tale of *hara-kiri*—were to be longish short stories. For the remainder of his life, however, with the exception of the last year, he alternated continually between writing plays and novels. In 1956, for instance, he wrote *The Temple of the Golden Pavilion* in the early part of the year and followed it with a play, which he completed in time for the autumn season—*Rokumeikan*. This drama, the most successful of all Mishima's plays, is a 'historical' work set in the 1880s in Japan. The events of the play are imaginary but the setting, the Rokumeikan ('The Hall of the Deer's Cry')—a hall which the Japanese Government built in Tokyo in 1883 for the entertainment of the foreign community—is true to life. The story of the Rokumeikan itself is central to Mishima's play. The hall was built by the government to provide a site for gaudy balls to be attended by Japanese and foreign dignitaries as part of a public relations campaign intended by the Japanese authorities to convert the diplomatic and foreign trading community to the view that the Japanese people were civilized. This strategy behind the Rokumeikan was naïve—it was part of a much broader official campaign to induce the Western powers to abandon the 'unequal' trade treaties which had been forced upon Japan thirty years before. It was also regarded as ill-considered, even ludicrous, by a section of Japanese public opinion, especially by devout nationalists who saw no reason for Japanese ladies to abandon their kimonos and order full-length dresses from Vienna—together with dancing masters to teach them to waltz.

The Rokumeikan provided Mishima with the setting for a play about unsuccessful revolutionaries and complex social relationships. The action takes place at a grand ball given on the occasion of the Emperor's birthday in 1886. At the denouement, one of the principal characters, the reactionary politician Kageyama, who shoots his opponent with a pistol, delivers the line: 'Politics is the ability to understand the hate of others.' There is naturally a good deal more to the play than this. This single line, however, was held to characterize Mishima's own critical attitude towards the craftiness of politicians, be they Japanese or Western. Certainly, he disliked party men (later he was to profess his admiration for a particular type of national leader, one who identified himself with the nation he led—General de Gaulle). The merit of *Rokumeikan* lay, nonetheless, in its strength as drama, not in any political message.

Toka no Kiku ('Tenth Day Chrysanthemums', 1961) was the other great triumph of Mishima's career as a dramatist. September the ninth is a day of festival in Japan, on which exhibitions of chrysanthemums are staged. 'Tenth day' flowers would be too late for the show—they would be wasted. The chrysanthemum is a symbol of loyalty in Japan (the Imperial crest is composed of a 32-petalled chrysanthemum). Thus, Mishima's play has as its theme wasted loyalty.

The principal character of *Toka no Kiku* is a politician, a former Finance Minister named Mori, who had once, in the 1930s, been the target of an assassination attempt by right-wing terrorists. Mori's attitude towards the incident is brought out during a visit paid to him by Kiku, the faithful maidservant who saved his life sixteen years before, who has not seen him since the time of the assassination attempt (described in the play as if it were a minor detail in one of the numerous unsuccessful *coups d'état* of the 1930s). The old man states that the most 'honourable' day of his life—a moment he prizes more highly than the day on which he was appointed Finance Minister, his greatest office—was that on which patriotic youths tried to kill him. The most fortunate accident that can befall a statesman, Mori implies, is to be struck down by the hand of an assassin. Death in the service of the nation and the Emperor is to be preferred to life, if that life has no meaning. Mori spends his days pursuing a lonely hobby, the growing of cacti; his activities as a cactus fancier are much dwelt upon in Mishima's play. The old man is depicted as one who, like the cactus, has no 'blood'; his existence is without meaning. The political background to the play is the murderous struggle which took place in the 1930s between those whose prime objective was order—politicians, men of business and civil servants—and those who put a premium on 'honour'. Mori has belatedly realized that he belongs, at heart, to the latter camp. In Mishima's play, Kiku gives Mori short shrift at their meeting and

Toka no Kiku may be read as an assault upon sentimental conservatism; the dramatic action favours such an interpretation. The playwright himself, however, had a streak of sympathy for Mori's attitudes; the play was based on the *Ni Ni Roku* Incident of 26 February, 1936, carried out by rebel army officers with whom Mishima later claimed he had much in common.

Not that *Toka no Kiku* is a political play. The dramatic interest lies in the relationship between Kiku and her former master and employer, Mori. The part of Kiku was taken by Haruko Sugimura in the production given by the *Bungakuza* in November 1961, on the occasion of the twenty-fifth anniversary of the foundation of the theatrical group, and this was one of the most distinguished performances by an actress generally regarded as the finest of *Shingeki* players. How far the *Bungakuza*, whose dominant personality was Miss Sugimura, was from regarding *Toka no Kiku* as an ideological drama was made apparent two years later when the group rejected a fairly mild play of Mishima's on ideological grounds, precipitating a furious row between the *Bungakuza* and Mishima that ended in his resignation from the group with which he had worked, almost exclusively, for nearly a decade. Had *Toka no Kiku* been sympathetic to the Right in the eyes of the *Bungakuza* it would scarcely have been selected by them for performance at an anniversary.

The play which caused a rupture between Mishima and the *Bungakuza* was *Yorokobi no Koto* ('The Harp of Joy', 1964) and, although it is not one of Mishima's important plays, it must be examined here as it had so great an impact on its author's career in the theatre.

The play is set in post-war Japan and is based on the 'Matsukawa Incident'–the derailment of a train in 1949 by saboteurs whose identity was never established, although the authorities believed for a time that they were from the Left. The principal character is a senior police officer, Matsumura, a veteran who is popular with his subordinates, one of whom, Katagiri, he instructs to investigate the derailment of a train (the Matsukawa Incident is not identified as such in the play). The zealous Katagiri arrests several men and is astonished by their immediate release, when it has been ascertained that they are rightists. There are frequent left-wing demonstrations in the streets, the object of which is to show popular discontent with a government which is trying to pin the blame for the train derailment on the Left, without having any proof. A strange incident then occurs at the police station where Katagiri and his men work. A young policeman says that he has heard the sound of a *koto* (a classical Japanese musical instrument) while on duty. The others laugh at him—how, in the midst of noisy demonstrations, could he have heard such a thing? Shortly afterwards the investigation of the sabotage takes a totally unexpected turn. Matsumura, the man who is carrying out the police inquiry, is himself accused of having organized the sabotage; the police chief is said to have been an undercover communist agent. The faithful Katagiri is shattered by this turn of events. Later, the charges against Matsumura are shown to have been fabricated by the Right; nonetheless, the younger man loses his faith in his superior. One day, when Katagiri is on duty in the streets, with demonstrators surging about him, he hears the beautiful sound of a *koto*. A man who had placed his faith in absolute authority, in the impermeable system of the law, seeks refuge in fantasy after the collapse of his belief in Order.

The turning point in the play comes when Katagiri realizes that Matsumura, his revered leader, has exploited him for his own ends—though these are not political. The *Bungakuza,* after starting rehearsals of *Yorokobi no Koto* in mid-November 1963, and following the return of Haruko Sugimura from travels in China, suddenly suspended the rehearsals and informed Mishima that the production was cancelled. Some of the actors, it was explained to Mishima by a succession of delegations which visited him at his home to give reasons for the suspension of rehearsals, objected to the 'right-wing' lines spoken by the policemen in the play. Mishima was incensed. His angry rebuttal of the *Bungakuza* case was printed in an open letter to the group which appeared in the *Asahi Shimbun* a few days later, following his resignation from the *Bungakuza.* It read in part: 'Certainly *Yorokobi no Koto* is quite different from my other works and includes an element of danger. But what have you been thinking about me all this while that you should be astonished by a work such as this? Have you been making a fool of me, saying that Mishima is a playwright . . . who writes harmless dramas which gather large audiences? You set up such safe criteria as "Art" and conceal within yourselves a vague political inclination [to the Left], dropping the phrase "art for art's sake" from time to time . . . isn't this just hypocrisy and commercialism? I would like you to understand this: there is always a needle in art; there is also poison; you can't suck honey without the poison too.'[6] The *Bungakuza* had misunderstood Mishima's play. The break between them was complete, however. Shortly afterwards, he joined another theatrical group, the NLT. It was a sad moment for Mishima, who never again found a group as effective to work with as the *Bungakuza* and the *Bungakuza*, meanwhile, had lost their best playwright.

The quarrel is a puzzling one. Within three years Mishima was to profess political beliefs which would have fully justified the *Bungakuza* in breaking with him. He was to assert that *Toka no Kiku* had all along, in reality, been a play about the *Ni Ni Roku* Incident–a fact which he did not reveal in so many words at the time at which he wrote the play. He was also to state that he shared the patriotic attitudes of the fanatically imperialist young officers who staged the *Ni Ni Roku* Incident. Had the *Bungakuza* got wind of the change which was going on within Mishima as early as 1963? It seems not; otherwise the *Bungakuza* leaders would have cited their objections at the time of their row with Mishima. His imperialism did not surface clearly in his dramatic work until the summer of 1966 when he wrote *Eirei no Koe* ('The Voices of the Heroic Dead'). Another surprising feature of the squabble between Mishima and the *Bungakuza* was its violence. He had very few rows with people or with organizations during his life. There were disagreements, but Mishima avoided public hostility on almost all occasions. Like many Japanese–and however un-Japanese he may have been in many respects–he abhorred public fracas.

Madame de Sade, the next of Mishima's plays, chronologically, once again shows him to be a playwright far more interested in problems of structure than in political matters. This play, he wrote, 'might be described as Sade seen through women's eyes': 'Reading *The Life of the Marquis de Sade* by Tatsuhiko Shibusawa I was most intrigued as a writer by the riddle of why the Marquise de Sade, after having demonstrated such absolute fidelity to her husband during his long years in prison, should have left him the moment that he was at last free. This riddle served as the point of departure for my play, which is an attempt to provide a logical solution. . . . This play might be described as "Sade seen through women's eyes." I was obliged therefore to place Madame de Sade at the centre, and to consolidate the theme by assigning all the other parts to women. Madame de Sade stands for wifely devotion; her mother, Madame de Montreuil, for law, society and morality; Madame de Simiane for religion; Madame de Saint-Fond for carnal desires; Anne, the younger sister of Madame de Sade, for feminine guilelessness and lack of principles; and the servant, Charlotte, for the common people.'[7]

Mishima's fascination with structure is evident in this passage from his 'postface' to Keene's translation of *Madame de Sade*: 'I had to involve these characters with Madame de Sade and make them revolve around her, with something like the motions of the planets. I felt obliged to dispense entirely with the usual, trivial stage effects, and to control the action exclusively by dialogue; collisions of ideas had to create the shape of the drama, and sentiments had to be paraded throughout in the garb of reason. I thought that the necessary visual appeal would be provided by the beautiful rococo costumes. Everything had to form a precise, mathematical system around Madame de Sade.'[8] Keene has described the debt owed by Mishima to Racine: 'Mishima's classicism . . . is given its most extreme expression in the play *Madame de Sade*. . . . Here he adopted most of the conventions of the Racinian stage—a single setting, a reliance on the *tirade* for relations of events and emotions, a limited number of characters each of whom represents a specific kind of woman, and an absence of overt action on the stage.'[9]

Madame de Sade was a considerable success in Tokyo although the subject matter was a little too *recherche*. After its translation into English, Mishima hoped that it would be produced on Broadway and pressed his agent in New York, Audrey Wood, to find a theatre for it. *Madame de Sade*, however, proved to have no appeal to American actresses; the 'absence of overt action on the stage' was the major problem. Quite possibly, none of Mishima's long plays will ever be performed on the Western stage. Certainly it is unlikely that Mishima's subsequent major plays, *Suzaku Ke no Metsubo* ('The Fall of the House of Suzaku', 1967)—a play based on a Euripidean model—and *Wagatomo Hitler* ('My Friend Hitler', 1969) would have great appeal to Western audiences. The latter is a play set in Germany in 1934 in which Mishima describes the events before and after the Night of the Long Knives. It makes the point that Hitler steered a 'neutral' course between the Brownshirts and the conservative forces—the regular army and big business—on that occasion. Mishima neither praises nor criticizes Hitler; nor does he develop the character of the dictator in his play. He treats the Night of the Long Knives as an incident in a struggle for power, a technical operation. The title of the play refers to Roehm, the head of the Brownshirts, one of Hitler's victims on the Night. In the play Roehm believes that the

Führer is 'my friend'—until it is too late. At the *première* of the play, in Tokyo on 19 January, 1969, Mishima distributed a note to the audience: 'The dangerous ideologue, Mishima, dedicates an evil ode to the dangerous hero, Hitler.' His intention was to mock the critics and the vaguely leftist 'neutralism' of Japanese intellectuals. 'Neutralism', the play says, can lead anywhere.

Mishima's last play for the modern theatre was *Raio no Terrasu* ('The Terrace of the Leper King', 1969). He invited me to the *première*, and I remember how he looked that evening—he was wearing all-white evening dress and accompanied by Yoko. Tennessee Williams was supposed to put in an appearance and there was an empty seat next to Mishima where he should have been: 'His dog is ill, it seems,' said Mishima, 'and he's staying on board ship at Yokohama.' The performance itself went well enough. *Raio no Terrasu* is a play about the Khmer king Jayavarman III, the builder of the temple of Bayon at Angkor Wat. The monarch suffered from leprosy; Bayon is his monument. Mishima used the tale to make the point that the material triumphs over the immaterial, the Body over the Spirit—Bayon alone remains. He was especially proud of the last scene of the play which is an exchange on the steps of the newly-constructed Bayon between the Body—the youthful image of the king—and the Spirit, represented by the voice of the dying, leprous king (a sepulchral, tape-recorded voice in the Teigeki production we saw).

BODY: King, dying king. Can you see me?

SPIRIT: Who is calling me? I remember the voice. That brilliant voice.

B: It's me. Do you see?

S: No. Of course not. I'm blind.

B: Why should the Spirit need eyes? It has been your source of pride that you see things without using your eyes!

S: Such harsh words. Who are you?

B: I'm the king.

S: Absurd! That's me.

B: We share the same name. King, I am your Body.

S: Who am I then?

B: You are my Spirit. The Spirit that resolved to build this Bayon. What is dying is not the Body of the king.

S: My Body was rotten and has vanished. You cannot be my Body, speaking so proudly and boldly.[10]

The actor who played the part of the Body was heavily sun-tanned and wore a short tunic with straps across his bare chest. As he spoke his lines he strode about the terrace of the temple, flourishing his arms. Behind him was a giant face made of foot-high blocks of stone, one of many such faces at the temple of Bayon. The actor, Kinya Kitaoji, was slightly over-weight; his voice boomed out cheerfully, while the groaning Spirit endeavoured to reply:

B : It's not true. Your Body was never rotten. Your Body is here, shining with youth, full of vigour, like an immortal golden statue. The cursed illness is an illusion of the Spirit. How could such a triumphant king as I be affected by illness?

S : But what could the Body achieve? What imperishable things can he construct? It is not stones that planned and constructed this imperishable Bayon. Stones are nothing but materials. It's the Spirit that made this.

B: (*laughing aloud with pride.*) The Spirit cannot see Bayon any more, because even the Spirit depended on the Body.

S : No. I don't need to see it. The finished Bayon shines in my spirit.

B: Shining? It's only a small streak of light, which is about to be put out. Think, if it is enough to be shining in the Spirit, why was it necessary to construct Bayon with such an enormous quantity of stones?

S: The Spirit always longs for a shape.

B: That's because you are shapeless. Shape always takes its model from a beautiful Body like me. Did you use as a model of this temple the rotten body of a leper?

S: Rubbish! The body of a leper is nothing.

B: Nothing? You suffered for so long.

S: No, nothing. The Spirit is everything.

B: What are they, the rotten, shapeless and the blind? They are the shape the Spirit takes. It's not you that suffered from leprosy. Your very existence is leprous. You are a born leper.

S : Sharpness, clarity and the power to see through to the bottom of this world constructed Bayon. The Body cannot have such power. You are only a slave captured by the Body.

B: You say that you are more free than me? Are you? More free because you cannot run, cannot jump, sing, laugh nor fight?

S: I run through one hundred years. You run only in space.

B: There is light in space. Flowers bloom, bees hum. A beautiful

summer afternoon stretches ahead. But what you call time is
a damp and dark underground tunnel.

S: Oh, Bayon, my love.

B: Why do you leave it here? Bayon is the present. The forever
shining present. Love? Were you ever so beautiful as to be loved?

S : I'm dying. Each breath is agony. Oh, my Bayon.

B: Die! Perish! . . . You planned and constructed. That was your
illness. My breast, like a bow, shines in the sun. Water flows,
sparkles and is still. You didn't follow me. That was your illness.

S: My Bayon. . . .

B: The Spirit perishes, as a kingdom perishes.

S: It's the Body that perishes. The Spirit is imperishable.

B: You are dying. . . .

S: Bayon. . . .

B: You're dying.

S: . . .

B: What has happened?

S: . . .

B: No answer. Are you dead?

S: . . .

B: You are dead.

(*The sound of birdsong.*)

Look. The Spirit has died. A bright blue sky! Beautiful birds, trees
and Bayon protected by all these! I will reign over this country again.
Youth is immortal. The Body is imperishable. I won. It is I that am
Bayon.[11]

Early in 1970 Mishima surprised his friends by announcing that he
would write no more plays. The drama had been such an important
part of his life for so many years that his decision was incompre-
hensible; some put it down as a foible, others believed that he was
tired by his struggle with *The Sea of Fertility* and had decided to
concentrate all his strength on that single novel.

Not long before he killed himself, Mishima arranged a shelf of
objects in his upstairs sitting room at home in Magome. There were:
a Greek vase, a small bronze nude of himself, a collection of translations of his books, and a stage model for the last scene of *Raio no
Terrasu*. One evening he showed this display to some friends. 'How do
you like it?' he asked them in an ironic tone. 'This really sums up
my life, don't you think?' And he burst into laughter.

VI

The River of Body

This is a young River that suddenly began flowing at the mid-point of my life. I had been dissatisfied for quite some time by the fact that my invisible spirit alone could create tangible visions of beauty. Why could not I myself be something visibly beautiful and worthy of being looked at? For this purpose I had to make my body beautiful.

When at last I came to own such a body, I wanted to display it to everyone, to show it off and to let it move in front of every eye, just like a child with a new toy. My body became for me like a fashionable sports car for its proud owner. In it I drove on many highways to new places. Views I had never seen before opened up for me and enriched my experience.

But the body is doomed to decay, just like the complicated motor of a car. I for one do not, will not, accept such a doom. This means that I do not accept the course of Nature. I know I am going against Nature; I know I have forced my body onto the most destructive path of all.

YUKIO MISHIMA—*the catalogue to the Tobu Exhibition.*

Mishima was physically a small man. His height was 5 foot 4½ inches, somewhat below the average for Japanese men of his generation, though the Japanese as a race are physically smaller than other Asian peoples. His body was slim; even after he had taken up body-building—which he did at the age of thirty—he did not spread outwards very much. In a suit, he looked a man of average build for one of his height. His shoulders did not seem large nor did his chest stick out. He simply held himself straight, in the manner of a professional soldier. He had, however, a fine, well-proportioned, strong body. Shoulders, arms and legs were heavily muscled, and the muscles lay well on his small-boned frame. His waist was slim, the stomach perfectly flat and strong, and his chest—showing signs of training with weights—was well-developed and powerful. Unusually for a Japanese he had a lot of black hair on his body, mainly on his chest—for which he was teased by other Japanese. His body had one defect: the legs were much too short in relation to the trunk–a not uncommon feature amongst Japanese men and women. This was one subject on which Mishima, who often mocked himself, was never known to make jokes. He considered himself to be beautiful, and when he stated, in an introduction written for a book containing pictures of young Japanese body-builders–*Young Samurai*–that he was the ugly duckling amongst them (he also appeared in the volume) he was in fact trying to say the opposite: that he was the finest-looking of them all. Actually, he was right. Professional body-builders, with their masses of bulbous muscles, are not beautiful. By comparison, the amateur Mishima was sleek and trim.

Mishima started intensive physical training in 1955. He had always been ashamed of his weak physique, of 'being skinny and having a bad stomach'. As he began to make his way as a writer he became aware that this 'unhealthy pursuit' would make his plight even worse. He began to fear that he would be a physical wreck before he had reached the age of thirty. He started to ride and set up a bar in his garden, from which he would swing, but neither pursuit had much effect upon his physical state. Then in 1955, in the summer of his thirtieth year, he came across a picture in the Waseda University physical culture club's magazine. Accompanying the picture was the sentence: 'YOU TOO CAN HAVE A BODY LIKE THIS.' Mishima at once got in touch with Hitoshi Tamari, the coach at Waseda.

In *Sun and Steel*, Mishima gives a second description of the genesis of his decision to take up physical training. Early in his life, he says, he felt a loathing for his body. He put all his emphasis on 'words', on the pursuit of literature; 'words' tended to corrode his being–as if white ants were eating into his person–and he sought a second 'language', 'the language of the flesh'. It was the sun that opened his eyes to this possibility: 'The sun was enticing, almost dragging my thoughts away from their night of visceral sensations, away to the swelling of muscles encased in sunlit skin. And it was commanding me to construct a new and sturdy dwelling in which my mind, as it rose little by little to the surface, could live in security. That dwelling was a tanned, lustrous skin and powerful, sensitively rippling muscles. . . . It was thus that I found myself confronted with those lumps of steel: heavy, forbidding, cold as though the essence of night had in them been still further condensed.'[1]

For Mishima, lying on the deck of the *President Wilson* in 1952, the sun came as a personal revelation. Three years later he took up body-building.

As he explained in an article he wrote for the American magazine *Sports Illustrated* shortly before his death, Mishima attached considerable importance to his choice of sports coaches. He was immediately impressed by Tamari, the Waseda coach, when the latter demonstrated to Mishima how he could ripple his chest muscles so that 'their activity was apparent even beneath his shirt'. Mishima came very late to the sport of body-building. The ideal age at which to begin is twenty. However he applied himself diligently and began to see results. After training for a year he realized, suddenly, that his stomach disorder had disappeared, 'like something I had put down somewhere and forgotten'.

At the end of the first year, Mishima found a second coach, Tomo Suzuki; and he made Suzuki's slogan of 'exercises for everyday life' his own. Suzuki was a colourful character and he amused Mishima greatly. 'See, Mr Mishima,' he said one day, pointing to an exemplary trainee under his command, 'in a sound body you'll find a sound spirit. Look at the perfect suppleness of his body, the dexterity of his movements. There's a real human being for you.' Somewhat later the model youth absconded with Suzuki's earnings from the gym.

In addition to training at the gym, Mishima engaged in a number of other physical activities. In the summer of 1956 he joined a team of local youths in the district of Jiyugaoka, the outlying part of Tokyo where the Hiraoka family lived. The function of this group of young men was to carry about the heavy *omikoshi* (portable shrine) on the occasion of the summer festival. Escorted by a Shinto priest, and attended by crowds of children with their own little *omikoshi*, the procession went up and down the narrow streets of Jiyugaoka with Mishima jostling and struggling amongst the youths who carried the shrine. For the occasion he wore a *hachimaki* round his head and a light tunic; a photograph shows Mishima with an expression of child-like glee on his face. The ambition to carry an *omikoshi* on a summer's day had been with him since childhood when he had first seen such a spectacle and had been fascinated by the raw, sweaty men who had stampeded in and out of Natsuko's front garden in the house at Yotsuya where Mishima was born (the scene is described at length in *Confessions of a Mask*). Mishima's exploit at the summer festival was duly reported in the gossip magazines in Tokyo. It was the start of a stream of publicity given to his non-literary exploits, a stream which was to become a great torrent in later years.

Mishima also began to make stage appearances. In a production of *Rokumeikan* he appeared briefly as a gardener, and in a production of Racine's *Brittanicus*, the translation of which he had supervised, Mishima played another small part—that of a soldier carrying a spear. A photograph was taken of him in the second role, standing together with two fellow soldiers on stage. Mishima is in front of the other two and has a set expression on his face. Behind him are two taller men, professional actors with a softness about the jowls. The picture is intriguing; it was amongst the first of many group photos of Mishima in which he appears as a man of the same stature as tall men in his company. In fact, he would arrange that the photographer shoot from a low angle, or use some other device to give the impression that Mishima was of equal height to his companions. One of the best devices he contrived for this purpose was to wear an extraordinarily tall pair of *geta* (wooden shoes). *Geta*, which are wooden platforms on two parallel, rectangular sections of wood—one under the heel, the other under the ball of the foot—can easily be made taller. On one occasion Mishima appeared in a duel scene with Shintaro Ishihara, a tall, graceful actor, stepping upon *geta* five-inches-high, waving his sword vigorously.

Mishima's ambition was to become a great athlete but he never quite succeeded. In 1956 he joined the training sessions of Nippon University's boxing team, having fallen under the spell of Tomoo Kojima, the boxing coach there. Kojima was a quiet, austere man whose life was dedicated to his sport. 'In the literary world,' wrote Mishima, 'I had the reputation of being rather severe with myself but compared to the preternatural austerity practised by Kojima, I conducted myself like an unbridled wastrel.' Mishima did not make a great boxer, but he enjoyed the hard training and discipline of the training camp: 'During the first day . . . I thought every minute my breath was going to give out, but my earlier training had taught me I would become used to this sort of hardship, too. By the third day I felt myself starting to become accustomed to the rigorous drills. I will never forget the excitement I felt the first time I entered the ring for a sparring session. The truth was that my first adversary was Kojima himself, and he took it extremely easy on me. Though I was formidable enough to look at, stepping into the ring, I took little pride in the headgear, which felt so strange, and the heavy gloves, which stirred so odd a sensation. After I put them on I gave my chin a light tap, and the coach laughed beside me. "That's what everybody does the first time," he said. When I heard this I felt an extravagant happiness at the thought that I had become, after all, without my realizing it, not too much different from other men who liked sports. During my first or second sparring session a novelist friend visited the camp with an eight mm ciné camera and captured my wretched performance on film. Sometime later, when the literary crowd gathered at my house, he showed his film to a mambo accompaniment, to the hilarity of all. And, indeed, my on-screen figure making its desperate evasive actions to the Latin rhythm seemed like something out of a cartoon.'[2]

Mishima was witty enough about his misfortunes in the boxing ring–this willingness to make himself a butt of humour was an attractive feature of the man. I used to think, when I met him years after these experiences, that this ironical Mishima was real. In other words, I believed that his physical training was an aspect of his physical exuberance and that he did not take this part of his life seriously. His narcissism sometimes got out of hand. I regarded this as a quirk of character. Many others must have taken a similar attitude. He was obviously a little ill; he suffered from romanticism. It was hard to believe, however, that so intelligent a man could regard himself–his body–as a temple of beauty for more than a few seconds in a day.

Had one read his books more carefully, had one believed that he meant what he wrote, the mistake would have been avoided. In *Sun and Steel* he describes his attitude towards body-building quite clearly; concerning his reasons for pressing on with *bodei-biru* he re-marks : firstly that it was part of an educational process–his argu-ment is that of *mens sana in corpore sano* and he expounds the merits of classical education like an earnest English public schoolboy; secondly that he needed a 'classical' body to achieve his aim in life, which he describes thus: 'Beyond the educative process there also lurked another, romantic design. The romantic impulse that had formed an undercurrent in me from boyhood on, and that made sense only as the *destruction* of classical perfection, lay waiting within me. Like a theme in an operatic overture that is later destined to occur throughout the whole work, it laid down a definitive pattern for me before I had achieved anything in practice. Specifically, I cherished a romantic impulse towards death, yet at the same time I required a strictly classical body as its vehicle; a peculiar sense of destiny made me believe that the reason why my romantic impulse towards death remained unfulfilled in reality was the immensely simple fact that I lacked the necessary physical qualifications. A powerful, tragic frame and sculpturesque muscles were indispensable in a romantically noble death. Any confrontation between weak, flabby flesh and death seemed to me absurdly inappropriate. Longing at eighteen for an early demise, I felt myself unfitted for it. I lacked, in short, the muscles suitable for a dramatic death. And it deeply offended my romantic pride that it should be this unsuitability that had permitted me to survive the war.'³

Here is the most probable explanation of Mishima's faking of his army medical in 1945, though this is a matter to which Mishima apparently never alluded later in life. A straightforward reading of *Sun and Steel* leads one to the conclusion that Mishima, while he mocked his wretched performance as a sportsman, took his body for a work of art: 'Muscles, I found, were strength as well as form, and each complex of muscles was subtly responsible for the direction in which its own strength was exerted, much as though they were rays of light given the form of flesh. Nothing could have accorded better with the definition of a work of art that I had long cherished than this concept of form enfolding strength, coupled with the idea that a work should be organic, radiating rays of light in all directions. The muscles that I thus created were at one and the same time simple existence and works of art; they even, paradoxically, possessed a certain abstract nature. Their one fatal flaw was that they were too closely involved with the life process, which decreed that they should decline and perish with the decline of life itself.'⁴

Mishima had found an alternative to literature—what he called 'a true antithesis of words'. And, as has been shown, he governed the latter years of his life according to his *Bunburyodo*, the dual way of Art and Action, which ended with his suicide. One might ask: how did he arrive at such a system as his *Bunburyodo*? How did he make the move from the River of Body to the River of Action? The clue may be found in the passage above. His 'muscles' had 'one fatal flaw'. He was bound to get old. In order to achieve his romantic apotheosis he had to die while his body was still beautiful, while he was still a comparatively young man. Such is the argument of *Sun and Steel*.

Does one take it seriously—as a description of what went on in

Mishima's mind in the mid-1960s? I think so. One test is that of
intellectual coherence. The essay is consistent throughout–unlike
Mishima's 'political' writing in the late 1960s. A second criterion is
my personal one. *Sun and Steel* has, for me, a passion that is–in
retrospect–sincere, however unpleasing it may be. Talking with
Mishima about the book I discovered that he cared a great deal for
what I had taken to be a mere diversion; this was not a discovery
upon which I acted during his life–I did not look up *Sun and Steel*.
It was hard, while he was alive, to read more than a few pages of his
romantic thoughts without falling asleep, hard to take seriously a
tome full of dire threats when its author–so 'intrepid, dispassionate
and robust' in his own words–seemed a living refutation of his
romanticism.

During the 1960s Mishima's narcissism was obvious. After his disappointment with the novel *Kyoko no Ie*, he plunged into a whirl of
activity. Early in 1960, as I have already mentioned, he took the lead
part in a gangster film, *Karakkaze Yaro* ('A Dry Fellow'), in which
he appeared, at the start of the film, exercising, stripped to the waist,
in a prison yard. The film ended with the murder of the black-
jacketed thug played by Mishima. (He also wrote and recorded the
theme song of the film.) He appeared to be indulging his narcissism
a little, no more. For the most part he led a highly-controlled, hard-
working life and poured most of his energy into his writing and
relentless training in gyms and *kendo* halls. Three years later he
posed for an album of photographs taken by the fashionable photographer, Eiko Hosoe. In these pictures he appeared in a number of
extraordinary poses–lying on his back in his garden against a baroque
ornament, stripped naked with a white rose in his mouth, or lying
upon his hairy chest. The album, *Barakei* ('Torture by Roses'), gave
Mishima a bad reputation in some quarters. Critics and other writers
who disliked him said that Mishima was going off his head at last.
And the appearance of pictures of the novelist lying totally nude on a
rocky foreshore gave encouragement to a class of correspondents for
whom Mishima had made no preparations–anonymous 'friends' who
wrote passionate notes to him requesting still bolder nude portraits. Yet these pictures were generally felt to reflect only one part,
and not a very vital part, of the man. His narcissism seemed, to most
people, to be irrelevant to his literary work. Besides, it was said,
he was doing such things in jest, seeking to irritate the critics whom
he so despised, not only for their scrawny chests, but more on

account of their flabby intellectual attitudes. Other Japanese got used to Mishima's exhibitionism, and not a great deal of attention was paid to the startling photographs which appeared in cheap weekly magazines.

Not even the famous portrait of Mishima as St Sebastian aroused more than a flicker of interest. This was a photo taken in 1966 by Kishin Shinoyama, the leading young Japanese photographer. It shows Mishima in the pose selected by Guido Reni for the portrait of St Sebastian which–as Mishima had described in *Confessions of a Mask* –had inspired his first ejaculation. By the time this picture appeared in Japan, the public was inured to Mishima's buffoonery. The other photographs taken by Shinoyama at this time–one of them portraying Mishima in boots, black jock-strap and sailor cap, leaning against a massive motorcycle–did not create a lasting impression either. This reaction, which may now appear obtuse in the West, where Mishima's portraits are well-known, is understandable. Most of the time, Mishima was engaged in 'serious' pursuits; above all, his writing. No one paid much attention to his foibles. 'What trick will he think up next?' was the most common reaction. Not long after posing for the Shinoyama pictures, he appeared in the cabaret act with Akihiro Maruyama, singing his song *The Sailor Who Was Killed by Paper Roses*, at the end of which the two men, Mishima and Maruyama, exhanged a kiss. 'Mishima has done it again,' the weekly magazines announced, and the little incident was quickly forgotten. One who underestimated Mishima's energy might make the mistake of thinking that he spent all his time posing for photographers; in fact, Mishima was engaged in a thousand other activities and would rush off a series of pictures with a skilled photographer in a matter of minutes. The photographs amused him, but he was not prepared to waste a great deal of time over them.

As he neared the age of forty, Mishima began to worry about his age, yet he was still extremely fit five years later, showing little sign of slowing down physically. His figure was almost as good as it had been fifteen years earlier, though his shoulder muscles had a slight tendency to sag and he did not look so impressive when he inflated his chest in the style of a body-building fanatic. According to his father, Mishima's wrist was stiff and he had frequent massage to enable him to do *kendo*. There were other signs of encroaching middle-age. During the training at Camp Fuji he could not keep up with the *Tatenokai* youths; he would join them only in those exercises at which he was best, press-ups, for example. On the whole, however, he was still in extraordinarily good condition for a man of forty-five, and two months before his death he posed for a last series of photographs taken by Shinoyama. These, he declared, should be published in a volume to be entitled *Otoko no Shi* ('Death of a Man'). Amongst the poses which Mishima struck for this unpublished volume were a number in which he committed *hara-kiri*. There were also portraits in which he appeared as a traffic accident victim, covered in blood. This was his last journey down the River of Body.

9 Mishima as St Sebastian.
   (*Photo Shinoyama*)

10 Mishima with sword
    and *hachimaki*.
    (*Photo Shinoyama*)

11   Mishima (centre) with the author (right) on Mt Fuji.

VII

The River of Action

The River of Body naturally flowed into the River of Action. It was inevitable. With a woman's body this would not have happened. A man's body, with its inherent nature and function, forces him towards the River of Action, the most dangerous river in the jungle. Alligators and piranhas abound in its waters. Poisoned arrows dart from enemy camps. This river confronts the River of Writing. I've often heard the glib motto, 'The Pen and the Sword Join in a Single Path.' But in truth they can join only at the moment of death.

This River of Action gives me the tears, the blood, the sweat that I never begin to find in the River of Writing. In this new river I have encounters of soul with soul without having to bother about words. This is also the most destructive of all rivers, and I can well understand why few people approach it. This River has no generosity for the farmer; it brings no wealth nor peace, it gives no rest. Only let me say this: I, born a man and alive as a man, cannot overcome the temptation to follow the course of this River.

YUKIO MISHIMA–*the catalogue to the Tobu Exhibition*

1

A mysterious aspect–perhaps *the* most impenetrable feature–of the Japanese tradition is the imperial system of that country. This was crucial to Mishima's 'River of Action'.

The role of the Emperor has been a varied one in Japanese history. Throughout feudal times the Emperors lived in Kyoto, the ancient capital, and their temporal powers were minute. The Emperor was respected as a religious and cultural symbol of state. As such, he had an important part to play in Japanese society; he was a mysterious, unseen presence. However, the actual rulers of Japan, the so-called Shoguns or Tycoons–the English word has a Japanese derivation–

G

allowed the Emperors very little part in government. Only after 1868, when the Imperial Court was moved to Tokyo and a young Emperor installed on the Chrysanthemum Throne–the Emperor Meiji (1868– 1911)–was the Japanese sovereign accorded the trappings of power. Even then, he remained largely in the hands of his senior officials, his 'advisers'. Meiji is not known definitely to have been responsible for a single major policy decision during his long reign. Taisho, his son, who reigned from 1912 to 1926, and who was mentally deficient, also remained aloof from policy matters. The present Emperor– known in the West as Hirohito–who succeeded Taisho after a period as Regent, took only two decisions during his reign, but they were important ones. He stamped out the revolt known to the Japanese as the *Ni Ni Roku* Incident–the rebellion of February 1936–and he took the decision to end the Pacific War in 1945.

To this day the role of the Emperor in Japan is a mystery. Accord- ing to the law–the post-war Constitution drafted by General Mac- Arthur and his advisers in 1946 and ratified the following year–the Emperor has no temporal authority. He is the symbolic head of state; his functions are limited to opening sessions of Parliament and to making occasional public appearances. His powers were drastically cut back under the Allied Occupation of 1945–52–first, by the declara- tion called the *ningen sengen*, in which he formally disclaimed the cardinal beliefs of twentieth-century Japanese imperialism (see Chapter Three), and second–implicitly–by the treatment accorded him by the US authorities. The Emperor was not consulted by the occupying ad- ministration on matters of state nor was he treated as a figure with anything more than nominal power. His children, also, were sub- jected to unprecedented treatment–his eldest son, the Crown Prince, was found an American governess. This was all in accordance with the US understanding of *demokurashi* in Japan. The marriage of the Crown Prince to a commoner in 1959–this was the first occasion on which a future Emperor or even an Imperial prince had married outside the traditional aristocracy–seemed to mark Japanese accept- ance of the system of government introduced to the nation during the Occupation. There has in fact been a considerable change in the position of the Emperor in post-war Japan. The post-war Emperor has been a popular figure rather than a divine symbol of authority; the pre-war practice of keeping the Emperor hidden within his palace, except for rare occasions on which he emerged as a man on a white horse, has been abandoned. The change might be compared to that which took place in England between the reigns of Charles I and Charles II. The Emperor of Japan still has a very special atmosphere about him but he is no longer a figure of ultimate authority, armed with divine rights.

The change, however, has not been a complete one. There are still many aspects of the imperial system which remain out of sight of the public. There is a taboo on discussion of the Emperor's position in the press. Mishima's attitude towards this taboo was aggressive. Whether he was truly an imperialist or not, he was in fact more out-spoken on the subject of the Emperor than any well-known man since the end of the Pacific War. Sometimes he lauded the imperial system; sometimes he castigated the present incumbent, Hirohito. At times, he appeared to be an out-and-out nationalist, on other occasions he seemed to have delivered deadly assaults on the Emperor. My im-pression is that Mishima's imperialism—contradictory as it was—had its roots in both a genuinely felt worship of the Emperor system and in his personal aesthetic. His aesthetic, I believe, was the strongest influence on Mishima, and the wellsprings of his decision to commit *hara-kiri*—traditionally an action undertaken by a *samurai* wishing to demonstrate his loyalty to his lord (who could be the Emperor)— were individual and were connected to this long-held aesthetic, his 'heart's leaning toward Death and Night and Blood'. Mishima was an imperialist, of course, but he was also a great deal more than that —a cold, self-obsessed creature given to fits of passion, a novelist, a playwright, a sportsman. He was a man with many sides to his character, and his imperialism cannot be regarded as central; Emperor-worship was only one facet of Yukio Mishima.

The River of Body, Mishima remarked, flowed into the River of Action. For an illustration of his meaning one may look at his writings on *kendo*, Japanese fencing, which he took up in 1959. It was this sport, he wrote, that 'finally satisfied that nostalgic yearning that I have so long felt towards athletics.' In *kendo* he believed that 'the ideal harmony between the body and spirit is realized.' In his *Sports Illustrated* article he explains how he hated the sport at school: 'I felt a hot flush of special mortification whenever I heard the rude, barbaric, threatening cries of *kendo*.' He was affronted by their 'gross shamelessness, their animality.' 'They threatened culture. They threatened civilization.' But, 'now thirty years later, I feel quite otherwise. The sound is pleasant to me; I have fallen in love with it. This sound is the cry of Nippon itself buried deep within me. . . .

It is a cry that present-day Nippon is ashamed of and desperately tries to suppress, but it breaks out, shattering all pretence. It is something bound up with memories that are dark, something that recalls the flow of new-shed blood. But whatever recollections it provokes, they are ones that recall most truthfully our nation's past. It is the cry of our race bursting through the shell of modernization. This ghost of Nippon Past has been long confined in chains, denied sustenance and so reduced to weak groans. But in the *kendo* drill halls we lend it our throats to come alive, giving it its chance to break free.'[1]

Anyone who has visited a *kendo* hall will understand Mishima's first reaction to the wild shouts used in the sport. These are blood-curdling and very loud, and as the combatants sweep back and forth at one another in their black armour and dark blue cotton skirts, faces covered by grilles and heads protected by heavy helmets, one imagines oneself back in the feudal past. Mishima was not especially good at *kendo*. His form–a Japanese expert could see at a glance –was quite poor. After years of practice he could not hold the *shinai* (lance) correctly. He was given a high ranking in the sport because he had lent his prestige to *kendo*. Much as an eminent statesman is awarded a doctorate and tasseled hat by an ancient university, Mishima was given his fifth *dan* in August 1968.

Mishima's nostaglia for 'Nippon Past'–a romantic ideal–was catalyzed by the political events of the year 1960. His father, Azusa Hiraoka, said after his son's death that the riots and disorders of the summer of 1960 played a part in turning Mishima's mind towards romantic imperialism. The evidence is impressive. Mishima took a keen interest in political events for the first time in the post-war period after the onset of the *Anpo* (US-Japanese Security Treaty) demonstrations in the spring of 1960–the worst civil disturbances in Japan in the post-war era. Up to this time he had shown no response to political developments in Japan, even to the spectacular changes of the early 1950s, when the Occupation ended and the Japan Communist Party made an abortive effort to prepare the way for violent revolution. During the *Anpo* riots Mishima went out onto the streets, observed events at first hand and reported on them for the national press. Commenting on the position of Nobusuké Kishi, the unpopular right-wing Prime Minister who was thrown out of office as a result of the *Anpo* disturbances, he recounted how he had spent an entire night on a balcony of the building next to the Prime Minister's office looking down on the place while crowds surged about it. He thought of 'the thin, lonely old man [Mr Kishi] who must have been sitting in the darkness of the official residence, all windows of which were shrouded by night. Kishi is a tiny, tiny nihilist whom people instinctively dislike because they can indentify themselves with such a person . . . how easily the psychology that "somehow I don't like Kishi" could be transformed into the psychology that "I like some-body somehow". While one hates a tiny nihilist, one may accept a nihilist on the grand scale such as Hitler.'[2]

Shortly after the *Anpo* disturbances ended, Mishima wrote the short story 'Patriotism'. Mishima was an excellent critic and a fair judge of his own writing. He remarked of 'Patriotism' that the story con-tained 'both the best and the worst features of my literature'; it may also be regarded as representative of his entire *oeuvre*. 'Patriot-ism', which Mishima wrote in the early autumn of 1960, is the story of a young Imperial Army lieutenant at the time of the *Ni Ni Roku* Incident of February 1936. There were two principal factions in the Japanese armed forces at the time. Both were expansionist, wanting Japan to pursue a policy of foreign conquest. One faction, the *Kodo-ha* ('Imperial Way faction'), favoured a 'strike north' against the Soviet Union. The *Tosei-ha* ('Control faction'), favoured a 'strike south' against Britain and other European colonial powers. The conflict came with the *Ni Ni Roku* Incident, which was triggered by *Kodo-ha* officers seeking to forestall seizure of power by their *Tosei-ha* rivals. Their action was spurred on by a plan for the despatch of the First Division, many of whose officers were *Kodo-ha* members, to Manchuria—this would have greatly reduced the strength of the *Kodo-ha* in Tokyo. The *Kodo-ha* adherents, led by a handful of young officers—Takatsugu Muranaka, Asaichi Isobe, Teruzo Ando, Yasuhide Kurihara and others—decided to strike against the authorities before that happened. Early on the morning of 26 February, when the capital lay under a fresh fall of snow, the officers mobilized 1,400 men and seized control of the centre of Tokyo after assassinating three leading members of the government. They declared that their action was carried out on behalf of the Emperor and was aimed at his evil advisers. After a brief hesitation, Hirohito himself ordered them to surrender and the revolt collapsed after four days.

The protagonist of Mishima's story, Lieutenant Takeyama, is an officer in a regiment stationed in Tokyo at the time of these events. He is a friend of the rebel officers and sympathizes with their aims.

He is omitted from the plans for revolt because he has recently married. After the outbreak of the *Ni Ni Roku*, he is ordered to lead an attack on the rebels. His way out of the moral dilemma created for him by this order is to commit *hara-kiri*. In 'Patriotism' Mishima describes the *hara-kiri* of the young man in extraordinary detail; this is probably the most elaborate account of the former *samurai* rite in the whole of Japanese literature. It is all the more striking in that the author appears to endorse the ideology of Lieutenant Takeyama and his associates. The *hara-kiri*, subtly idealized by Mishima in the story, appears as a grisly act justified by a high ideal:

> By the time the lieutenant had at last drawn the sword across to the right side of his stomach, the blade was already cutting shallow and had revealed its naked tip, slippery with blood and grease. But, suddenly stricken by a fit of vomiting, the lieutenant cried out hoarsely. The vomiting made the fierce pain fiercer still, and the stomach, which had thus far remained firm and compact, now abruptly heaved, opening wide its wound, and the entrails burst through, as if the wound too were vomiting. Seemingly ignorant of their master's suffering, the entrails gave an impression of robust health and almost disagreeable vitality as they slipped smoothly out and spilled over into the crotch. The lieutenant's head drooped, his shoulders heaved, his eyes opened to narrow slits, and a thin trickle of saliva dribbled from his mouth. The gold markings on his epaulettes caught the light and glinted.
>
> Blood was scattered everywhere. The lieutenant was soaked in it to his knees, as he sat now in a crumpled and listless posture, one hand on the floor. A raw smell filled the room. The lieutenant, his head drooping, retched repeatedly, and the movement showed repeatedly in his shoulders. The blade of the sword, now pushed back by the entrails and exposed to its tip, was still in the lieutenant's right hand.
>
> It would be difficult to imagine a more heroic sight than that of the lieutenant at this moment, as he mustered his strength and flung back his head.[3]

One other surprising feature of the story is that Lieutenant Takeyama kills himself first, leaving Reiko, his wife to follow him in death. She stabs herself in the throat with a knife, having firmly secured her skirts so that she shall not be found dead in an indecorous posture. The reason given for the husband taking precedence–instead of the wife dying first as would have been normal–is that 'it was vital for the lieutenant, whatever else might happen, that there should be no irregularity in his death.' The point is not easy to follow. What is clear is that the officer wants to be watched as he performs *hara-kiri*.

'Patriotism' emerges, from this detail alone, as a work by an abnormal man.

In the years which followed, Mishima wrote twice more about the *Ni Ni Roku* affair. In his play *Toka no Kiku* and in his unclassifiable work *Eirei no Koe* ('The Voices of the Heroic Dead', 1966), an elegy for the war dead and also an assault upon Emperor Hirohito for deserting the souls of the departed by making his intervention in the *Ni Ni Roku* Incident and by announcing his *ningen sengen* in 1946, Mishima endorsed the 'ideology' of the rebel officers of 1936. In saying this I am not forcing the issue; Mishima himself put the three works—*Patriotism, Toka no Kiku* and *Eirei no Koe*—together in one volume, which he called his *Ni Ni Roku* triology. In a postscript to the triology he describes his conclusions, which I condense a little here:

> I wrote 'Patriotism' from the point of view of the young officer who could not help choosing suicide because he could not take part in the *Ni Ni Roku* Incident. This is neither a comedy nor a tragedy but simply a story of happiness. . . . If they [husband and wife] had waited one more night, the attack on the Imperial Army [the rebels] would have been called off and the need for their deaths would have decreased, although the legal authorities would have caught up with him [Takeyama]. To choose the place where one dies is also the greatest joy in life. And such a night as the couple had was their happiest. Moreover there was no shadow of a lost battle over them; the love of these two reaches to an extremity of purity, and the painful suicide of the soldier is equivalent to an honourable death on the field of battle. Somewhere I obtained the conviction that if one misses one's night one will never have another opportunity to achieve a peak of happiness in life. Instrumental in this conviction were my experiences during the war, my reading of Nietzsche during the war and my fellow feeling for the philosopher Georges Bataille, the 'Nietzsche of eroticism'. . . .
>
> Surely some great God died when the *Ni Ni Roku* Incident failed. I was only eleven at the time and felt little of it. But when the war ended, when I was twenty, a most sensitive age, I felt something of the terrible cruelty of the death of that God, and this was somehow linked with my intuition of what had happened when I was eleven. For a long time I was unable to understand the connection but when I wrote *Toka no Kiku* and 'Patriotism' there appeared a dark shadow in my consciousness as I wrote—and then it disappeared again without taking definite shape. This was a 'negative' picture of the *Ni Ni Roku* Incident; the positive picture was my boyhood impression of the heroism of the rebel officers. Their

purity, bravery, youth and death qualified them as mythical heroes;
and their failures and deaths made them true heroes in this
world. . . .

In the meantime, the melancholy within me became enlarged and
I was astonished by the realization that the endless fatigue,
which I used to take as a condition of 'collapse' common to the
young, metamorphosed into something the reverse of the corrupt
—something which urged me on. I fell in love with *kendo*, and found
true significance only in the clear echo of bamboo sword on
sword and the fierce, fanatic shouts. After that I wrote my short
story *Ken* ['Sword']. How can I explain my mental condition? Am
I rotten or in a state of exaltation? Slowly, a purposeless sorrow
and anger pile up within me; sooner or later these had to combine
with the intense cry of the young officers of the *Ni Ni Roku*
Incident. This Incident has been with me for the past thirty years,
going back and forth between my conscious and sub-conscious. . . .
The desire to console the spirits of the true heroes who had influenced me for so long, to restore their reputation and to
reinstate them was always deep within me. But whenever I consider the matter further I am at a loss how to treat the Emperor's
ningen sengen. The history of the Showa period [the reign of
Hirohito] is divided in two by the defeat in war, and one like me
who lived through both parts [of the Showa era] continuously
cannot help desiring to find a real continuity and a basis for theoretical consistency. This seems perfectly natural for a man, whether
he is a writer or not. The *ningen sengen* declaration by the Emperor
himself was more important than the new Constitution which
provides that the Emperor be a symbol. I was forced to the point
where I could not help but describe the shadow of the *Ni Ni Roku*
Incident; thus I started *Eirei no Koe*. It may seem strange if I
use the word 'aesthetics' in this context. But I came to realize that
there is a hard, huge rock at the very foundation of my aesthetic—
the emperor system.[4]

Whatever one may feel about Mishima's imperialism—which I reject
—there is no denying his passion. Early in 1966 he shut himself up in
a hotel room in Tokyo for three days and poured out his feelings in
Eirei no Koe, a work of eighty pages in length. This was undoubtedly
a turning point in his life. 'It was after writing *Eirei no Koe*,' he told
me three years later, 'that I decided to create the *Tatenokai*.' His
frame of mind in early 1966 is vividly illuminated by *Eirei no Koe,*
the refrain of which runs : '*Nadote Sumerogi wa hito no naritamaishi*'
('Why did the Emperor have to become a human being?'). The
work, most Japanese critics agree, was not a fine piece of literature;
the chantings of the souls of the war dead are akin to rantings. The
book was quickly forgotten, once the scandal of its publication died

down. It is important to know more, however, about Mishima's attitudes at this time. He expressed himself forcibly in an interview which he gave to the *Sunday Mainichi* magazine early in March 1966:

Q. Do you think that the pre-war Emperor system is the only one for the nation?
A. Yes. The *kokutai* ('national system') had collapsed since the Emperor made his *ningen sengen*. All the moral confusion of the post-war period stems from that. Why should the Emperor be a human being? Why mustn't he be a God at least for us Japanese? If I explain this matter, it all boils down to a question of 'love' in the end. In modern times nations have moved forward from the physiocratic to the capitalist system. This is unavoidable. Feudalism collapses, the nation industrializes and then cannot but become a modern welfare state–the most desperate of conditions. In the meantime, the more a nation modernizes, the less meaningful, the cooler, become personal relationships. For people who live in such a modern society love is impossible. For example, if A believes that he loves B, there is no means for him to be sure of it, and vice versa. Therefore love cannot exist in a modern society–if it is merely a mutual relationship. If there is no image of a third man whom the two lovers have in common–the apex of the triangle–love ends with eternal scepticism. This is what D. H. Lawrence calls agnosticism. From ancient times the Japanese have had an image of the apex of the triangle (God), which was a God in a physiocratic system; and everyone had a theory of love, so that he should not be isolated.
The Emperor was the absolute for us Japanese.[5]

A reading of the interview suggests that Mishima was an orthodox Japanese imperialist. After the publication of *Eirei no Koe* he did indeed become a favourite of the *Uyoku* (the violent Right) and also of the right wing of the LDP, the ruling conservative party. He did not associate with the former, which has criminal elements. He did, however, become friendly with many conservative leaders, including Prime Minister Sato and his sharp-witted wife. But his imperialism was unique; it had the same narcissistic quality which characterized all Mishima's thoughts and actions–as one may see from these selected quotations from a long dialogue which took place in 1966 between Mishima and the notorious right-wing bigot, Fusao Hayashi:

[The leaders of the Meiji Restoration] succeeded in Westernizing Japan ninety-nine per cent. The remaining one per cent was the definition of the Emperor as sacred and untouchable–this was the fort against Westernization.

The Emperor is infallible. He is the most mysterious existence in the world.

To me, the Emperor, works of art and Shinpuren are symbols of purity. I want to identify my own literary work with God.[6]

The first two statements are orthodox enough. The last is true to Mishima. I think that he sometimes confused himself with God or with the Emperor. He remarked to me once: 'There is no one I can respect in Japan today, the situation is hopeless, there is no one to take account of. . . .' There followed a long pause. A strange expression flitted across his face. 'Except perhaps the Emperor. . . .'

In other writings he revealed a masochistic side to his character. This matters, for it showed that *hara-kiri* was not simply an act of loyalty towards the Emperor, an act of *kanshi* ('the suicide of remonstration'); Mishima also wanted to hurt himself. So much is apparent from the autobiographical essay I have often quoted, *Sun and Steel*: 'Pain, I came to feel, might well prove to be the sole proof of the persistence of consciousness within the flesh, the sole physical expression of consciousness. As my body acquired muscle, and in turn strength, there was gradually born within me a tendency towards the positive acceptance of pain, and my interest in physical suffering deepened. Even so, I would not have it believed that this development was a result of the workings of my imagination. My discovery was made directly, with my body, thanks to the sun and the steel.'[7]

Mishima classified various of his writings–'Patriotism', *Eirei no Koe* and *Sun and Steel* amongst them–under the heading of his 'River of Action'. They outlined his reasons for committing himself to action. The commitment itself came in the latter part of 1966, when he applied to train at *Jieitai* camps after his completion of *Spring Snow*. The second stage of his commitment began in the early summer of 1967 when he began to look round for young men to join his 'private army' or 'militia'–he preferred the second term. This was a time when the left-wing student *Zengakuren* had begun their campaign against the government in earnest, and right-wing student bodies, though very small and joined on the whole by the less intellectually gifted students, had sprung up in opposition to the ultra-Left. Mishima had therefore a number of places to look for potential recruits. He settled on two groups of youths: a small contingent of students who published a little-known, right-wing maga-

zine, the *Ronso Journal,* whose leader was a student named Kuramochi; and a group of students at Waseda University, the Tokyo
university at which the ultra-Left was most active. Among these was
a twenty-one-year-old from Yokkaichi, a coastal town near Nagoya,
whose name was Masakatsu Morita. Mishima kept in touch with
both sets of students during 1967 and, though he had preferred the
Waseda group of the two—perhaps because they were a cohesive, well-
defined group—he was forced to settle for the support of the *Ronso
Journal* youths, as the former would have nothing to do with Mishima
at first, taking him for an exhibitionist, an odd fellow.

Mishima inaugurated his activities with the *Ronso Journal* youths
—these activities were at first confined to meetings and long conversations only—at a session held in the office of the magazine. One
of those present later described the scene to Azusa Hiraoka, and we
are indebted to Mishima's father for this second-hand description
of a scene which might have come straight from a morbid passage in
Confessions of a Mask. There were about a dozen people present,
gathered round a table in the seedy office of the building in Kami-
Itabashi where the *Ronso Journal* had its headquarters. 'On a piece of
paper he [Mishima] wrote in Chinese ink: "We hereby swear to be
the foundation of *Kokoku Nippon* [Imperial Japan]." Then he cut
his little finger with a pen-knife and asked everyone else to follow his
example. They dripped blood from their fingers into a cup, all
standing round, until it was brimful; then each signed his name on
the piece of paper, dipping a brush into the cup and signing in
blood. . . . Some of the people felt faint and one had to rush out of
the door to vomit. Mishima then suggested that they should drink
the blood . . . he picked up the glass and asked: "Is anyone here ill?
None of you have VD?" All seemed well. He called for a salt cellar
and flavoured the cup; then he drank from it. The others followed his
example. "What a fine lot of Draculas," said Mishima, looking round
at the youths with their red mouths and teeth, laughing his raucous
laugh.'[8]

Afterwards the students placed the cup with any blood which remained in the safe of the *Ronso Journal.* Then Mishima called for
coffee and cakes and they sat down to eat.

From start to finish, the nascent organization which was to become
the *Tatenokai* had little promise of being very much more than a
personal vehicle for Mishima. The only real challenge to Mishima's
authority appears to have come from Morita, who joined forces with

Mishima, together with a number of other Waseda students, in the early spring of 1968. At this time Mishima, who was organizing his first party to train at Camp Fuji with the *Jieitai*, appealed to the Waseda students to send a dozen of their number as members of his party. A number of his own men had dropped out—youths who had enjoyed association with a famous man but whose desire to participate in any form of action with him was minimal; some had been put off by the requirement that they cut their hair. The Waseda students were reluctant to follow Mishima and only at the last moment did half a dozen students join Mishima in the party which trained at Camp Fuji in March 1968. Morita, who had broken his leg a month beforehand in an accident, joined the group last of all. Mishima took an immediate liking to him and singled him out for praise in front of the others, commending him for his willingness to train despite the fact that his leg was in plaster. In a letter written to a friend from Camp Fuji, Morita referred to Mishima by the honorific term *sensei* ('teacher'), a clear sign that he acknowledged him as leader. The two men became friends.

Morita is the key to subsequent events. He was born the youngest child in the family of a poor secondary-school headmaster two weeks before the end of the war. His first name, Masakatsu, which is 'Victory by all Means' in a literal rendering of the characters, reflected his father's patriotic belief that Japan would win the war. The boy was orphaned at the age of two, looked after by his elder brother, Osamu, and sent to a Catholic missionary school at Yokkaichi, where he proved himself to be a leader. He was made head of his class in the senior school, although his academic work was no better than average. He entertained the ambition of becoming a conservative politician, an extraordinary aim in one so young. Most young Japanese of his age were radical or *non-pori* (unpolitical) in their attitudes. Morita, advised by a younger brother of Ichiro Kono, the leading independent conservative politician of the day, to attend university before taking part in politics, entered Waseda at his third attempt, in the spring of 1966, at a time when left-wing students had overrun the university. Waseda, the place of Morita's dreams, was the centre of ultra-Left student activity in the nation. He reacted against the *Zengakuren* by joining a new, right-wing student club in the university, the *Nichigakudo* ('Japan Students Movement'), a tiny organization.

Morita and Mishima came together, originally, because their political views were similar. Both were among the few Japanese who held the view that the *Zengakuren* must be opposed by force. Both wanted to lead groups to do battle with the left-wing students; both were zealous imperialists and wrote pamphlets–independently–calling for Japan to have the H-bomb. People of such character were bound to drift into contact with one another, as they were so few, and Mishima and Morita, realizing how much they had in common, co-operated with each other after the spring of 1968. Mishima attended rightist student meetings at which Morita took the chair, while Morita ensured that the Waseda students stayed with Mishima. Kuramochi, the *Ronso Journal* man, was the official student leader of the *Tatenokai* at its foundation on 5 October, 1968, when its principles were established:

(i)   Communism is incompatible with Japanese tradition, culture and history and runs counter to the Emperor system.

(ii) The Emperor is the sole symbol of our historical and cultural community and racial identity.

(iii) The use of violence is justifiable in view of the threat posed by communism.

However, Morita gradually emerged as the effective student leader of the *Tatenokai* under Mishima. He had unshakeable determination, and his slow, steady character appealed to the other students. He was not disturbed by Mishima's flashiness, though many of the best recruits left the organization in the summer of 1968 when Mishima showed them the new *Tatenokai* uniform. He was also untroubled by the in-fighting that went on between the students under Mishima. Morita's stolid temperament and the fact that he was a favourite of Mishima ensured that he did not become embroiled in the bitter disputes that raged between the factions within the *Tatenokai*.

Mishima organized the *Tatenokai* into eight independent sections, whose leaders were responsible to him alone. Each section had roughly ten members, making a total membership of about eighty. Almost all the recruits were students at universities in the Tokyo region; Mishima would have liked working men as well, but the demands which he made on his members' time made it inevitable that most of his men would be students. Mishima's organization of the *Tatenokai* into sections, each one of which he controlled independently, was skilful; but his leadership was poor. The 'private army' was nominally imperialist, but as Mishima's thinking about the Emperor was muddled, he could not give his students the kind of realistic leadership which would have made a reality of the *Tatenokai*.

In the summer of 1968 he had an essay published which revealed clearly how muddled he was about the Emperor. This essay was *Bunkaboeiron* ('On the Defence of Culture'), which he laboured over for nearly a year. It concludes: 'Military honours, also, must be awarded by the Emperor, as a cultural concept. As I think it legally feasible under the present Constitution, the Emperor's prerogative to grant honours should be revived in substance. Not only should he receive military salutes, he should award regimental colours in person.'[9]

The weakness of the *Bunkaboeiron* is that Mishima makes no attempt to connect the main theme of the essay–that the Emperor is a 'cultural symbol'–to this militaristic conclusion, reminiscent of pre-war imperialism, when the Emperor was the divine symbol of the nation and also supreme commander of the armed forces (and did in fact present regimental colours).

A second problem for Mishima, as leader of the *Tatenokai*, was that his concept of the function of the organization was hazy, as he showed in an essay written for *Queen* magazine in England: 'My Shield Society (SS) [the literal translation of '*Tatenokai*' is 'Shield Society'] has only one hundred members: it is the smallest army in the world, and I do not intend to enlarge it. My men receive no pay, but twice a year they are given a new uniform, cap and boots. The uniform, especially designed for the SS, is so striking that passers-by stop on the street in amazement. I designed the flag, which shows two ancient Japanese helmets in red against a white silk background; this simple design also appears on our caps and on the buttons of our uniforms.

'Members of the SS are usually college undergraduates. . . .

'The SS is a stand-by army. There is no way of knowing when our day will come. Perhaps it will never come; on the other hand, it may come tomorrow. Until then, the SS will remain calmly at the ready. No street demonstrations for us, no placards, no Molotov cocktails, no lectures, no stone throwing. Until the last desperate moment we shall refuse to commit ourselves to action. For we are the world's least armed, most spiritual army.

'Some people mockingly refer to us as toy soldiers. Let us see. When I am on duty, the bugle-call gets me out of bed at the crack of dawn. . . .'[10]

Mishima was never very far from making a fool of himself with the *Tatenokai*.

2

In the aftermath of Mishima's suicide it was surprising to remember
how little attention had been paid to him and his *Tatenokai* before
his final action. No Japanese newspaper had reported the formation
of the organization and very little had been written about it in the
magazines. In the account which follows—excerpts from a description
of a visit I paid to Camp Fuji to see Mishima and the *Tatenokai* in
training—I have attempted to recapture the bemused surprise with
which I regarded the exercise, a reaction which any other person who
witnessed that occasion might well have shared. There was nothing
especially hideous or frightening about the *Tatenokai* close up. So far
as I know, no other journalist or foreign writer ever saw the *Tatenokai*
in training. After my visit to Camp Fuji, which led to an article in *The
Times*, to which the *Jieitai* objected, the *Tatenokai* training programme
was closed to visitors.

I

I was in a reluctant frame of mind as I made my way through the
crowds at Shinjuku Station in Tokyo on an early afternoon in March,
1969. I was *en route* to Mount Fuji, where I was to observe an 'all-
night exercise' conducted by Mishima's *Tatenokai*; and my worry,
the source of my reluctance, was the weather. On the previous night
18 inches of snow had fallen in Tokyo. The snow hung heavily
from the trees in my garden in central Tokyo, and had begun to drip
about midday; but on Mount Fuji it would be much colder and really
bitter at night—these were not ideal conditions for an 'all-night
exercise'. There was a second reason for my reluctance to undertake
the journey; I was not sure that the excursion would yield anything
of great use to me as a journalist. I could see Mishima virtually any
time in Tokyo; it was not necessary for me to go all the way up to
Mount Fuji to meet him. The only argument for going there had been
to see the *Tatenokai* in training, but was it worth it in such
weather?

At that time, like almost everyone else in Japan, I knew very little
about this recently created organization, beyond what Mishima had

told me in a short conversation or two. '*Tatenokai*' he had translated as 'Shield Society', from *tate*, meaning 'shield', and *kai*, 'society'. He had also named the *Tatenokai* after a short poem taken from the eighth-century classical Japanese anthology, the *Manyoshu*, in which a warrior pledges his life to 'shield' his lord and master, the Emperor, from the enemy. It was a poem which had been popular with soldiers during the war. The *Tatenokai* was to 'shield' the Emperor from the threat of communism. What this meant in practice, Mishima did not say.

I knew that the *Tatenokai* had been founded by the writer not long beforehand, and was largely financed by him; that the membership was small; and that the *Jieitai* were training members of the group. It was that fact which intrigued me. From what Mishima had said the training programme was a unique one—but why should the *Jieitai* be training such an organization as the *Tatenokai*? It seemed odd because, by doing so, the *Jieitai* appeared to be breaking the basic rule which had governed relations between the armed forces and civilians since the end of the war: that the *Jieitai* should have no political role of any kind. However one looked at it, the *Tatenokai* had the odour of a right-wing organization. Although the novelist was not connected with the traditional Right in Japan, who tend to be not much more than highly refined gangsters, he had established a reputation for holding right-wing political views, and it was *he* who had founded the *Tatenokai*. The *Jieitai* was in fact giving training facilities to a group organized by a writer whose views on politics in Japan, if accurately expressed by his writings, were in many respects virtually indistinguishable from those held by the Japanese military before and during the war.

I was aware that a 'political' view of the *Tatenokai* was only one possible attitude to take, and that many people doubted the seriousness of Mishima's politics. In Tokyo the *Tatenokai* tended to be dismissed as a wild joke. One view was that the organization had been created by Mishima on a personal whim, and was nothing more than a colourful toy of one much given to exhibitionism. A second theory, retailed by Japanese journalists, was that the *Tatenokai* was simply a homosexual club. Accustomed as I was, however, to allowing for the playful extremes to which Mishima would go in his non-literary enterprises, I could not quite imagine that he had created the *Tatenokai* in order to meet beautiful boys; it would have been altogether too roundabout an exercise. As a journalist, my question was whether the *Tatenokai* was (a) a right-wing organization or (b) merely the writer's toy. I had in fact almost made up my mind on the subject on a hunch, and had more or less decided that it was the former; but it hardly seemed necessary for me to participate in an 'all-night exercise' on Mount Fuji in order to check my conclusion at that stage. There was no urgency about the matter; even the Japanese press was ignoring the *Tatenokai* completely, and *I* had got interested only because I knew Mishima personally.

Mishima, however, had anticipated my reluctance to push through to a conclusion the eccentric idea of midnight reporting on Mount Fuji. Regarding me as unpunctual and unreliable, which I certainly was by his rigid standards, he had made arrangements which made escape out of the question. He had told me that I would be the only journalist taking part in the proceedings. Having lured me with this bait, and confirmed my intention to participate in the *Tatenokai* exercise, he had then sprung the trap. In five years of reporting in Japan I had never before been given such detailed instructions, a multitude of arrangements and safety checks, including an escort from Tokyo to the *Jieitai* camp.

Honoured as I was by the extreme care being taken to ensure my arrival at Gotemba, I wondered why Mishima was going to so much trouble. The explanation could only be that he quite violently desired publicity for the *Tatenokai* and regarded *The Times*, for which I worked, as a suitable vehicle. Having failed to have his *Tatenokai* taken very seriously in Japan, he hoped to have a little attention overseas.

II

Right on time, at a quarter to five, we arrived at regimental headquarters, a long, nondescript building, into which we were led. Once inside the building, I was taken down a corridor to a door at which my escort knocked loudly. We entered a small office with a large desk. On the walls were a regimental standard and some plaques, one of which commended '*chiimu-waaku*' in the large *kata-kana* letters which I had learnt to read: 'team-work'. A man in uniform, whom I took to be the regimental commander, rose to meet me with a smile. He was Hiroshi Fukamizu, the colonel in command of the infantry regiment based at Camp Fuji, and he was responsible for the Fuji military school. With the manner of a Japanese well accustomed to meeting foreigners, he gestured towards the empty chair at my side and instructed the sergeant to leave my bag with me.

The third man in the room was Mishima. No matter how many times I met him, I was always surprised by his small stature. He came up to above my shoulders, but he always seemed shy about his height, as if feeling dwarfed. The well-known head, with its heavy black brows, large staring eyes and ears sticking out a fraction, seemed for a moment to sit ill upon his shoulders. He drew himself in, and we shook hands. I quickly accepted the colonel's invitation to be seated and watched Mishima relax as he also took his chair and reached for a cigarette from a tin which he was carrying with him. He smiled as he surveyed my ski-ing clothes and my boots. For my part, I was seeing him in the role of military man for the first time, clad in denims and brown polo-neck jersey, with his hair cut even shorter than usual; only short black bristles remained on his large skull.

III

It was to my great relief that I heard, finally, the news that the *Tatenokai* 'all-night exercise' had been cancelled, because of the bad weather conditions and the deep snow. Mishima's plans had for once been thwarted. It was the first time in our acquaintance that he had been forced to change his plans completely, but he took the reverse in his stride. In a loud voice he discussed the training programme of the *Tatenokai* at the camp, equating Camp Fuji to Fort Benning in the US. The comparison between the two leading military-training establishments in the two countries was somewhat far-fetched, as the latter is very much bigger, but Mishima, as usual, wanted everything to be larger than life, in accordance with his romantic view of the world. The *Tatenokai* training was going very well, he said. There were two parties at the camp, one of two dozen men doing a refresher course of one week, and a second which would be in the camp with him for an entire month. Mishima would boast how they 'ran a mile a day and marched twenty-eight miles a day', but they would not be doing so under these conditions. We were all being given a break on this occasion, thanks to the weather.

I had escaped from the 'all-night exercise' after all, but Mishima had in store for me an experience which, if different, was quite as severe as scrambling about the forests of Mount Fuji at night. After the evening meal he suggested that we pay a visit to the *Tatenokai* billeted nearby. We left the regimental headquarters and trudged through the snow outside. Lights were shining in a barracks close at hand, and Mishima led the way there, and along a corridor inside. He stopped at a door, opened it briskly and we entered the room. It was full of young Japanese men in denims. Some sat at a long table close to us, and others were lying on their bunks, double-decker beds which occupied much of the room, where they were reading comics or chatting. This was an hour of relaxation, and there was none of the activity which I associated with a barracks, no polishing of boots or pressing of uniforms. One or two of the young men came forward and joined Mishima and me as we took our seats at the table by the door, and others moved into the background. This was no doubt by pre-arrangement; Mishima did not leave such things to chance.

I asked Mishima if I could put questions to the *Tatenokai* members, and he introduced me to the few who sat with us as 'Stokes-san' of the *'London Times'*, taking a cigarette from his tin as he did so; he was going to translate for me. Most of the *Tatenokai* members were university students. This was the first fact which I established, talking to a twenty-two-year-old from Waseda University in Tokyo. I asked this youth, Ikebe, why he had joined the *Tatenokai*. His reply was that he had been attracted by what he described as Mishima's *jintoku*, a word which the writer translated as 'personality'. He added that I should understand that the *Tatenokai* was 'not a code organization', by which I took him to mean that it was not secret, and in no way dangerous; Mishima's English was usually excellent, but on this occasion we were having problems with translation. There was, I suspected, a second barrier to communication. I had the feeling that Mishima had briefed the students about what to tell me, and that he had told them to say that the *Tatenokai* was 'not dangerous'. The writer, if this was so, had correctly anticipated that I had come to Camp Fuji with the idea that the *Tatenokai* was an extremist group.

The next student to whom I spoke took, however, a recognizably independent line of his own, and my reservations about the way the meeting was going disappeared. Mishima had introduced him as Morita; he was a twenty-three-year-old student from Waseda. Morita's appearance was not unusual in any way, and he made no impression on me at all; later, I could not even remember what he had looked like. He was serious and at first sight dull, and I put him down simply as a conscientious student who was playing a leading role in the *Tatenokai*. (When I looked at photographs of Morita later, after his suicide with Mishima, I could recall his features: the heavy jowls which one finds in a few Japanese faces, big lower jaws, thickening towards the ears and suggestive of strength of character. He was not good-looking; there was no trace of sensitivity about his heavy face, nor any mark of intelligence on his brow; but there was no doubt about his strong personality, he was a born leader.)

Morita chatted about himself, giving a long explanation of his reasons for having joined the *Tatenokai*, in reply to my question. Too few people in Japan cared about the national interest, he said. At Waseda he had been shocked to find how active the *Zengakuren* students were, and how destructive their demonstrations at the university. He had also felt it wrong that they should be taken by the general public in Japan to be representative of students as a whole at Waseda. He had joined the anti-Leftist student groups at the university, and had become the leader of one of these small organizations, the 'Counter-Protecting Club', as Mishima translated its name from the Japanese. This move had not given him satisfaction, as such student groups actually did very little, and he had read the works of Japanese nationalist writers to enhance his understanding of the situation. Once again his efforts had been frustrated, however. He had not been able to develop himself as a man, and he had turned, eventually, to the *Tatenokai* to study 'military techniques'. He concluded by saying, via Mishima, who used the third person in translating: 'In his way he wants to follow Mishima . . . Mishima is related to the Emperor.'

I asked Morita what he meant by these words, and in particular what was the meaning of the expression 'related to the Emperor'. In what way was the writer linked with the Emperor, in his view? Morita appeared troubled and confused when Mishima translated my questions back to him. He looked about him as if at a loss for a reply, and for a while it seemed that he was going to say nothing. When his answer eventually came, it may have been meaningless; the phrases which Mishima translated were in any case disconnected. Morita talked of 'Japanese culture' and 'his own emotions'; it was through these that he could grasp 'the relation between the Emperor and Mishima's mentality'. Books, however, had been of no assistance in this process; he had 'never tried to catch through book-reading' what he understood by feeling. As for Mishima, Morita praised him because 'he keeps a sense of tradition', 'not through politics' but by his own 'personal approach'.

Hard as it was to understand Morita, I thought I could grasp his two main points. The first was the importance of the concept of the Emperor to the *Tatenokai*; the second, his strong personal feeling towards Mishima. It was the first point which interested me. If Emperor-worship was central to the *Tatenokai*, then the organization *had* to be taken seriously, and was not a toy of Mishima's. (As a matter of course, those who exalt the Emperor in post-war Japan are assumed by most Japanese to be heirs to the tradition of the militarists of the 1930s.)

My feeling was that if the Emperor was the central value of the *Tatenokai*, as Mishima's choice of the name of the organization had suggested in the first place, and as Morita was asserting, then the organization *was* a dangerous one. Emperor-worship had once before in this century led Japan along the path of war, and it was hardly desirable that militarism should be revived. Worship of the Emperor had supplied both a motive and a justification for the most grave actions: the annexation of Korea in 1910; the invasion of Manchuria in 1931 and the creation of the 'independent republic' of Manchukuo; the invasion of northern China in 1937; and finally the attacks against the Allies in December 1941, which had precipitated the Pacific War. Behind these acts of aggression had lain a form of Emperor-worship which had poisoned men's minds. If the *Tatenokai* was imbued with the war-time spirit, then my original suspicions had been amply confirmed. And yet I felt that it could not be as simple as that, not in 1969, and with Mishima involved.

Morita's second point had been his strong feeling for Mishima as an individual. I could not easily understand at the time, however, what he was saying, or, beyond that, what Mishima's role was as leader of the *Tatenokai*. It was natural that much younger men should look up to Mishima. The writer was twenty years older than the eldest of the *Tatenokai* students, he had been educated before and during the war, and he shared their presumably nationalistic views, unlike most of his contemporaries. It was not surprising that they should admire one of the best-known men in Japan. What was puzzling was the 'relation' which Morita had insisted on, between the Emperor and Yukio Mishima. The student leader was a prosaic-seeming person in his way, and Mishima a careful translator; there could be no doubt that Morita had twice spoken of such a 'relation'. Mishima was the only person,

I reasoned, who could have put such an idea into the heads of the *Tatenokai* members; *he* must have told the students this, persuading them that in some mysterious way he was connected with the Emperor. The question was *how* one of Mishima's great intelligence had put this point to the students. However he had done it, I had the feeling that it was in this manner that he had secured the affections of such a stolid student as Morita, and those of other members of the *Taten-okai*, who had been willing to follow Mishima to Camp Fuji.

After the talk with Morita and a few others, Mishima suggested that we should pay a visit on the second group of *Tatenokai* members, those who had come to Camp Fuji for an entire month, and were comparative newcomers to the group. Mishima took me along to them straightaway. We found the students in a long room similar to the one which we had just left; there was the same high ceiling, rows of bunks, and young Japanese in denims sitting on the beds talking to one another. I decided not to ask questions this time, and Mishima started to tell me about some of the students in the room with us. They were, I noticed, paying attention to our conversation, and listening to what Mishima said; unusually for Japanese students, some of them could follow English. One student, said Mishima, had waited for two nights outside the Imperial Palace in order to be the first of 200,000 to sign the Emperor's book at the New Year. The students around us listened carefully, and I felt that they were a much more lively and intelligent group than those with whom we had just been talking. One of them asked me : 'Do you think that war must come every twenty years? Quite recently more and more students have wanted to fight, just look at the streets of Tokyo. . . . What do you think about it?' Giving a brief answer, I asked the student his opinion of the *Zengakuren*, hoping to provoke my questioner.

'They are very childish,' said one in a loud voice. There was a little burst of applause. 'We have guns,' said another, 'and all they have are *gewabo*'; he referred to the '*Gewalt* sticks' carried by the left-wing students during their street battles with the police. Mishima at once qualified what he had said, adding that, while the *Tatenokai* might carry rifles in the camp, they were not permitted to fire them under *Jieitai* regulations. The students were chattering loudly and the room became distinctly noisy; some unfriendly faces looked down on me from the bunks, and other students laughed and joked as they looked across at us, sitting at a table. Mishima at this point introduced to me the student who had waited outside the Imperial Palace for two nights, Tanaka from Asia University. 'Why did you wait for two days and nights outside the Palace?' I asked him. Mishima almost had to shout in order to make me hear the reply: 'Because he respects and loves the Emperor from his heart.' Others were shouting, too. 'Don't compare us to the *Sampa*,' said a tall student in English, Fukuda from Waseda University. He was referring to the most militant of the *Zengakuren* factions, the *Sampa Zengakuren*. My answer should have been that Mishima himself had made such a comparison when talking about the 'spirit' of the *Tatenokai*, but for a moment I was lost for a reply. 'What do *you* think of the *Tatenokai*?' the tall student shouted. 'Are you terrified of us?' 'Yes, I am scared to death,' I replied, wondering if I did not mean what I said. There was something odd about this tense questioning, an atmosphere of sexual excitement amidst all the shouting.

I had been in Japan for almost five years, but I had not encountered a reception like this before. It was usually hard to get much of a response from a group of Japanese at a first meeting; the first *Tatenokai* contingent had been typical in this respect: slow and stodgy and hard. The second group could not have been more differ-ent. 'Are you a *gaijin* spy?' shouted one, using the word for 'foreigner' which has either a familiar or a pejorative meaning, when used by an adult. There was more laughter and chattering amongst the *Tatenokai* students, and also one or two distinctly sour faces to be seen. '*Gaijin* spy! *Gaijin* spy!' Some were treating it as a joke, and others definitely not. I wondered if Mishima could control them.

It was a hard experience to analyse, but at the back of my mind there lay the question: What was the meaning of the Emperor to this second group of *Tatenokai*? It was as if Mishima read my thoughts. Sitting close to me at the table, he said: 'In the *Tatenokai* A relates to B, and B relates to me, and I to the Emperor.' It was precisely what he must have told the *Tatenokai* members. And he added: 'The whole thing is built on personal relationships.' I did not have the wit at that moment to ask Mishima how his 'personal relationship' with the Emperor had been established. I felt fuddled and ill at ease. 'You all scare me to death,' I tried to joke once more, and I half meant it. 'That boy,' said Mishima, pointing to a student, 'has been arrested eight times by the police for attacking *Sampa* barricades.'

Before I left the barracks that night, I talked to Mishima about the organization of the *Tatenokai*. He told me then that finance was supplied entirely by him. The students bought their train tickets and paid for travel; the *Jieitai* gave them free accommodation at the barracks, and also paid for such items as petrol for the armoured personnel carriers which they used at Camp Fuji; apart from this, the entire burden fell on the writer. For this reason, Mishima said, the organization would have to remain a small one, the membership would go no higher than 100. He also told me about the recruiting of the *Tatenokai*. Practically all the members were students, as students, unlike working men, had time to train with the *Jieitai* for a month at a time. The first-year members had been found through advertisements put in the *Ronso Journal* and through Kuramochi, the 'student leader' of the *Tatenokai*. The requirements had been stiff, he claimed, 'only five out of 150 applicants' had been admitted in the first year. For the second year members had been found by 'personal introduction', though Mishima had also put up a notice about the organization on the board at Waseda University. That was after the *Tatenokai* had become a publicly-known affair, in the autumn of 1968, when it had been formally inaugurated and the first report about the *Tatenokai* had appeared in a Tokyo magazine.

IV

When I arrived back at the camp the next morning just before 7 a.m., I found that a full-day exercise had been planned. It had been decided that Mishima and I would play the parts of 'local collaborators' or 'spies'. We would lead a column of *Tatenokai* 'guerillas' through 'enemy territory', and finally make an attack on an 'enemy camp'. I summoned up memories of military training at an English public school fifteen years before; essentially, this was to be an exercise in map-reading, moving across ground and attack. I would observe these events through the eyes of one trained in the Winchester College Cadet Corps. Images of 'flank attacks' and 'smoke bomb charges' flitted through my mind, and a recollection of my last field exercise, at the age of eighteen, lying in a wood in East Anglia and being tormented by suicidal flies.

The weather was extraordinary. Instead of the murky skies of the day before, they were a brilliant blue, not a trace of cloud anywhere. The air was dry and cold and the snow sparkled everywhere.

I had found Mishima in his little room at the barracks and after coffee there and a chat about the novel *Spring Snow*, which had just been published, he led me outside, where we waited for a jeep to pick us up. Mishima had dressed for the role of 'spy' with a good deal more care than I had anticipated. He wore a pair of blue jeans with a fashionable fade, and gaiters to keep the snow out of his plain army boots. He had also put on a black leather jacket, a double-breasted and belted garment of the kind he had once worn to play the lead in a gangster film, *Karakkaze Yaro*. His chief ornament on this occasion, however, was a big khaki-brown hat. It was round, the shape of the head, and lined with white fur. Two heavy flaps of white fur hung down over the ears, and he was letting these fly in the air, as he exercised in the brilliant morning sun to keep warm. The flaps jumped and swung as he leaped into the front seat of the jeep, telling me to get into the back with a sergeant. We left the compound and went east, travelling along a narrow road that had been cleared of snow, with Mount Fuji on our left.

We soon arrived at our rendezvous point. There we would meet the *Tatenokai* column which had set out from the barracks before us, on foot. We were then to take over as 'guides', according to the theory of the exercise. We had some time to wait, and the sergeant, who carried a poacher's sack, took dry wood from it, and busied himself with a fire. Mishima chatted away to me about the nationalist leader, Masaharu Kageyama, as we warmed our backs against the fire. While I was listening to the curious tale of how the supporters of this person had committed *hara-kiri* to the last man at the end of the Pacific War, and how Kageyama had 'refrained' from following them, the *Tatenokai* came in sight, walking slowly up the road towards us. They were well equipped for their roles as 'guerrillas', I had to admit. Some had walkie-talkie sets, a model known as a P–6, which had a long waving aerial. Everyone in the group, a dozen or more men, carried the 1964-type Japanese army rifle, a good weapon, and on their heads they wore American-style fibre helmets. Mishima and I swung in line in front of the *Tatenokai*, and the sergeant, who was the one among us who knew the ground, led the way. We began to trudge up the narrow road, straight towards Mount Fuji. The students were at first spread out; but as the road dwindled to a narrow path and the snow got deeper, we began to plunge in up to our waists and the students started to follow one after another in the holes made by the energetic sergeant. Even so it was slow, and it took us more than two hours to reach the forest ahead, where we stopped in the first trees, a scattering of silver birches. We were going no further than this up Mount Fuji, to my disappointment.

Mishima looked up towards Mount Fuji, round which one or two clouds had begun to form at high altitude, increasing the beauty of the mountain. There was no sound but that of our feet crunching through the snow, and an occasional swoosh as someone knocked snow off the branch of a tree. We were small black and brown figures in a vast expanse of white; in this deep snow we seemed to swim and then to fall back rather than to make progress. Mishima swung his head round and began to shout across the snow at me: 'It's a good excuse to walk in this beautiful snow. If you go alone, you feel crazy.' As he turned back and bounced forward in his stride again, the earpieces of his hat spun in the air, jumping and banging against the sides of his close-shaven head. The sun caught the white fur, as if he had two great dandelion clocks dancing over his shoulders.

We were coming close to our target, the 'enemy camp', but the entire party seemed careless of this fact, infected by good spirits. The *Tatenokai* members trudged along in a line in the open, making no effort to spread out or to conceal themselves; they were in fact all bunched together close to the edge of the forest. Vague memories of the Meads at Winchester and of schoolmasters shouting 'Spread out' came to my mind. Did one not spread out, in case everyone was machine-gunned at once? Was this not one of the most basic rules? It occurred to me that in fact we *were* just going for a walk; it *was* 'a good excuse to walk in this beautiful snow'! Even the army officers who were with us seemed to take the event in a most light-hearted way. They waded along in the snow parallel to us, in their white anoraks and dark glasses, chatting and laughing; they might have been ski instructors. As we walked on I recalled the conversation I had had with Mishima that morning over coffee; he had compared the *Tatenokai* to the *Zengakuren* and had asserted that the former had more 'spirit' and were closer to 'the *samurai* spirit'. Yet it had to be admitted that the *Zengakuren* fought, while the *Tatenokai* only trained, and that the standard of training, I could now see, was low. It seemed that the *Tatenokai* had little to do with the traditional *samurai*, except in the romantic ideals of their leader; he wanted to be a kind of Japanese Lord Byron. Indeed, that morning he had talked with envy of Byron, of how the poet had been able to afford to gather 300 men in his service and repair ships.

We had been following the lower edge of the forest for about two hours, when an order came via the army instructors that Mishima and I were to detach ourselves from the 'guerrilla' column and to make our way to the 'enemy camp'. From there we would view the final assault by the *Tatenokai* on the enemy position. When we arrived at this point, well in advance of the students, we found that the army NCOs who occupied the camp had built a couple of rough igloos and a snow wall, keeping themselves warm in the process; it was a snug place. For a long time we waited; sometimes there were shouts and we would catch sight of an army instructor. It was late afternoon when the attack finally came. Streaming down a nearby hill the students came at us in twos and threes, while smoke bombs fizzed in the snow. They had all been 'dead men' at a range of 200 yards, the way they had come over the skyline, but on they came, making no attempt to keep low, exposed to 'fire' in the form of thunderflashes hurled from our igloos. When they eventually struggled through the snow, already tired, they were set upon by the NCOs, who wrestled them to the ground and ripped off their boots in a flash, trussing them up tightly, one to another. Mishima joined in the skirmish, and rolled over in the snow, shrieking with laughter as he grappled with the sergeant. It was all over in ten minutes.

V

When I woke the next day, I felt far from lively. The weather had changed again; it was a close, muggy day with clouds, a lot warmer than the day before. I had to breakfast quickly and leave the inn before I was properly awake, to be at the barracks by 7.30 a.m. Though this was the last day at the camp, I had not thought out the questions I must put to Mishima before we parted. It was too early in the morning for that, and we still had time; Mishima and I were not to leave the camp until midday, when we would return to Tokyo by train together.

I had been summoned to the camp at this early hour to witness a *Tatenokai* ceremonial parade. It was to take place in a large hut close to the entrance of the camp. Normally, it would have been staged on the regimental parade-ground in the open air, but on this particular morning the snow was too slushy for that. I walked into the hut, and found there a number of *Tatenokai* members forming up in their yellow-brown uniforms; there were also army NCOs and one or two officers. Mishima came up to me; he was also dressed in the *Tatenokai* uniform with its large cap and badge composed of ancient *kabuto* (*samurai* helmets). We discussed briefly—he was short of time—where I should stand to observe the proceedings. I was in favour of an inconspicuous position to the side, but Mishima wanted me to stand in the front, on the extreme left, where I would be able to see the whole parade, the rostrum from which the colonel would speak and also the brass band which was just then forming up. The NCOs then held a short rehearsal, with Mishima standing by; he did not give orders, it seemed, either on exercises or on parade at Camp Fuji. The twenty-five men on parade were kept at attention for only a couple of minutes, but, to my surprise, two of them keeled over, and had to be carried away. The atmosphere was too close in the hut, and I felt uncomfortable myself.

At eight o'clock precisely the *Tatenokai* were brought to attention once more, and Colonel Fukamizu made his entrance from the far side of the hut, accompanied by officers. An order was given, and the entire parade faced in my direction. As the national anthem was played—and it seemed to last for an interminable time—twenty-five pairs of *Tatenokai* eyes looked through me. I realized what was going on. The students had faced towards Tokyo, because that was where the Emperor lived. It was just unfortunate that I, clad in ski-ing clothes, none the more elegant for three days of continuous wear, happened to be in the line of fire. Should I also have made a gesture, by turning in the direction of the Imperial presence? I contemplated the idea for a second, but it was too late. . . . I cursed Mishima for having overlooked what would happen. At last the anthem came to an end, and the parade once again faced the front. This time the colonel took the salute, and, as instructed by Mishima at the outset of the proceedings, I bowed twice in his direction, wondering whether this was really necessary. The colonel then inspected the parade (what *did* he make of those uniforms?), and took his place on the rostrum, from which he gave a short speech on *riidashippu* ('leadership'). A few minutes later we were all trotting out of the hut into the open air again.

My visit to Camp Fuji was at an end. I waited for Mishima to tell me about our travel arrangements, watching him and the *Tatenokai* members line up outside the hut for the last time, in order to have their photographs taken. Mishima told me that he had changed the travel plans and had hired a taxi to take us back to Tokyo at midday; he would pick me up at the *Fujimotoya* inn where I had been staying.

I was grateful for this extravagant arrangement, which meant that I would have the opportunity to prepare my questions in advance, and would also be able to talk to Mishima without fear of interruption. I had seen two sides of the *Tatenokai*. In the evening, two days before, I had been exposed to all manner of wild ideological talk, centering on the Emperor, and suggesting that the *Tatenokai* was an alarming organization, right-wing and nationalistic. The following day, when we had exercised in the snow, I had seen a completely different side of the organization—essentially, the students were untrained, and unlikely to be effective as a force. My original question, at the start of the proceedings, and before I had set foot in Camp Fuji, had been whether the *Tatenokai* was a right-wing organization or simply a toy of the novelist's; I had been inclined to think it was the former. Seeing the men in the field, however, had made me doubt my original conclusion. My questions to Mishima, therefore, must simply revolve around the original problem: the nature of the *Tatenokai*, fascist club or writer's plaything?

The interest of our drive back to Tokyo was nothing more nor less than the scenery. From the hills round Hakone we had our best view of Mount Fuji; we had really been too close to the mountain at Gotemba to get the proportions right. As the Toyota taxi began to drop down towards Odawara, however, we were both in more of a mood to talk. I asked Mishima why he had created the *Tatenokai*. The *Tatenokai*, he replied, as our car began to run into heavy traffic above Odawara, was 'the first example of a National Guard'; he was reaching for a phrase to express the essence of the organization—it was a show. He wanted to 'inspire people with a sense of national pride,' he said, as if imagining the sound of brass bands and cheering multitudes of onlookers. When talking to *me*, I realized, Mishima was inclined to stress that aspect of the *Tatenokai* which was personal to him, non-ideological and romantic, and no more than this. I tried to press him on the right-wing nature of the organization by asking him to confirm that it had unique training privileges with the *Jieitai*. Yes, this was true; the *Tatenokai* alone could exercise with guns. Tens of thousands of civilians passed through *Jieitai* camps, but they mostly stayed only a few days under a holiday programme designed for *Jieitai* public relations.

They were not allowed to touch rifles. 'How had the exceptional arrangement been made for the *Tatenokai*?' I asked. 'It was very difficult,' Mishima replied. He had had to go and see a great number of people in the *Jieitai*, but in the end it had been arranged with the help of the civilian head of the Defence Agency, Kaneshichi Masuda—and, I suspected, the Prime Minister or those close to him.

And what did the *Tatenokai* amount to, in practical terms? I put the question while we were still stuck in slow-moving traffic. Mishima was trying to bully the driver into taking a short-cut, and the man was replying firmly that the expressway which the novelist wanted to take had not yet been opened to the public. Mishima fell back into his seat, shrugging his shoulders. Well, he wanted to increase the size of the *Tatenokai* to 100 members in all, and then each of his men might take charge of 20, making a total force large enough to take effective action. 'To stage a *coup*?' I might have asked. But I did not put the question. I did not believe in such fantasies. Talking to Mishima about the *Tatenokai* one felt the conversation bordering on his dreams, and I again sensed that with *me* he would prefer to stress the personal aspect of the organization, not the ideological. I adopted a different approach, and asked Mishima when he had decided to create the *Tatenokai*. It had been after completing his book *Eirei no Koe* ('The Voices of the Heroic Dead'), he replied, 'three or four years ago' (in June 1966). I had not read the work. As we passed on down the increasingly steep road, swinging round hair-pin curves and under the boughs of great trees, Mishima began to talk instead of Goethe and his essay on suicide: 'If literature is not a responsible activity, then action is the only course,' he paraphrased. On this trip, I concluded, I was not going to be able to understand the nature of the *Tatenokai*.

As we left Odawara, and reached the coastal expressway beyond, the car passed the first of a succession of big industrial plants which we would see on our return to the capital, still an hour away at least. There was no beach below us, only a dreary series of massive reinforced concrete tetrapods, intended to break the force of the sea, as it hit the mighty wall below us. 'I believe in culture as form and not as spirit,' said the writer. The Emperor, he said, was 'the supreme cultural form'; his 'physical body' was *the* form of culture. In the unique Japanese Imperial institution, with its long tradition of poetry, he found the ultimate value. And he added: 'I do not believe in the non-material, only in the actual.' A few minutes later, he cradled his head in his left arm, leaning back in his seat, and went fast asleep. The car sped swiftly on towards Tokyo, which we would reach in another half-hour. I felt that I was worlds away from understanding this extraordinary person, and I, too, tried to sleep. From time to time I caught sight of buildings, new factories, other expressways. As we passed Chigasaki there was an occasional pine tree to be seen by the road, still remaining on what had once been the historic Old Tokaido Road to Osaka, 300 miles to the west. That was all that was left of the old Japan, perhaps, a few pine trees. While I entertained such banal thoughts, Mishima slept on. Only when we reached that ugly road, the Tamagawadori, did he wake up, and instruct the driver to go first to my home.

3

A month after his return from training with the *Tatenokai* at Camp Fuji, Mishima was invited to take part in an open debate with ultra-left-wing students at his old university, *Todai*. Mishima went to the hall where the debate was to take place—in the Komaba grounds of *Todai*—wearing a black shirt with a string front; outside the hall he found a large cartoon on a bill-board depicting him as a gorilla. Both he and his student hosts were in an aggressive mood and the two-and-a-half-hour debate between them was a success, as entertainment. The *Todai* students, prompted by Mishima, showed a remarkable interest in the subject of the Emperor:

Student: 'Mishima writes a great deal about the Emperor. The reason for this is that the Emperor does not exist. His non-existence constitutes absolute beauty for Mishima. Why, then, does he play the fool all the time? He should stick to aesthetics. Instead he starts fooling around and the beauty which the Emperor embodies is thus destroyed.'

Mishima: 'I am touched by your patriotic remarks. You want to keep your beautiful image of the Emperor and for that purpose wish me to remain in my study. . . .' (*Laughter*)

Another student: 'I want to ask you about the Emperor. If he happens to fall in love with a woman other than the Empress what should he do? He must be restricted in so many ways. One must feel sympathy for him.'

Mishima: 'I really think the Emperor had better keep mistresses. . . .'
(*Laughter*)[11]

Mishima had had a moment of paranoia when he approached the
hall at Komaba, fearing that the students would seize and murder
him on the spot. Afterwards he remarked: 'I was as nervous as if I
was going into a lions' den but I enjoyed it very much after all. I
found we have much in common—a rigorous ideology and a taste for
physical violence, for example. Both they and I represent new
species in Japan today. I felt friendship for them. We are friends
between whom there is a barbed wire fence. We smile at one another but we can't kiss.' He also commented: 'What the *Zengakuren*
students and I stand for is almost identical. We have the same cards
on the table but I have a joker—the Emperor.'

I had numerous discussions with Mishima about events in Japan
at this time, and in mid-summer I asked him if he would write a
short article for me, summing up his thoughts. I proposed to send
this to *The Times* in London. In the middle of August he told me
that the piece was ready and invited me down to Shimoda, where he
was staying with his family for the summer holidays. I stayed there for
a couple of days, swimming with the Mishimas on the beach, and
returned to Tokyo with his contribution for *The Times*. It represented
a crystallization of our conversations and was one of the clearest
summaries Mishima ever made of his 'political' views. I give the
article in full.

A PROBLEM OF CULTURE

Not long ago, in early August, a young Japanese tried to attack the
American Secretary of State, Mr William Rogers, with a knife at
Tokyo airport. The reaction of the Japanese press was to heap
abuse on this individual and totally to condemn his action.

The man explained that he had intended to injure an American
representative by way of retaliation; Japanese who took part in the
anti-American [military] base campaign on Okinawa had been
wounded by American bayonets, he claimed. He had held no
personal grudge against Rogers, he said. Nor had he belonged to
any right-wing organization.

I do not myself support terrorism; nor do I support the spirit
of this young man's action. However, the fact that every Japanese
newspaper heaped abuse on him, all displaying the same hysterical
reaction, interests me a great deal. Whatever the political per-

12   The last picture of Mishima, used for Tobu exhibition in November 1970.

13   The public funeral. From the right: Kawabata, Yoko Mishima, Azusa Hiraoka, Shizué Hiraoka. (*Photo Kyodo*)

suasion of the paper–left, neutral, right-wing–the reaction was the same. Such hysteria is displayed only by people who have something to hide. Just what is the Japanese press trying to hide under all this anger and abuse?

Let us look back a little. For the past one hundred years the Japanese have been making enormous efforts to make their country a paradigm of Western civilization. This unnatural posture has betrayed itself many times; the cloven hoof has been all too visible! After the Second World War people thought that Japan's biggest defect had been exposed. Thereafter Japan came to rank among the leading industrial nations, and need no longer fear self-betrayal. All that is felt to be necessary is for our diplomats to advertise Japanese culture as peace-loving–symbolized by the tea-ceremony and by *ikebana* (flower-arrangement).

In 1961 when Inejiro Asanuma, chairman of the Socialist Party, was assassinated in Tokyo, I was in Paris. Asanuma was stabbed to death by a 17-year-old right-winger, Otoya Yamaguchi; the boy killed himself almost immediately afterwards in jail. At that time the Moulin Rouge in Paris was showing a *Revue Japonaise* which included a swordfight scene. The Japanese Embassy in Paris hurriedly proposed to the Moulin Rouge that the scene should be cut from the revue, in order that 'misunderstanding' be avoided. Fear of misunderstanding is sometimes fear of disclosure.

White Fans Over Heads

I always recall the Shinpuren Incident of 1877–that incident which retains today among Japanese intellectuals the reputation of having displayed Japanese fanaticism and irrationality; a shaming thing indeed, which should not be known to foreigners. The incident occurred during a revolt led by about one hundred stubborn, conservative and chauvinistic former *samurai*. They hated all things Western, and regarded the new Meiji Government with hostility as an example of the Westernization of Japan. They even held white fans over their heads when they had to pass beneath electric lines, saying that the magic of the West was soiling them.

These *samurai* resisted all forms of Westernization. When the new government enacted a law abolishing swords, collecting up these very symbols of *samurai* spirit, one hundred rebels attacked a Westernized Japanese army barracks with nothing but their swords and spears. Many were shot down by rifles–imported from the West; and all the survivors committed *hara-kiri*.

Arnold Toynbee wrote in *A Study of History* that nineteenth-century Asia had only these alternatives: to accept the West and to survive after complete surrender to Westernization; or to resist and perish. This theory is correct, without exception.

Japan, in fact, built a modern and united nation by accepting Westernization and modernization. During this process the most

H

striking pure act of resistance was that of the Shinpuren revolt. Other resistance movements were more political, lacking the ideological purity and cultural element of Shinpuren.

Thus Japanese ability to modernize and to innovate, sometimes in an almost cunning way, came to be highly praised—while other Asian peoples could be looked down on for their laziness. Yet people in the West understood little of the sacrifices that the Japanese were obliged to make.

Rather than attempting to learn about this reality the West prefers to stick to the idea of the yellow peril, sensing intuitively something dark and ominous in the Asian soul. What is most exquisite in a national culture is tied closely to what may also be most disagreeable—just as in Elizabethan tragedy.

Japan has tried to show only one side of herself, one side of a moon, to the West, while pushing on busily with modernization. In no era of our history have there been such great sacrifices of the totality of culture—which must embrace lightness and darkness equally.

In the first twenty years of my life national culture was controlled by the unnatural puritanism of the militarists. For the past twenty years pacificism has been sitting heavily on the *samurai* spirit, a burden on the easily stimulated 'Spanish' soul of the Japanese. The hypocrisy of the authorities has permeated the minds of the people, who can find no way out. Wherever national culture seeks to regain its totality, almost insane incidents occur. Such phenomena are interpreted as the undercurrent of Japanese nationalism, intermittently bursting out like lava through cracks in a volcano.

Conspicuous radical action of the kind taken recently by the youth at Tokyo airport may be explained in such terms. Yet few people notice that both the right and left wing in Japan are exploiting nationalism under all kinds of international masks. The anti-Vietnam War movement in Japan was predominantly left-wing, and yet appealed strongly to nationalism—a strange kind of nationalism by proxy. Until the war began few Japanese would even have known where Vietnam was.

Nationalism is used one way or another for political purposes, and thus people often lose sight of the fact that nationalism is basically a problem of culture. On the other hand the hundred *samurai* who attacked a modern army barracks with swords alone recognized this fact. Their reckless action and inevitable defeat was necessary to show the existence of a certain essential spirit. Their ideology was a difficult one; it was the first radical prophecy of the danger inherent in Japanese modernization, which must damage the totality of culture. The painful condition of Japanese culture, which we feel today, is the fruit of what could only be vaguely apprehended by Japanese at the time of the Shinpuren Incident.[12]

What was Mishima to do with his *Tatenokai?* On 3 November he invited a few foreign correspondents, including me, to witness the only public parade ever given by his 'private army'. It was held on the roof of the National Theatre on a cold, blustery day. A striped tent had been put up on the roof of the building and chairs had been placed there for the VIPs who were to attend. The *Tatenokai* members streamed onto the roof in their yellow-brown uniforms. While Mishima watched from the side of the 'parade-ground', Morita gave the orders; for several minutes the men marched back and forth across the roof; they were inspected by a retired general. At the end of the parade, all faced east across the moat of the Imperial Palace, which runs below the National Theatre, and gave a salute to His Majesty. Thereafter, everyone trooped downstairs into the theatre where a reception was held. While his audience nibbled at sandwiches, Mishima gave two short speeches, one in Japanese and one in English: 'My reason for creating the *Tatenokai* is simple. Ruth Benedict once wrote a famous book, *The Chrysanthemum and the Sword*. Such are the characteristics of Japanese history: the chrysanthemum and the sword. After the war the balance between these two was lost. The sword has been ignored since 1945. My ideal is to restore the balance. To revive the tradition of the *samurai*, through my literature and my action. Therefore I asked the *Jieitai* to give my men basic training, one month at a time. The *Jieitai* is composed of volunteers. A quarter of a million men is insufficient to defend this country. Therefore some civilian co-operation is necessary. This is needed because twentieth-century war is fought by guerrillas; this is a new type of warfare, conducted by irregulars. . . . My ideal is to give Japan a system like the Swiss system of military service.'[13]

Early in December 1969, Mishima set off for South Korea. The purpose of his journey was to see the South Korean army in action. On his return he wrote to me that he was irritated by the calm situation he found in Korea. He said that he had been to the east coast to see the place where guerrillas had landed from the north, the training of anti-guerrilla forces and the coastguard militia. The same YS–II plane which had taken him to Seoul was hijacked to North Korea on the following day. If only, he said, he had been kidnapped to North Korea, he wouldn't be so bored.

This letter gave a misleading impression of his actual state of mind. He was, in fact, secretly preparing himself to take the plunge, getting ready to stage his miniature *coup d'état* less than a year later.

So much is apparent from a remark he made to a friend, Ichiro Murakami, in December 1969: 'One has to take responsibility for what one says—once one has said it. The same is true of the written word. If one writes: "I will die in November," then one has to die. If you make light of words once you will carry on doing so.'[14] His words are scarcely ambiguous.

Early in April 1970, Mishima secretly formed the group of students (within the *Tatenokai*) who were to assist him in his twentieth-century version of the Shinpuren Incident. The members of the group were—in addition to Morita—Masayoshi Koga and Masahiro Ogawa, both twenty-one and students at universities in Tokyo. 'Chibi-Koga', as he was known to other members of the *Tatenokai* (the nickname served to dinstinguish him from another Koga in the organization), was the only son of a tangerine farmer from Arita in Wakayama prefecture; his father had died in 1953 and his mother had brought him up alone. She introduced the boy, at the age of twelve, to a religious organization with a strong nationalist creed, the *Seicho no Ie*, and he had developed right-wing views. He met Mishima in August 1968 and became a member of the *Tatenokai* after completing a month's training at Camp Fuji. He was made a section leader in April 1969. Chibi-Koga was tiny but energetic; he was devoted to the *Tatenokai* and considered completely trustworthy by Mishima and Morita. Masahiro Ogawa was a different kind of person, the son of an office employee, who lived at Chiba, close to Tokyo. Ogawa was Morita's closest friend and had been introduced to Mishima by Morita; he was made a section leader of the *Tatenokai* in April 1970. Tall and pale, with a toothbrush moustache, Ogawa was the standard-bearer of the *Tatenokai*. Although he made a conspicuous figure on parade, he was physically weak. This group of four—Mishima, Morita, Koga and Ogawa—met in secret, frequently changing their rendezvous in order to avoid arousing the slightest suspicion. They began to lay their plans.

The chief planners were Mishima and Morita. At the beginning of April, Mishima met Chibi-Koga at a coffee-shop in the Imperial Hotel and asked him if he was willing to commit himself 'to the very end'—without explaining what he was asking. Chibi-Koga immediately agreed. A week later Mishima put the same question to Ogawa at his home in the suburbs of Tokyo. Ogawa hesitated and then agreed. In mid-May, during another meeting at his home, Mishima proposed to the three students that the *Tatenokai*, as a whole, should

stage an uprising with the help of the *Jieitai* and occupy Parliament;
then they would call for a revision of the Constitution. Mishima,
however, was vague and seemed to have no precise plan of action.
About three weeks later, on 13 June, Mishima met the three students
again, this time in Room 821 of the Hotel Okura. He explained that
they would have to carry out their plan by themselves because they
could not rely on the *Jieitai*. He had presumably made soundings
within the *Jieitai* with discouraging results. Mishima then proposed
a drastic change of course; instead of acting with the army, they
would attack the army. He still lacked a definite plan, however, and
suggested a number of proposals. One idea was to attack a *Jieitai*
arsenal; another suggestion was to take an army general hostage—
he proposed that their target might be a very senior general who had
his HQ at a place of historical importance to the Imperial Army of
pre-war days: General Kanetoshi Mashita, commander of the Eastern
Army at Ichigaya in central Tokyo. His aim was to find a means of
forcing a *Jieitai* command to assemble an audience of young soldiers.
He had confidence in the young soldiers and officers and was sure that
if he could make a speech to them they would join in an uprising
with him and the *Tatenokai* students.

I assume that Mishima had forced himself into a state of mind
in which he could believe this incredible scenario. But at the same
time there must have been a cold and logical element within him that
was quietly asserting that he was talking rubbish. One can only
make sense of Mishima's determination to ignore this contradiction
if one assumes that his ultimate purpose was to die, and that the
means by which he would achieve this aim, provided that they had
a theatrical quality, were not especially important. In any event,
Mishima and the students agreed at this meeting that they would make
their move at the second anniversary parade of the *Tatenokai* to be
held in November. General Mashita would be invited to review the
parade and there they would seize him.

The next meeting was held at another Western-style hotel in central
Tokyo. This time Mishima chose a writers' hotel, the *Yamanoue*
('Hill Top') Hotel. It took place eight days after the meeting at the
Okura. He informed the students that he had obtained permission
for the *Tatenokai* to hold an exercise on a heli-pad at the Ichigaya
military base, but that they would have to change their target from
General Mashita to the commander of the infantry regiment stationed
at Ichigaya, a Colonel Miyata. This was an altogether more modest

target, but Miyata's office was closer to the heli-pad than that of Mashita. He also proposed that they should be armed with swords and asked Chibi-Koga to buy a car for their use, in which the swords would be carried into the base. Everyone agreed.

What was Mishima's real goal? The three students believed him to be an ardent patriot, but this is much too simple a view. At this time, Mishima was on the verge of his final decision to commit *hara-kiri*. The timing of his decision can be specified exactly, for at the *Yamanoue* meeting he had proposed that the weapons they would use at Ichigaya would be swords. I presume that he realized that there was no guarantee that he would die if he simply staged an attack within a *Jieitai* base (even if he used firearms). The army would not shoot him down as, since the war, they had been forbidden to fire on civilians under any circumstances. Thus he was propelled into the decision to use swords in the attack at Ichigaya. Whatever happened there, with a sword in his hand and a dagger within reach, he could be virtually certain that he would die–by his own hand.

While all this was going on, I met Mishima, but I saw no sign of it. I met a different Mishima, the usual cordial and outgoing host. I saw him during his summer holiday at Shimoda and he was showing no particular signs of tension. He relaxed by the swimming pool, his body being turned a deep brown by the sun, and each afternoon he would accompany his family to the beach. One day there was a phone call from Shigeru Hori, the Prime Minister's right-hand man, proposing a meeting with Mr Sato; another day Yasuhiro Nakasone, the head of the Defence Agency (which controls the *Jieitai*), telephoned to ask Mishima to give a speech to a group of his supporters –his 'faction' within the ruling conservative party. I was surprised by these signs of Mishima's popularity with conservative politicians. Mishima was caustic about them. He denounced Nakasone as a 'fraud' and said that he had no intention of accepting either invitation. There was an element of *shibai* ('theatre') in all this.

His boisterous talk of suicide also seemed to be an act. As he lay by the side of the pool, basking in the sun and confidently predicting the suicides of other writers (Truman Capote, for example), speculating about the mysterious deaths of writers (for instance, St Exupery, who, he insisted, had flown his plane straight out into the Atlantic until he crashed), it was unimaginable that he was serious. One night I accompanied the Mishimas to a *yakuza* (gangster) film and he insisted afterwards, standing up in a coffee-bar, that the *yakuza* were the only Japanese who still possessed 'the *samurai* spirit'. I thought that he was being silly.

Behind this frivolous mask Mishima continued with his plotting. From Shimoda he kept in constant touch with the three members of the *Tatenokai* group. He sent them to Hokkaido, the northern island of Japan, and paid for their holiday there. He also asked them to recruit one more member, having appreciated that the group was too small for the task he envisaged. He had decided to take only one more man as he gave top priority to security. His choice was Hiroyasu Koga, 'Furu-Koga' as he was known in the *Tatenokai*, the son of a primary school headmaster in Hokkaido who was a lecturer at the *Seicho no Ie* headquarters and had introduced his son to right-wing thinking. He was twenty-three, a year older than Chibi-Koga and Ogawa, and was studying to be a lawyer. On 9 September Mishima met him at a restaurant in the Ginza and told him the whole plan in strictest confidence. Mishima said that it would be impossible to find *Jieitai* men who would rise with them, and that he himself would have to die whatever happened. The date would be 25 November. Furu-Koga agreed to join the group.

On 15 September the five had dinner together at *Momonjiya* in Ryokogu on their way back from watching a display of *ninja-taikai*, a feudal martial art. Ten days later they met again, at a sauna club in Shinjuku, and Mishima said that the arrangements for the monthly *Tatenokai* meeting in November must be tightened up. Members who had relatives in the *Jieitai* must be excluded from the meeting; he would personally sign all invitations. A week later they met at a Chinese restaurant in the Ginza and Mishima described the plan in detail. The monthly meeting would start at 11 a.m. At 12.30 p.m., Mishima and Chibi-Koga would leave the meeting on the excuse that they had to attend a funeral. They would drive off and fetch the swords and also two reporter friends of Mishima, who would be waiting for them at the Palace Hotel, but would be totally ignorant of the plan. They would return to Ichigaya and would park the car at the headquarters of the 32nd Infantry Regiment. The reporters would wait in the car. The group would then take Colonel Miyata hostage. Meanwhile, the rest of the *Tatenokai* would have started the exercise at the heli-pad.

On 9 October another meeting was held. Furu-Koga was absent. He was in Hokkaido saying good-bye to his family. Ten days later they had a group portrait in full uniform taken at the Tojo Hall, where wedding parties are the usual customers. Mishima joked to the others that the Tojo Hall cameramen always made everybody look beautiful.

Mishima's planning entered a final stage on 3 November, when the group met at *Misty*, a sauna club at Roppongi in central Tokyo. They took their baths in the grotto which is the pride of this club and adjourned to the lounge at the top of the building. Mishima had an announcement to make: 'I appreciate your firm resolve to die, all of us together. But I must ask the two Kogas and Ogawa to ensure that the colonel does not also commit suicide, and to hand him over safely to his men.' He added: 'Morita must do *kaishaku* (the beheading) at the earliest possible moment. Please don't leave me in agony too long.' Thus Mishima completely reversed the plans for the three youngest members of the party to die with their leaders. They protested vehemently and Mishima and Morita calmed them. Mishima said: 'It is much harder to go on living than to die. What I am asking you to do is to take the hardest course of all.' The three students agreed to abide by his instructions.

Three days later the group travelled up to Gotemba near Mt Fuji to say good-bye to the other members of the *Tatenokai*, who were on a course there. The rest of the *Tatenokai* were not aware that this was a final farewell, when they all met at an inn in the town. Mishima poured toasts of *saké* for all forty people present, drinking with each student and *Jieitai* training officer, and becoming very intoxicated for once in his life. On their return to Tokyo Morita and the other three visited Ichigaya to check a parking space for the car on 25 November and reported back to Mishima. On 12 November Morita asked Ogawa to do *kaishaku* for him. Ogawa agreed to do so. On 14 November the group met again at *Misty*. Mishima said that they would send their pictures and a copy of the *gekibun*, the last manifesto, to his two reporter friends, the NHK reporter Daté and the *Sunday Mainichi* journalist Tokuoka, on the morning of the 25th. On the following day, at another sauna club, they discussed their timetable. It would require twenty minutes to take Miyata hostage and to get the *Jieitai* garrison to assemble. Mishima's speech would take thirty minutes; each of the others would speak for five minutes; another five minutes would be allowed for a speech by another *Tatenokai* member and the meeting would end with *Tenno Heika Banzai* ('Long Live the Emperor').

At the last moment there was a major change of plan. On 21

November Morita visited Ichigaya to confirm that Colonel Miyata would be there on the 25th. He found that in fact the colonel would be away on manoeuvres. At a meeting at a Chinese restaurant in the Ginza, they decided to take hostage General Mashita, commander of the Eastern Army, as had been planned originally. Mishima telephoned Mashita's office and made an appointment with the general for 11 a.m. on the 25th. That day and the following day, a Sunday, the four students bought supplies while Mishima was busy with his family. They purchased rope with which to tie up the general, wire and pincers to make barricades, cotton cloth on which to write their demands and to be hung from the balcony, and brandy and a water bottle. Mishima gave them the money for these purchases. On the evening of 22 November, Morita, who had been worrying that he would be unable to behead Mishima properly, asked Furu-Koga to act instead of him, if he should fail. Koga, a trained swordsman, agreed to do so.

On 23 and 24 November the group met in Room 519 at the Palace Hotel. They held eight complete rehearsals of their plan. The plan was this: Mishima would introduce the four students to the general, explaining that he was going to give them awards; he would then show the general his sword. When Mishima said: 'Koga, a handkerchief'—in order to wipe the sword—Chibi-Koga would step behind the general and pin him down. Furu-Koga and Ogawa would help him. Mishima and Morita would make barricades at the doors. If the *Jieitai* officers attempted to enter they would bar the way. Then they would read their demands to the officers. Once a large crowd of soldiers had gathered in front of the main building Mishima would make a speech from the balcony, followed by the other four who would introduce themselves briefly. Thereafter Mishima and Morita would commit *hara-kiri*. The others would behead them.

They cut rope into suitable lengths, wrote their demands on the cotton cloth and also wrote farewell *tanka* (31-syllable poems, which were written by soldiers before going into battle in the Second World War). Mishima rehearsed his speech with the television switched on in the room so that he could not be heard from outside; finally they packed up their supplies. Among these were wads of cotton wool. Morita asked Mishima what these would be used for; the latter smiled and said that the two of them must pack their anuses with cotton wool, in order that they should not evacuate their bowels when committing *hara-kiri*. Finally, Mishima phoned his two reporter friends, telling them to have cameras ready for the morrow and also armbands. They must be ready by 11 a.m. He told them that he would call again at 10 a.m. on the following day to give them final instructions. That evening, on the 24th, the group had their farewell party at a little restaurant called *Suegen* in the Shimbashi quarter. There is only one large room at *Suegen* and the *Tatenokai* party took the room for the evening.

After the meal the group drove to Mishima's home. He left them there and they went on to Morita's lodging house in the Shinjuku district. After dropping him there the three younger students continued to Chibi-Koga's lodging house, where they spent the night.

Mishima then paid a short visit to his parents. Shizué was out and Mishima found himself alone with his father. Azusa grumbled about his son's smoking habits—Mishima was chain-smoking *Peace* cigarettes —and then Shizué came in. Mother and son talked for a short while and then Shizué saw him out: 'I watched him leaving and I couldn't help thinking how tired he looked, how stooped was his back,' she said later. In his own house, Mishima sorted through his papers until late. He signed the final instalment of *The Decay of the Angel*, putting on it the date 25 November 1970. He also sealed two letters to foreign scholars—Ivan Morris and Donald Keene. And, on his desk, he put a short note: 'Human life is limited, but I would like to live forever.'

VIII

The Decay of the Angel

> Finishing the long novel (*The Sea of Fertility*) makes me feel as if it is the end of the world.
>
> YUKIO MISHIMA to the author,
> October, 1970

Why Mishima chose 25 November as the day he would die is a matter for speculation. One view is that he chose that day because it was the anniversary of the death of the nineteenth-century hero Shoin Yoshida. During my visit to Shimoda in August 1970 I discussed Yoshida with Mishima, mentioning that there was a large statue of Yoshida in a shrine close to the inn where I was staying–the Mishima shrine (so named after a shrine in the town close to Mt Fuji from which Mishima had derived his *nom de plume* almost thirty years before). In conversation, however, Mishima showed little interest in Yoshida, and I doubt whether he was deeply interested in the man.

My guess is that Mishima chose to die on 25 November because that was the day on which he was to hand over the last instalment of the fourth book of his long tetralogy, *The Sea of Fertility*. It was the deadline for the manuscript, and Mishima as a rule stuck rigidly to his schedule. He had calculated that at the end of November he would deliver the final section of *The Decay of the Angel*, the fourth book in the tetralogy, to the magazine *Shincho*. The magazine was publishing the work in instalments and had been receiving each one on or about the twenty-fifth of each month. Mishima had in fact completed the final part by August 1970, for another guest at Shimoda, Donald Keene, had seen it at that time. Thus Mishima could plan far ahead so that his death would coincide with the handing over of the conclusion of his last book, and his literature would officially end on the same day as his life. It was also typical of Mishima that he controlled his last actions to the final

detail. The man who maintained a smiling face throughout his last
summer holiday at Shimoda, while secretly planning his bloody end,
faithfully kept his literary schedule to the last.

What kind of book was he able to write at the same time that
he was planning his death? It might be seen as an attempt at
justifying and explaining what he did—a last message to posterity—but
that is only one aspect of a very complex book. It certainly reflects
his desperate state of mind in the last year of his life; it ends
with a 'catastrophe', as Mishima put it to the literary critic, Takashi
Furubayashi, on 18 November in the last interview he ever granted.
Replying to a question about his use of the theme of reincarnation in
The Sea of Fertility, Mishima said: 'One of the reasons [I used the
theme] is technical. I thought the chronological novel outdated. Using
[the idea of] reincarnation, it was easy to jump in time and also in
space; I found that convenient. But, with the notion of reincarnation, the novel became a fairy tale. That is why I argued the philosophy
of reincarnation so strongly in the early part of *The Temple of
Dawn*. This was a preparation for the fourth volume. In the last
book I wrote episodes only and went straight through to the catastrophe.' Mishima had written the book rapidly—once he had made
up his mind to die in 1970—and it rounded off not only his view
of reincarnation but of the course of a human life. And the catastrophe? The whole of *The Decay of the Angel* is the answer to that
question.

The action of this last novel takes place in Japan in the early
1970s, starting in the early summer of 1970 and ending in the late
summer of 1975. Honda is once again a main character and is again
related to the chief protagonist, another boy of remarkable physical
beauty—Toru. The plot is very simple in comparison with the first three
volumes of the tetralogy. Honda adopts Toru as his son when he,
the ageing lawyer, is seventy-six and the boy is sixteen. The two live
together in Tokyo where Toru, a highly intelligent youth, passes his
entrance examinations for Tokyo University.

As Honda becomes older and Toru grows more aggressive, the old
man waits for Toru's death at the age of twenty, for the boy has the
physical mark on his body to show that he is the reincarnation
of Kiyoaki and the others—three moles on the side of his chest.
Toru, however, looks forward to inheriting Honda's money. He becomes vicious and finally assaults Honda with a poker, inflicting super-
ficial wounds. Honda can do nothing about the situation—he fears

that if he makes a complaint to someone, Toru will have him shut
up in a home for the senile. At the end of *The Decay of the Angel*
Toru and Honda both endure misfortune. The boy, tormented by
Keiko, Honda's old friend and the ex-countess who in *The Temple of
Dawn* was the lover of Ying Chan, tries to kill himself by drinking
industrial spirits but only succeeds in blinding himself, a symbolic
incident which takes place just before his twenty-first birthday. At
twenty-one could he be the true reincarnation? The movements of
the heavenly bodies had left Honda aside. 'By a small miscalculation,
they had led Honda and the reincarnation of Ying Chan into
separate parts of the universe. Three reincarnations had occupied
Honda's life and, after drawing their paths of light across it (that
too had been a most improbable accident), gone off in another burst
of light to an unknown corner of the heavens. Perhaps somewhere,
some time, Honda would meet the hundredth, the ten thousandth,
the hundred millionth reincarnation. There was no hurry. . . .'[1]
Toru lives on miserably in his foster father's home. Honda himself is
publicly disgraced. He is caught by the police after an incident in a
public park where he has been peeping at lovers, and it is reported
in the press: 'Famous Judge Turned Peeping Tom'.

He also begins to suffer from pains in the abdomen. 'General
debilitation and rhythmical attacks of pain brought new powers to
think. His ageing brain had lost all ability to concentrate, but now it
returned, and pain even worked aggressively upon it, to bring certain
vital faculties other than the purely rational to bear. At the age
of eighty-one Honda attained to a wondrous and mysterious realm
that had before been denied him. He knew now that a more comprehensive view of the world was to be had from physical depression
than from intelligence, from a dull pain in the entrails than from
reason, a loss of appetite than analysis.'[2] He had by himself 'reached
that honing of the senses, achieved by few in this world, to live
death from within. When he looked back upon life from its far side
other than as a journey over a flat surface, hoping that what had
declined would revive, seeking to believe that pain was transient,
clinging greedily to happiness as a thing of the moment, thinking
that good fortune must be followed by bad, seeing in all the ups
and downs and rises and falls the ground for his own prospects—
then everything was in place, pulled tight, and the march to the
end was in order. . . .'[3]

He makes an appointment at the Cancer Research Institute, and on the day before takes one of his rare looks at television. There is a shot of a swimming-pool with young people splashing about in it. 'Honda would end his life without having known the feelings of the owner of beautiful flesh. If for a single month he could live in it! He should have had a try. . . . When admiration passed the gentle and docile and became lunatic worship, it would become torment for the possessor. In the delirium and the torment were true holiness. What Honda had missed had been the dark, narrow path through the flesh to holiness. To travel it was of course the privilege of few. . . .'⁴

After being examined for a week, Honda is told the result—'There seems to be no more than a benign growth on the pancreas.' The doctor adds, 'All we have to do is cut it away.' Honda does not believe him, but fears it is malignant. He asks for 'a week's reprieve' before going into hospital.

He visits Toru. Earlier in the novel we have been given the five signs of the decay of an angel, the five marks that death has come. According to *The Life of Buddha* fifth fascicle, 'The flowers in the hair fade, a fetid sweat comes from under the arms, the robes are soiled, the body ceases to give off light, it loses awareness of itself.'⁵ He seems to discover all these signs in Toru. 'There was no smell of flowers'; 'the dirt and oil on the kimono had mixed with the sweat into the smell as of a dank canal that young men put out in the summer'; 'the smile had left him'; 'Toru had abdicated control of the regions above his neck.'⁶ We see the decay of the angel. And we also see the decay of Honda, but it has taken much longer. ('He who had had no such awareness to begin with lived on. For he was no angel.')

He also decides to fulfil a lifetime's ambition—for there may be little time left—to see again Satoko Ayukura, Kiyoaki's mistress in *Spring Snow*, who has become abbess of the nunnery in which she sought refuge from the world sixty years before. Satoko is now eighty-three. In July of 1975 Honda obtains an appointment with her and travels down from Tokyo to Kyoto, where he books into a hotel. The following day he sets off for Gesshuji, the nunnery. It is a fine summer day and Honda is driven by a chauffeur. He refuses the chauffeur's suggestion that he should be taken right up to the front gate of Gesshuji; his intention is to suffer the pains which Kiyoaki experienced sixty years earlier. Countless cicadas are singing in the woods. Honda goes slowly up a long flight of stone steps

with his stick; sometimes he stoops and fights the pain in his
body, and finally reaches the door, covered in sweat. He clearly
remembers the scene sixty years before; the years seem no more than
a moment. He feels as if he were young once more and Kiyoaki were
waiting for him, back at their hotel, with a high temperature and
a dangerous fever. At the nunnery he is allowed to enter and is
guided to a guest room. He expresses his profound gratitude to the
nun who has escorted him and experiences great happiness as he
reflects that the scandal about him in Tokyo has proved no obstacle
to his meeting. At the same time he thinks to himself that, if he
did not feel shame and a consciousness of his evil and of death, he
would not have come to the nunnery.

An aged nun enters the room, escorted by a younger nun who holds
her hand. The old nun wears a white kimono and over this a deep
violet robe (a *hifu* or mid-length gown). This must be Satoko. Honda
cannot look directly at her for a while; he feels tears welling in his
eyes. She must really be Satoko, Honda thinks, looking at her face
finally–at her nose and the shape of her mouth; she has even kept
her beauty. Age has purified Satoko; her eyes are clear. The old
abbess has the quality of a precious stone, crystallized in old age.

She admits she has seen his letter. It seemed 'almost too earnest'.
She thought 'there must be some holy bond between us'.

Honda reminds her that sixty years before he had not been allowed
to see her. He had been angry. 'Kiyoaki Matsugae was after all my
dearest friend.'

'Kiyoaki Matsugae. Who might he have been?' she replies.

Honda looks at her in astonishment.

She might be hard of hearing but she could not have failed to
hear him.

She repeats her question, 'Who might he have been?'

Scrupulously polite, he recounts his memories of Kiyoaki's love
and its sad conclusion. When he has finished, the abbess says coolly:
'It has been a most interesting story, but unfortunately I did not know
Mr Matsugae. I fear you have confused me with someone else.'

Honda's persistence 'passed a reasonable limit'. But she does
not seem to resent it. 'For all the heat, her purple cloak was cool.
Her eyes and her always beautiful voice were serene.'

'No, Mr Honda, I have forgotten none of the blessings that were
mine in the other world. But I fear I have never heard the name
Kiyoaki Matsugae. Don't you suppose, Mr Honda, that there never

was such a person? You seem convinced that there was; but don't you suppose that there was no such person from the beginning, anywhere? I couldn't help thinking so as I listened to you.'

'Why then do we know each other? And the Ayakuras and the Matsugaes must still have family registers.'

'Yes, such documents might solve problems in the other world. But did you really know a person called Kiyoaki? And can you say definitely that the two of us have met before?'

'I came here sixty years ago.'

'Memory is like a phantom mirror. It sometimes shows things too distant to be seen, and sometimes it shows them as if they were here.'

'But if there was no Kiyoaki from the beginning . . .', Honda is groping through a fog. His meeting with the abbess seems half a dream. He speaks loudly as if to retrieve the self that 'receded like traces of breath vanishing from a lacquer tray.' Honda remarks: 'If there was no Kiyoaki, then there was no Isao. There was no Ying Chan, and who knows, perhaps there has been no I.'

For the first time there is strength in the eyes of the abbess. 'That too is as it is in each heart.'

After a long silence the abbess calls her novice. She wishes to show Honda the south garden. 'It was a bright, quiet garden, without striking features. Like a rosary rubbed between the hands, the shrilling of the cicadas held sway.'

'There was no other sound. The garden was empty. He had come, thought Honda, to a place that had no memories, nothing.'

'The noontide of summer flowed over the still garden'.⁷ This is the last we know of Honda and the final line of *The Sea of Fertility*.

This is presumably the 'catastrophe' to which Mishima alluded in his last interview. Reincarnation is thrown into doubt, so is Honda's whole life: '. . . who knows, perhaps there has been no I.' The tetralogy as a whole has been dependent on the idea of reincarnation, exemplified by the lives of Kiyoaki, Isao, Ying Chan, and, finally, Toru. And then, at the close of the 1,400 page novel, Mishima seems to explode the notion that the three successors of the beautiful youth Kiyoaki are reincarnations; the theme which links the four books of *The Sea of Fertility* is questioned with classical irony. Such is my interpretation of the ending and of Mishima's use of the word 'catastrophe' in reference to it.

It is an appropriate ending. Mishima himself did not believe in reincarnation and his writing on the subject in *The Sea of Fertility* is lacking in conviction; it was reasonable that he should doubt and even discard the idea at the end of the work. Through his emphasis on reincarnation in the earlier parts of the tetralogy, he works up to a climax in which he questions the entire structure of the story. He even leaves his chief character at the very end of his long life doubting that it had any meaning. And yet nothing in the novel is that simple. Honda, it seems, has entered Nirvana, or extinction, in Buddhist terms—a cold and comfortless place 'that had no memories', a place akin to the surface of the moon. This is the ironic ending of the ironically titled *The Sea of Fertility*, and no doubt the exact interpretation will long be disputed. How like Yukio Mishima to have left his last work of literature—and his comment on life—in this way. One can almost hear his familiar laughter behind the final pages: Huh-huh-huh.

After Mishima's suicide events conspired to give me a privileged view of all that took place in Tokyo. I found myself the only foreign reporter at the press conference held by the *Jieitai* at the Ichigaya headquarters some fifteen minutes after Mishima's death there. On the following day I visited Mishima's home to leave a note for his widow, and to my surprise, because I had expected the family would not want visitors, I was invited in. The Mishima home was full of white chrysanthemums and elegant women in black silk kimonos, family or very close friends. I was the only non-Japanese person there and I stayed only a short time to chat with a friend of Mishima's. The private funeral service took place half an hour later, followed by cremation.

In December, in my capacity as a reporter, I attended a memorial meeting held in a hall at Ikebukuro, not far from the department store where Mishima's last exhibition had been staged; and in January I was present at the public funeral at the Tsukiji Honganji temple in Tokyo. The funeral was attended by over ten thousand people and was the largest of its kind ever held in Japan. Before the general public was allowed to look into the temple (no one from the public was admitted inside the building itself), there was a short service for about three hundred people. The altar was a beautiful sight—huge spheres made up of small white chrysanthemums, by which flickered tall candles. Members of the family were seated at the front with Yasunari Kawabata, who acted as principal mourner; behind them were the *Tatenokai*, all eighty members, in uniform. After the service, Kawabata, looking old and frail in his morning coat, made a short, very restrained speech, asking those present to do everything they could to help the widow and children.

I was apparently the only non-Japanese invited to the funeral (if there were others they did not come); and I was also the only Western person on hand when the trial of the three survivors of the action at Ichigaya opened in the Tokyo District Court in March 1971. The authorities would not admit more than one foreign reporter to the court, and he had to be someone with a better command of Japanese than I, as he was to take notes for the entire foreign press. (Takeshi Oka of *The New York Times*, a Japanese, accepted this responsibility.) To get into the court, I lined up with about five hundred other people at seven in the morning, taking my chances in the ballot that determined who would be admitted. The odds were ten to one against success, but I was one of those who received a piece of paper with a cross on it: I would be allowed in to the Mishima trial.

The beginning, as it happened, was the only interesting part of the trial, which lasted until April 1972 (and ended with sentences of four years imprisonment for the *Tatenokai* students). For the first time, the two Kogas and Ogawa made a public appearance; they wore Western suits and open-neck shirts or polo jerseys and looked neat and alert. What amazed me was their size—they looked so *small*—and their seeming frailty and youth. The two Kogas had fresh boyish faces and were quite short; Ogawa, the standard-bearer of the *Tatenokai*, was taller and had a toothbrush moustache that made him appear slightly older; but, beside my memory of Mishima, they all seemed very young and undeveloped. The three were asked to make speeches at the opening session. Fura-Koga, a youth with a sensitive face, proved to be the most eloquent: chauvinism, imperialism and loyalty to Mishima were his themes. A change had taken place after Mishima's death; the chauvinistic tone of Furu-Koga's speech was in contrast to everything Mishima had stood for as a writer and as a man. I sensed that Mishima's occasional anti-foreign sallies in his novels and in his conversation had been blown up out of all proportion by his self-appointed right-wing allies. As I listened to the evidence in court, it seemed as ironic an ending to the life story of Yukio Mishima as *The Sea of Fertility* had been to his writing.

Post Mortem

He committed suicide to complete his literary work.

TAKEO OKUNO, literary critic

He died to defend what he loved.

SHINTARO ISHIHARA, author and right-wing politician

An act motivated by a sense of phantom crisis

DAIZO KUSAYANAGI, sociologist

The heightening of his sexuality produced an increasing urge to commit suicide by disembowelment.

TADASU IIZAWA, playwright

A suicide brought about by an explosive self-exhibitionistic desire.

SHIGETA SAITO, psychiatrist

A gorgeous mosaic of homosexuality, *Yomeigaku*, and Emperor worship.

A Japanese friend three months after Mishima's death[1]

1

The image of Mishima's head with the *hachimaki* headband still secure about it, propped on the blood-soaked carpeted floor of General Mashita's office–the photograph was published by the Japanese press and in *Life* magazine–remains indelibly in my mind. That powerful head had been torn from its shoulders! How had Mishima justified this action to himself?

In *The Decay of the Angel*, Honda, the chief character, regrets that he is the kind of person who is 'unable to stop time' and therefore cannot enjoy the 'endless physical beauty' which is 'the special prerogative of those who cut time short.'

'As he grew older, awareness of self became awareness of time. He

243

gradually came to make out the sound of the white ants. Moment by moment, second by second, with what a shallow awareness men slipped through time that would not return! Only with age did one know that there was a richness, an intoxication even, in each drop. The drops of beautiful time, like the drops of a rich, rare wine. And time dripped away like blood. Old men dried up and died. In payment for having neglected to stop time at the glorious moment when the rich blood, unbeknownst to the owner himself, was bringing rich drunkenness.'[2]

Mishima adds that 'just before the pinnacle when time must be cut short is the pinnacle of physical beauty.' In his last novel, he seems to be explaining that he knows he has passed the first pinnacle and reached the second, and, unlike Honda, he has no intention of ignoring 'the glorious moment.' If this is true of his purpose in *The Decay of the Angel*, his *hara-kiri* simply stopped time for him: endless physical beauty therefore would be his 'special prerogative.'

This is a literary explanation in keeping with many of the ideas that had obsessed Mishima for most of his life, but it seems too simple when one remembers Mishima's delight in role playing—how he must have enjoyed explaining the 'glorious moment' to posterity—and especially the events of that last day. We have seen how his plans changed, how Morita provided essential support, how the police and the army failed to intervene effectively—it is easy to imagine how that last day might have turned out differently, and Mishima would have missed his 'glorious moment' and perhaps lived on like Honda (and yet he was such a determined man and rehearsed his death so many times that it now seems to have a certain inevitability about it). Even in *The Decay of the Angel*, there is a certain ironic undertone throughout. Honda's failure to stop time and his slow ageing seems to bring certain compensations, as if the narrator is perhaps questioning his earlier soliloquy about the 'glorious moment.' Nothing is straightforward: is everything in doubt? At least in Mishima's last novel, one is wary of seizing on a simple message in case it is merely another confession of a mask and not the true meaning of the real man, that complex, very perceptive student of human nature, including his own. Perhaps even unknown to himself, at an unconscious level, his last novel may have been expressing some doubts of what he was to do. Do we sense a growing sympathy, even envy, for Honda who missed the 'glorious moment' but went on living?

Certainly many of Mishima's contemporaries did not accept a simple explanation for what had happened even months after the conclusion of *The Decay of the Angel* had been published. In the spring of 1971 the *Japan Quarterly* published an article by Junro Fukashiro entitled 'Post-mortem' which summarized the popular theories about Mishima's motives: 'The "insanity theory", which needs no further explanation; the "aesthetic theory," which holds that the beauty sought by Mishima in his literary pursuits could only be completed by his own ultimate dramatic death; the "exhausted talent theory," which suggests that Mishima had written himself out in the course of almost thirty years of writing and had nothing left to look forward to but despair; the "love-suicide theory," which asserts that he was a homosexual who committed a *shinju* [double suicide for love] with [Morita] in pursuit of some ultimate eroticism; and, finally, the "patriotism theory," which postulates that Mishima sought to incite members of the *Jieitai* to carry out a *coup d'état* which would realize Mishima's personal ideal of Japan as a nation-state united under the Emperor.'

2

Even if one accepts that Mishima in his own eyes had chosen the 'glorious moment,' one must relate it to his narcissism and his homosexuality, two complex aspects of the man. Homosexuality, I believe, was a key to his suicide. My speculation is that he was having an affair with Masakatsu Morita and that the two decided to commit a *shinju*, or lovers' suicide. The evidence is circumstantial: Mishima and Morita planned the incident at Ichigaya together and then brought in the three other *Tatenokai*. They decided that only they would commit suicide and they communicated their decision to the others afterwards—at the meeting at Misty sauna club on 3 November, 1970.

After the suicides, two people who had known Mishima personally made statements to me, in response to general questions, which supported the idea that it had been a *shinju*. One of these was a senior police officer who had access to the huge police dossier on the Mishima Incident. A number of outsiders interested in the suicides sought his help because he was known to have been close to Mishima and because of his high rank. The day before I called on him at his office in February 1971, he had had a phone call from the conservative politician, Shintaro Ishihara, who questioned him about the relationship of Mishima and Morita. The police officer was eager to talk about Mishima provided I did not quote him by name, and I was impressed by the humorous, ironical way he answered my questions. He remarked that Mishima and Morita were probably lovers, although only the two dead men knew for certain and so we could never be sure.

My other informant was a very different kind of person—a woman who had known Mishima all his adult life, an elegant and accomplished patroness of the arts and the wife of one of the leading politicians in Japan. I met her over lunch at a Western hotel in Tokyo in the early spring of 1972 and my secretary was present to interpret, if necessary, as all our conversation was in Japanese. She was someone I knew only slightly, but she showed no lack of trust and talked freely about Mishima. He had once proposed marriage to her and she had a voluminous correspondence, part of which she later showed me. 'Mishima was deeply in love with Morita,' she claimed. In her view, Morita had had a considerable influence on Mishima; she believed that Mishima alone would not have committed suicide (and missed the 'glorious moment'?). She saw Morita as a conventional, not very bright right-wing student, and Mishima as the man he was—a brilliant, intelligent, charming writer with a streak of instability, a man whose ideal was a beautiful death. The interests of the two men had coincided. Morita was in fact the first to propose that the *Tatenokai* stage a *coup d'état* (the police confirmed this); he made the suggestion in the autumn of 1969 and Mishima then turned him down, only to endorse the idea a few months later. Thus the 'Mishima Incident' had its genesis in the mind of Masakatsu Morita. It was adopted wholeheartedly by Mishima as it suited his ends perfectly once he knew that he was to finish *The Sea of Fertility* within a short period of time. In a sense, Morita stepped into a ready-made drama and unwittingly triggered off the mechanism which began it.

When I saw the two men together at Camp Fuji in 1969, they were obviously on close terms. Morita remarked that he could understand the ideal of the Emperor only through Mishima, who was mystically related to the Emperor. The Emperor was Morita's ideal and his worship presumably carried over to Mishima, too. This is crucial to an understanding of the relationship between the two men—if one follows Mishima's thinking about the Emperor. In his essay which accompanied the trilogy of works on the *Ni Ni Roku* Incident, Mishima stated that love was only possible under the aegis of the Emperor. A might love B and B might love A, but their relationship would only be meaningful if the Emperor existed; otherwise it would be hollow. He compared the situation to a triangle, in which the apex was the Emperor and the two lower angles were the lovers.

Mishima's thinking on the subject of leadership also throws light on his relationship with Morita. He was rough and autocratic in his ways in the *Tatenokai*, but he was also ready to accept criticism. One of his favourite books, the *Hagakure*, the eighteenth-century record of *samurai* ethics–Mishima once called it his favourite reading –explains the relationships between *samurai* warriors in terms of love; indeed, the *samurai* often were homosexual lovers. The *Hagakure* also states that subordinates, or followers, have the principal duty of 'remonstrating' with their supporters or feudal lords if the latter stray from the path of righteousness. Mishima, so Morita thought, was not serious about the *Tatenokai*, and would not commit the private army to action. Morita, the faithful follower and passionate admirer, goaded Mishima into action.

Eros and 'Blood' had a close connection in Mishima's literature, and it must surely have been his dream to achieve this ideal combination in reality. Although Mishima and Morita were both careful to destroy correspondence and diaries that might have told us for certain, the person with whom Mishima died, by whom he was killed, has to have been his lover.

3

The 'insanity theory'? Some of the anecdotes and conversations I have described towards the end of his life show that he was under considerable strain. I remember particularly that strange dinner at which he described Japan as being menaced by a 'green snake'. Many of the later photographs he posed for show him acting out his fantasies. Surely, for example, Mishima as St Sebastian was crossing the pathological border, and in the famous photograph brandishing the giant sword with which he was to be killed, his expression seems demented. But Mishima was such an incredible actor and stage-manager in life that one must still wonder to what extent even there was he still playacting.

The testimony of experts on Mishima's mental condition is not very helpful. The one psychologist who ever examined him, Dr Kataguchi, who subjected him to Rohrschach ink-blot tests in 1962–a long eight years before his death–came up with no clear opinion beyond the fact that Mishima was homosexual. After Mishima's death, however, he wrote an article describing Mishima as paranoid, psychopathic, and schizophrenic; this was not a great contribution to a deeper understanding of the man. I prefer a more commonsense approach based on what we have seen of his childhood. For the rest of his life he attempted to compensate for his frailty by prodigious actions. He had a consuming desire to prove that he was *not* weak, and in his battle to do so, he sought to control everything about him. This must over the years have been a tremendous strain on him. And if those close to him, through seeing him regularly, missed the signs (though his widow said afterwards she thought something was going to happen but perhaps the next year), outsiders and particularly those who knew him only through his books noticed. About a year before he died, an incident took place at Mishima's home which reflects this. Early one morning a young man took up a vigil outside the house (which is a standard technique in Japan for introducing oneself, and the longer the petitioner waits the more his sincerity is respected and the better chance he has of meeting the famous man). He waited there for an entire day, and towards evening, Mishima, whose family had seen the young man, relented and sent his maid to invite the young man in. Mishima greeted him with the remark: 'I am a busy man and I will let you ask one question, no more. Right?' The visitor paused for a moment. '*Sensei*,' he asked, 'when are you going to kill yourself?'

One remembers the reflection of the ageing Honda in *The Decay of the Angel*: 'He knew now that a more comprehensive view of the world was to be had from physical depression than from intelligence . . .' Was this a reflection of his own state of mind? Did his image of an ugly, materialistic Japan in this last novel mirror an unbalanced despair? As Edward Seidensticker, the translator of the novel, has written of Toru: 'The hero is a young boy given over to glittering and utterly empty cerebration. It is obvious that Mishima hated the boy, who is withal a brilliant creature of fiction, and who reminds one of no one so much as Mishima himself.' But to an adherent of *Yomeigaku*–the neo-Confucian philosophy which inspired Isao to commit *hara-kiri* in *Runaway Horses* and played a part in

Mishima's own decision to die–it would not be enough to recognize the rot within himself in a fictional confession; he also had to take action to escape hollow cerebration, and it must be a real suicide not a botched one like Toru's.

The importance of *Yomeigaku* to Mishima was underlined in a letter he wrote to one of his translators, Ivan Morris, just before his death, in which he asserted that he had been influenced by *Yomeigaku* and believed that 'knowing without acting' was not sufficient knowledge and that the act itself did not require any effectiveness. It was not enough for Mishima, in my interpretation of his last letter to Morris (he wrote a similar one, also mailed after his death, to Donald Keene), to regret the vanishing of Japanese tradition by 'mere verbal expression'; he could only truly 'know' the situation in his country if he took action. As he believed that Japan was in such a disastrous condition, only the most extreme response, suicide– an act of remonstration–would represent a 'consummation of knowledge'. And he had to kill himself in dramatic style, for drama was the keynote of the actions of the well-known nineteenth-century heroes of Japanese history who espoused *Yomeigaku*. What could be more dramatic than to hand over the end of his last novel and then commit *hara-kiri* virtually on television? As he wrote to Ivan Morris, he parted with *The Decay of the Angel* 'on the very day of my action in order to realize my *Bunburyodo*.'

No, the 'insanity theory' is far too simple and convenient an explanation. A Japanese friend of mine has claimed that three principal factors were homosexuality, *Yomeigaku* and Emperor worship, and that together they formed a 'gorgeous mosaic'. He thought no one element was decisive. What mattered was the overall effect, for even in his work–particularly in his plays–Mishima had often been far more interested in form than content. Like many an artist with suicidal tendencies, he saw his death as his final and most important work of art. 'I want to make a poem of my life,' he wrote at twenty-four. This was part of the strong Narcissus quality in him. His overriding aim was to die beautifully, and his life-long aesthetic of 'Death and Night and Blood' dictated that swords and knives, not guns, be the weapons. *Hara-kiri* for him was a supreme sexual act –the 'ultimate masturbation', as he told a visitor in the summer of 1970. By that time, believing that the supremely beautiful event was the violent death of a young man, he could not afford at forty-five to wait much longer.

But this too seems an oversimplification: the explanation for Mishima's death lies in his whole life and therefore this whole book is my explanation.

4

It was certainly an event which had a great effect—many effects—on a vast number of people. It greatly affected the men of Mishima's own generation in Japan, not because they respected his arguments, as laid out in the *gekibun* or before that in *Eirei no Koe*, but because his action reminded them of the Emperor worship which they had espoused during the war, when all of them had expected to die for the Emperor. In war-time the highest virtue had been to sacrifice oneself on the battlefield for the Emperor; hence the prestige of the *kamikaze* pilots whom Mishima praised in *Eirei no Koe*. Mishima for many had revived the old ideal of the Emperor, and therefore his death moved many of his contemporaries more deeply than any event since 1945. It was a measure of the sincerity of his imperialism in their eyes.

A newspaper poll showed that about one third of students had a degree of understanding for Mishima, though they condemned his *hara-kiri*. The entire press commented unfavourably on it, and he was condemned not only by the opposition parties but by the conservatives as well. Scarcely anyone was prepared to say a favourable word for him in public. But although the vast majority of Japanese said they disapproved of what Mishima had done, there were a great many people who had a kind of sympathy for him, and this increased the more the shock of that grim event faded into the past.

Even people who were close to Mishima were often critical of his action. Shortly afterwards Yasunari Kawabata arrived at the Ichigaya headquarters and was shown the corpses and was briefed by the police on the spot. Kawabata had very little to say to the press thereafter. 'What a waste!' he remarked. He was the first person to call on the widow and it would seem that both of them disapproved of the suicide. One indication of the widow's attitude was her choice of the photograph which hung above the altar at the public funeral. She avoided pictures of her husband in *Tatenokai* uniform, and selected one of him wearing a dark T-shirt. She also took swift steps to bring the *Tatenokai* to an end. On 28 February, 1971, a brief ceremony was held at a Shinto shrine in Tokyo, attended by Yoko Mishima, at which the *Tatenokai* was disbanded. This action implied that the *Tatenokai* had been a personal organization of Mishima's, a suicide vehicle; it suggested that with Mishima dead, the private army had no *raison d'être*.

Yoko Mishima in fact revealed herself as a veritable *samurai* widow, showing far more strength of character than her husband sometimes had done. She had a great deal of work to do as the heir to most of Mishima's literary estate, and she dealt with the problems which faced her with extraordinary strength of mind. Before long she was in a greater position of power in the publishing world than her husband had been. Practical and businesslike in her conduct of affairs she made all the necessary arrangements for Mishima's estate; this was growing rapidly as the sale of his books had greatly increased–in the first year after his death income on his estate was more than £100,000, mostly from sales in Japan.

Yoko, however, never spoke of her husband in public after his death. Little pieces of information came from the family through friends. Mishima had wanted, it was learned, to give his children a treat in early 1970 and had proposed to Yoko that they take the children on their first overseas trip in the summer–to Disneyland. Yoko, saying that he should finish his long novel first, had turned him down. What she thought, and what she thinks about her husband, may never be known. Quite possibly she was the only person outside the *Tatenokai* group who sensed that he was planning something major, but he apparently gave her no direct warning and let her go off that morning to school with the children without any final good-bye.

She wished above all to protect her husband's reputation. She wanted him to be remembered as an international writer, not as a right-wing extremist. At her home she put up the large photograph that had been displayed at the funeral, and by it she placed a smaller one of Morita–Mishima after all had been responsible for his death.

Other members of the family also disapproved of Mishima's suicide. His father objected; his son had not even said good-bye to the family, he grumbled. Mishima's younger brother, Chiyuki, who was serving in the Prime Minister's office at the time of the suicide, and who had the task of dealing with the press at Mishima's home, also refrained from saying a word of approval of the suicide. The only member of the family who took a sympathetic attitude was his mother. Shizué was bitterly critical of the rest of the family, saying that they had never understood her son. Shizué accused her husband, Azusa, of being a philistine and said that Yukio would have never killed himself if he had had a better wife than Yoko. The disagreements in the Hiraoka family were publicized by Azusa, who wrote articles in the press describing the quarrels. He told how Shizué wept at the Buddhist altar in their home, on which she had placed a volume of Nietzsche for her son to read; Azusa, beside himself with irritation, would step out into the garden to smoke a cigarette and calm himself.

To disapprove of Mishima's suicide was one thing, to prevent it dominating one's whole life another—so the case of poor Yasunari Kawabata demonstrated. In the year following Mishima's death he threw himself into a whirlwind of activities; he campaigned for the conservative candidate for the governorship of Tokyo, and he gave a press conference in which he said that he had been inspired to act by Mishima's example. Kawabata was in a depressed state of mind and told friends that he wished sometimes, when he went on a journey, that his plane would crash. He also mentioned that he was haunted by the ghost of Mishima; the spectre would visit him when he was alone at his desk or trouble his dreams. Although the old writer had more than once expressed disapproval of suicide, in April 1972 he gassed himself in his apartment.

5

My own attitude towards Mishima's suicide is ambivalent. I was both deeply moved and repelled by it. He had been a friend of great charm, generosity and wit; he had the gift of persuading people whom he met that they alone mattered to him; he was endowed with extraordinary energy and made those of us who had only a fraction of his vitality feel like pale worms. His outstanding asset was his intelligence. Almost alone among modern Japanese intellectuals he was familiar with Western and classical Japanese culture. He had also an enormous sense of humour and an evening with him passed quickly as he told one anecdote after another about events and personalities in Japan. His most striking feature, in my own experience, was his ability to empathize with others, to understand what they were thinking and to respond to it. No one of my Japanese friends had one fraction of his uncanny ability to know what was going on in my mind. That he had put an end to his life seemed for many months afterwards a totally inconceivable and unimaginable fact. When finally, after many attempts, I succeeded in writing a description of his suicide–which forms the first chapter of this book–I had a terrible nightmare. I dreamt that Mishima came to my home in Glastonbury and knocked on the door. When I saw him standing there, I struck him down with a mattock. I was in fact for a long time revolted by his suicide, his self-murder; I could see nothing beautiful in it. I loved him and I felt that I had been betrayed by his death (I had to master this feeling before I could be objective enough to start the research for this book). Many of those who knew him had similar reactions. His Japanese biographer, Takeo Okuno, has related how he had nightmares about Mishima for two or three hundred nights in a row! He was indeed an extraordinarily strong personality. How else could he have had such an impact on those who knew him–or read him?

One aspect of his charm was his self-knowledge and his ironic wit, and remembering this makes any simple interpretation of his actions suspect. In a conversation which he recorded with the older novelist Jun Ishikawa in the autumn of 1970, Mishima said–and his death was close at hand: 'I come out on the stage determined to make the audience weep and instead they burst out laughing.' He knew, in other words, how foolish–and how unbeautiful–his suicide would appear to the audience that beheld his last actions. What a farce his last speech was! There he was, derided by a large audience, up to the very last moment of his life. He appears to have known that this would happen, though he was disappointed by the *absolute* failure of his audience to respond.

How will Mishima be regarded by posterity?

He will be remembered, for one part, as a fascist agitator. The manner of his death, and the literature on imperialism which he left behind him, leave no doubt of his fascist tendencies. He resorted to violence in the name of the Emperor; he attempted to steer his country onto the path of militarism, demanding that the Emperor should once again be restored to a position of honour and that the Constitution be revised in order to sanctify the role of the armed forces in the State under the command of the Emperor, as in pre-

World War Two days. Alone among leading Japanese intellectuals of his generation he endorsed the benighted system of Emperor worship which led Japan into a futile war, from which it emerged with millions of dead and a devastated homeland. The fact that he committed *hara-kiri*, the ultimate spiritual action in the Japanese tradition, commended him to the right wing in Japan, which, though it remains weak, could well play a greater role in the affairs of state in the latter 1970s. There is already a powerful element in the ruling conservative party, the group known as the *Seirankai* ('Blue Storm Association'), which favours imperialism, rearmament and the colonization of Taiwan and Korea, and amongst whose members are to be found politicians who sympathized with Mishima's final action; one of them, Shintaro Ishihara, remarked after his death that Mishima had 'died to defend what he loved.'

I would prefer, however, that he be honoured as a novelist rather than denigrated as a right-wing fanatic. He spent the greater part of his life writing plays and novels—his *Collected Works* were published in thirty-six volumes after his death—and was regarded, in fact, until the late 1960s, as a writer with vaguely leftist sympathies, as he never expressed reactionary opinions until the last five years of his life. During his youth he was invited to join the Communist Party, and in his late thirties he remained intensely suspect to the *Uyoku*, the fanatical right wing in Tokyo. None of his novels suggests that he was in any way affiliated with the right wing in Japan—and he never had, in fact, any contact whatever with the *Uyoku*, whom he regarded as gangsters. His reputation as a novelist has meanwhile never stood higher in the West than at present. *The Sea of Fertility* is regarded as the best of his numerous novels; it is a panoramic vision of Japan in the twentieth century and tells more of modern Japan than any other work in translation. The descriptions of Japan in the early Taisho period, the chronicle of Isao, the right-wing terrorist of the early 1930s, and the depressing account of modern Japan in *The Decay of the Angel* are brilliant evocations of a country that is little understood in the West.

Mishima probably wrote best, however, about himself. He may be compared to André Gide, whom he resembled in so many ways, as an individual and as a writer. Like Gide, Mishima was born into an upper-middle-class family in which the mother had the dominant role; the fathers of both men were weak, ineffective figures, and their mothers were principally responsible for their upbringings (in

Mishima's case his formidable grandmother must be taken into account). Both men had strong narcissistic tendencies, both were homosexual and both enjoyed the game of double identities, appearing under their own names in private life, while adopting *noms de plume* in their literary activities. The most important of Gide's works was his *Journal*; and in my opinion Mishima's finest 'novel' was his auto-biographical *Confessions of a Mask*. Their limitations were that they found it hard, impossible perhaps, to put a distance between themselves and their work; their strained childhoods, when they were brought up alone, apart from other children, drove them into little worlds of their own from which they never really emerged. These were fascinating worlds, subjected to intelligent scrutiny, but they were limited.

One day someone will write a psychobiography of Yukio Mishima comparable to the classic work by Jean Delay, *La Jeunesse d'André Gide*. He will have access to family correspondence and will have the cool detachment that only the passage of time will bring—we are still too close to events. I thought at the start of my work on this book that I would be satisfied if I found in his life the hint of an explanation for his death. Now at the end I remember that last note he left on his desk on 25 November, 1970: 'Human life is limited, but I would like to live forever.' This book then has been an attempt to describe how he will live—in my memory at least.

WORKS BY YUKIO MISHIMA

This is a complete list of all Mishima's books, as published in Japan. It does not include articles, essays or short stories, except where these have been collected under one title and published in book form. I have omitted many various editions of Mishima's *Collected Works*, except the last. The translations of the Japanese titles were made with the assistance of Donald Keene. The date in each case is of the first Japanese edition.

1944	Hanazakari no Mori	The Forest in Full Bloom
1947	Misaki nite no Monogatari	A Story at the Cape
1948	Tozoku	Robbers
	Yoru no Shitaku	Preparations for Night
1949	Hoseki Baibai	Traffic in Precious Stones
	Kamen no Kokuhaku	Confessions of a Mask
	Magun no Tsuka	The Passage of Demons
1950	Todai	The Lighthouse
	Kaibutsu	Monster
	Ai no Kawaki	Thirst for Love
	Junpaku no Yoru	The Pure White Night
	Ao no Jidai	The Blue Period
1951	Seijo	The Holy Virgin
	Kari to Emono	The Hunter and His Prey
	Tonorie	Riding Club
	Kashiramoji	Initials
	Kinjiki (Vol. 1)	Forbidden Colours
	Natsuko no Boken	Natsuko's Adventure
1952	Aporo no Sakazuki	The Cup of Apollo
1953	Manatsu no Shi	Death in Midsummer
	Nipponsei	Made in Japan
	Yoru no Himawari	Twilight Sunflower
	Higyo (Kinjiki Vol. 2)	Secret Medicine
	Aya no Tsuzumi	The Damask Drum
1954	Migoto na Onna. Todai. Uma	Wonderful Woman. The Lighthouse. Horse
	Shiosai	The Sound of Waves
	Koi no Miyako	The Capital of Love

I

	Watakushi no Henreki Jidai	My Wandering Years
	Kinu to Meisatsu	Silk and Insight
	Daiich no Sei–Dansai Kenkyu Koza	The First Sex–Studies of Males
1965	Ongaku	Music
	Ame no naka no Funsui	The Fountain and the Rain
	Me–Aru Geijutsu Danso	Eye–Fragmentary Reflections on Art
	Sado Koshaku Fujin	Madame de Sade
1966	Han-Teijo Daigaku	The Book of Anti-Chaste Wisdom
	Yukoku	Patriotism
	Eirei no Koe	The Voices of the Heroic Dead
	Taiwa–Shin Nihonjin Ron	Dialogue on the Japanese People
1967	Areno yori	From the Desolate Fields
	Geijutsu no Kao	The Face of Art
	Hagakure Nyumon	An Introduction to Hagakure
	Yakaifuku	Evening Dress
	Suzakuke no Metsubo	The Fall of the House of Suzaku
1968	Fukuzatsu na Kare	A Complicated Guy
	Taidan–Ningen to Bungaku	Dialogue on Man and Literature
	Mishima Yukio Reta Kyoshitsu	Yukio Mishima's Classroom in Letter Writing
	Taiyo to Tetsu	Sun and Steel
	Wagamoto Hittora	My Friend Hitler
	Inochi Urimasu	I Will Sell You My Life
	Haru no Yuki	Spring Snow
1969	Honba	Runaway Horses
	Bunka Boeiron	On the Defence of Culture
	Kurotokage	Black Lizard
	Mishima Yukio vs Todai Zenkyoto	Yukio Mishima vs Tokyo University Student Struggle Association
	Raio no Terrasu	The Terrace of the Leper King
	Wakaki Samurai no tame ni	For Young *Samurai*
	Chinsetsu Yumiharizuki	Chinsetsu Yumiharizuki
1970	Akatsuki no Tera	The Temple of Dawn
	Shobu no Kokoro	The Heart of Martial Spirits
	Kodogaku Nyumon	On Action
	Gensen no Kanjo	Gensen no Kanjo
	Sakkaron	Essays on Authors
	Tennin Gosui	The Decay of the Angel
	Ranryoo	Ranryoo
1973-5	Mishima Yukio Zenshu	Collected Works (36 volumes)

NOTES

CHAPTER I

1 The account of Mishima's suicide is based on documents produced at the trial of the survivors of the 'Mishima Incident' in 1971 and on statements made to me by the *Jieitai* and police officers involved in the affair. I also visited the office of General Mashita where Mishima died. In certain cases I have invented dialogue, a course adopted nowhere else in the book; however Mishima's entire balcony speech was recorded on tape and many other passages in direct speech correspond to the words spoken by the actors in this drama.

2 The translation given here is a precis of the full *gekibun*. The 'Peace Constitution' is the 1947 Constitution, drafted by the American Occupation authorities. The idea that the *Jieitai* should have risen in 1969 was entirely Mishima's own, and was very far-fetched. However Mishima was strictly correct in remarking that that 'the *Jieitai* is unconstitutional'; Article 9 of the 1947 Constitution denies Japan the right to have armed forces.

3 *Bu*–the warrior ethic.

CHAPTER II

1 *Confessions of a Mask*, Peter Owen, 1960, p. 21. Translated by Meredith Weatherby. (Hereafter *Confessions*).

2 Ruth Benedict, *The Chrysanthemum and the Sword*, Routledge, 1967.

3 The reliability of *Confessions of a Mask* as a source is a subject to which I have devoted much attention. Before his suicide I discussed the matter with Mishima in general terms; he implied that the book was largely auto-biographical. After his death I asked Professor Donald Keene to what extent *Confessions* could be regarded as autobiography. His reply was that for the most part the book was authentic, but there were certain passages the accuracy of which could not be totally confirmed as Mishima was no longer alive. My next step was to consult Miss T. Etsugu, a leading authority on Mishima texts. She stated that the first two chapters of *Confessions*–which cover the pre-war period–might alone be depended upon entirely. In order to check this assertion I compared statements by Shizué Hiraoka, Mishima's mother, with *Confessions*; in every case the two corresponded. It is impossible to be 100 per cent certain of the accuracy of some of the pensées in the early part of the book; however, I consider them to be probably entirely authentic.

4 *Confessions*, p. 5.

5 Ibid., p. 4.

6 Ibid.

7 Ibid., p. 5.

8 Ibid.
9 Shizué Hiraoka, quoted in *Shokun* magazine, in a series of articles which appeared between December 1971 and April 1972. Translated by M. Shimizu. (Hereafter *Shokun*).
10 Ibid.
11 *Confessions*, p. 6.
12 *Shokun*.
13 Ibid.
14 Ibid.
15 *Confessions*, p. 6.
16 Dr Kiyoshi Nakamura to Michiko Shimizu, 1972.
17 *Confessions*, p. 7.
18 Ibid, pp. 7-9.
19 Ibid., p. 11.
20 Ibid.
21 Ibid.
22 Ibid., p. 12.
23 Ibid., pp. 13-14.
24 Ibid., p. 14.
25 Ibid., p. 15.
26 Ibid., p. 16.
27 Ibid.
28 Ibid., pp. 17-18.
29 Ibid., p. 19.
30 Ibid., p. 20.
31 Ibid., p. 21.
32 Ibid., p. 24.
33 Ibid., p. 26.
34 *Shokun*.
35 *Confessions*, p. 25.
36 Ibid., p. 26.
37 Ibid., p. 27.
38 Ibid., p. 28.
39 Ibid., p. 27.
40 *Shokun*.
41 From the catalogue to the Tobu Exhibition, November 1970. Tr. Shimizu.
42 'Isu', first published in *Bessatsu Bungei Shunju* magazine in March 1951. Collected with nine other stories in *Tonorikai*, pp. 78-9, Shinchosha, 1951. Tr. Shimizu.
43 *Confessions*, p. 37.
44 Ibid., p. 35.
45 Ibid., p. 36.
46 *Ajisai no Haha* ('Hydrangea Mother'), a magazine article, 1953.
47 *Shokun*.
48 *Confessions*, p. 37.
49 Ibid., pp. 38-9.
50 Ibid., pp. 40-1.
51 Omi, so Mishima told Donald Keene, was a real person.

52 *Confessions*, p. 61.
53 Ibid., p. 62.
54 Ibid., p. 65.
55 Ibid., p. 68.
56 Ibid., pp. 77-8.
57 *Shokun* magazine, January 1971. Tr. Shimizu.
58 *Confessions*, pp. 62-3.
59 Ibid., p. 90.
60 Ibid., pp. 92-3.
61 Ibid., p. 93.
62 Ibid., p. 97.

CHAPTER III

1 *Mishima Yukio Taikan*, Hyoron-Shinsha, January 1971. Tr. M. Shimizu.
2 Tr. M. Shimizu.
3 *Confessions*, p. 108.
4 Ibid., p. 109.
5 Ibid., p. 111.
6 Ibid., p. 115.
7 *Bungei Bunka*, September 1941. Tr. M. Shimizu.
8 *Confessions*, p. 116.
9 See the Emperor's surrender broadcast of 15 August, 1945.
10 *Shincho*, February 1971. Tr. K. Takamasu.
11 Masaharu Fuji, *Bungei*, February 1971. Tr. M. Shimizu.
12 From the introduction to *Hasuda Zenmei o Katura* by Jiro Odakane, Chikuma Shobo, 1970. Tr. K. Takamasu.
13 From a conversation with the author, 1972.
14 *Bunshi no Shosei ni tsuite*, November 1939.
15 *Shincho*, November 1938.
16 *Sun and Steel*, Kodansha International, 1970, p. 47. Translated by John Bester, Secker & Warburg, 1971.
17 *Confessions*, p. 117.
18 Ibid., p. 118.
19 Ibid.
20 *Bungei*, February 1971. Tr. M. Shimizu.
21 *Mainichi Shimbun*, December 1970. Tr. K. Takamasu.
22 Discussion with Zenkyoto students.
23 *Confessions*, p. 127.
24 Ibid.
25 Ibid., p. 133.
26 *Watakushi no Henreki Jidai*, Kodansha, 1964, p. 15. Tr. M. Shimizu.
27 Ibid., p. 18.
28 Ibid., p. 19.
29 *Confessions*, p. 135.
30 Ibid.
31 Ibid., p. 136.
32 Ibid.

33   Ibid., pp. 136-7.
34   Ibid., p. 138.
35   Ibid., p. 139.
36   Ibid.
37   Ibid., pp. 160-2.
38   *Sun and Steel*, p. 20.
39   *Confessions*, pp. 182-3.
40   Ibid., p. 188.
41   Ibid., p. 189.
42   *Sun and Steel*, p. 34.
43   *Confessions*, p. 217.
44   Ibid., p. 218.
45   Excerpt from official translation.
46   *Confessions*, p. 220.
47   Ibid.
48   A statement prepared by the occupation authorities.
49   *Oyuki no Hini (gakusei sakka Mishima Yukio)* by Utaro Noda, *Bungei*, February 1971. Tr. M. Shimizu.
50   Ibid.
51   Ibid.
52   Ibid.
53   Ibid.
54   See *Watakushi no Henreki Jidai*, p. 25.
55   *Confessions*, p. 231.
56   Ibid., p. 230.
57   Memoir by Nagaoka, quoted in *Shincho*, January 1971, p. 194.
58   A representative list of publications, not complete.
59   *Confessions*, p. 252.
60   Ibid., p. 253.
61   Ibid., p. 255.

PROLOGUE AND CHAPTER IV

1   From notes written at the time when Mishima was working on *Confessions of a Mask*.
2   *Watakushi no Henreki Jidai*, pp. 54-5. Tr. M. Shimizu.
3   Ibid., pp. 52-3.
4   Ibid., p. 53.
5   Ibid.
6   Ibid., p. 54.
7   Ibid.
8   Donald Keene, *Landscapes and Portraits*, Kodansha International, 1971, p. 210; Secker & Warburg, 1972.
9   *Thirst for Love*, Tuttle, 1970, p. 4. Translated by Alfred Marks, Secker & Warburg, 1970.
10   Ibid., p. 7.
11   Ibid., p. 114.

12 *Tosho Shimbun.*
13 *Forbidden Colours*, Tuttle, 1969, p. 4. Translated by Alfred Marks, Secker & Warburg, 1968.
14 Ibid., p. 21.
15 Ibid., p. 90.
16 Ibid., p. 149.
17 *Watakushi no Henreki Jidai*, p. 56. Tr. M. Shimizu.
18 Ibid., p. 58.
19 *Asahi Shimbun*, December 1956. Tr. M. Shimizu.
20 *Watakushi no Henreki Jidai*, pp. 59-60. Tr. M. Shimizu.
21 Ibid., p. 60.
22 Ibid.
23 *Forbidden Colours*, p. 292.
24 *Pacific Community*, April 1971, p. 480.
25 *Landscapes and Portraits*, p. 213.
26 *Watakushi no Henreki Jidai*, pp. 63-4.
27 'Onnagata', in *Death in Midsummer and Other Stories*, New Directions, 1966, p. 140. Translated by Donald Keene; Secker & Warburg, 1967.
28 Ibid., p. 143.
29 Ibid.
30 Ibid., p. 145.
31 Ibid.
32 *Ratai to Isho*, Shinchosha, 1966, p. 59. Tr. Keene.
33 *The Temple of the Golden Pavilion*, Tuttle, 1959, p. 93. Translated by Ivan Morris; Secker & Warburg, 1959.
34 Ibid., p. 101.
35 Ibid., pp. 142-3.
36 Ibid., p. 144.
37 Ibid., p. 145.
38 Ibid.
39 *Ratai to Isho*, p. 163.
40 Told to Takao Tokuoka, 1971.
41 *Young Lady*, December 1970.
42 *Juhassai to Sanjuyonsai no Shozoga* ('Portrait of an 18-year-old and a 34-year-old') in *Mishima Yukio Shu*, Shueisha, 1962. Tr. M. Shimizu.
43 *Geijutsu Shincho*, July 1959, p. 261. Tr. M. Shimizu.
44 *Waga Hibungakuteki Seikatsu* ('My Non-Literary Life'), in *Bi no Shugeki*, Kodansha, 1961, p. 163.
45 *Ratai to Isho*, p. 204.
46 Ibid.
47 *The Journal of Asian Affairs*, 1964.
48 *Ratai to Isho.*
49 *After the Banquet*, Avon, 1967, p. 9. Translated by Donald Keene; Secker & Warburg, 1963.
50 Ibid., p. 11.
51 Ibid., p. 141.
52 *Fukei*, June 1962, p. 13. Tr. M. Shimizu.
53 *Landscapes and Portraits*, p. 221.

54 *Spring Snow*, Tuttle, 1972, p. 128. Translated by Michael Gallagher; Secker & Warburg, 1972.
55 Ibid., p. 383.
56 Ibid., p. 384.
57 *Sun and Steel*, p. 14.
58 Ibid., pp. 31-3.
59 Ibid., p. 49.
60 Ibid., pp. 57-9.
61 A condensed version.
62 *The Hudson Review*, Vol. XXIV, No. 2 (Summer 1971), p. 275. (Translated by Edward Seidensticker). Secker & Warburg, 1973. (Translated by Michael Gallagher).
63 Ibid., p. 276.
64 Ibid.
65 Ibid.
66 *Sun and Steel*, pp. 84-8.
67 *Queen*, January 1970, pp. 40-42.
68 *Hasuda Zenmei o Kataru* by Jiro Odakane, Chikuma Shobo, 1970. Tr. K. Takamasu.
69 *Asahi Shimbun*, 22 September, 1970. Tr. M. Shimizu.

CHAPTER V
1 From the introduction by Donald Keene to *Five Modern No Plays*, Tuttle, 1957, p. xi. Translated by Donald Keene; Secker & Warburg, 1957.
2 Ibid., p. xiii.
3 *Shibai to Watakushi* ('The Play and I') an essay, 1951. Tr. M. Murasugi.
4 *Kokubungaku*, 1955, p. 182. Tr. Shimizu.
5 Ibid.
6 *Asahi Shimbun*, 27 November, 1963. Tr. M. Murasugi.
7 *Madame de Sade*, Peter Owen, 1968, p. 107. Translated by Donald Keene.
8 Ibid.
9 *Landscapes and Portraits*, p. 213.
10 *Raio no Terrasu*, Chuo Koronsha, 1969. Tr. M. Shimizu.
11 Ibid.

CHAPTER VI
1 *Sun and Steel*, p. 23.
2 *Sports Illustrated*, 11 January, 1971. © 1971, Time Inc.
3 *Sun and Steel*, pp. 27-8.
4 Ibid., pp. 28-9.

CHAPTER VII
1 *Sports Illustrated*, p. 26.
2 *Mainichi Shimbun*, 25 June, 1960. Tr. M. Shimizu.
3 'Patriotism' in *Death in Midsummer and Other Stories*, New Directions, 1966, pp. 114-15; Secker and Warburg, 1967.
4 *Niniroku Jiken to Watakushi*, Shinchosa, 1966. Tr. K. Takamasu.
5 *Sunday Mainichi*, 8 March, 1966. Tr. K. Takamasu.

6   *Taiwa Shinhihonjinron*, Bancho Shobo, 1966. Tr. M. Shimizu.
7   *Sun and Steel*, p. 39.
8   *Shokun*, Spring 1972.
9   *Chuo Koron*, August 1968. Tr. American Embassy, Tokyo.
10 *Queen*, January 1970.
11 *Mishima Yukio–Todai Zenkyoto, Chuo Koron*, 1969. Tr. M. Shimizu.
12 *The Times*, 24 September, 1969.
13 From notes made at the time by the author.
14 *Shobu no Kokoro*, a discussion with Ichiro Murakami, 1970. Tr. M. Murasugi.

THE DECAY OF THE ANGEL

1   *The Decay of the Angel*, New York: Alfred A. Knopf, 1974, p. 211. Tr.
    E. Seidensticker. To be published in London by Secker & Warburg.
2   Ibid., pp. 212-3.
3   Ibid., p. 213.
4   Ibid., p. 215.
5   Ibid., p. 52.
6   Ibid., p. 219-20.
7   Ibid., pp. 233-6.

POST MORTEM

1   *Japan Quarterly*, spring 1971, with the exception of the final quotation.
2   *The Decay of the Angel*, p. 105.

INDEX